Pony trekking in the hills above the Mawddach Estuary

1

This book contains more than accommodation information. Much more...

Panoramic views along the mountain road from Dylife to Machynlleth.

Your Guide to Wales

In addition to its great choice of places to stay, you'll find details of Wales's holiday areas and resorts, its countryside, events, traditional crafts and places to visit — in a nutshell, all the information you'll need to choose and book a holiday, break or business stopover.

The best for beauty

Wales's number-one attraction is its scenery. It contains no less than three National Parks and five areas officially designated as being of 'Outstanding Natural Beauty'. Snowdonia, the Brecon Beacons and the Pembrokeshire Coast make up the trio of National Parks. Its areas of outstanding beauty are the Gower Peninsula, Wye Valley, Isle of Anglesey, Llŷn Peninsula and Clwydian Range. And that's not taking into account the huge tracts of unspoilt countryside and coastline in unexplored Mid Wales.

The best for attractions

What's more, this beautiful landscape is filled with fascinating places to visit. Wales is famous worldwide as a land of castles – over 100 are open to the public. Other historic sites, such as stone burial chambers, stretch back to the earliest times, while the recent past is recalled at mining museums and slate caverns.

Wales's range of attractions is kaleidoscopic. There are sea and mountain zoos, narrow-gauge railways, parks dedicated to wildlife, butterflies and the countryside, spectacular showcaves ... even an energy-efficient 'village of the future'.

The best for crafts

Craft workshops are another big attraction throughout Wales. Stop off on your travels at a pottery, woollen mill, woodturner's, leather-worker's, candlemaker's, jeweller's or slate workshop. Look out also for the craft centres at Ruthin, Corris and Hay-on-Wye where a number of craftspeople work together.

The Brynkir Woollen Mill, near Porthmadog

2

Llyn Brianne in the remote Cambrian Mountains north of Llandovery

Throughout 1995, the City of Swansea plays host to the largest literary festival ever to be staged. Some of the world's finest writers will join with local artists to create a unique event that promises to be truly international.

Captain Cat, from Dylan Thomas's Under Milk Wood gazes out across Swansea's Maritime Quarter

UK Year of Literature and Writing - Swansea

The breadth and vision of this major festival is reflected in its list of patrons, an illustrious group which includes the American literary giants Saul Bellow and Arthur Miller, crime writer P D James, Salman Rushdie, musicians Paul Simon and Bono from U2, and Wales's own Jan Morris.

Swansea will be buzzing with activity through 1995 as the entire city celebrates the written and spoken word. Events range from

the serious to the unashamedly light-hearted. The packed programme will appeal to everyone, from lovers of the classics to alternative comedy, Shakespeare to street poetry, crime writing to science fiction. And the city will look the part, with flags, banners and decorations adding to the colourful festival atmosphere. You'll even see fragments of favourite novels and poems appearing on the buses!

4

The programme is still taking shape. Here's a sample from the range of events planned:

January

1-7 Jan: In the Beginning was the Word
(myths and legends)

1-31: Storyboard - The Comic Show
(comic exhibitions)

13-16: Celtic Comedy Classic
(stand-up comedy)

25 Jan-14 Feb: Swansea with a Loving Kiss
(romantic and erotic writing)

February

22-26: Out of the Cold -
Writing from Scandinavia

March

1-11: Wales in the World

23-26: Latin American Writing

April

4-9: Beyond Belief
(writing inspired by religion/fixed belief)

18-23: Looking for a New England
(the changing English novel)

**28 Apr-1 May: Swansea Jazz Festival -
A Writer's Notes**
(literature meets jazz)

May

**4-6: Uncommon Wealth - The Richness of
Canadian Writing**

Mid-May: Sea Shanty Festival

19-21: Criminal Pursuits
(crime writing)

26-29: Folk Writes

June

1-30: Dylan Thomas Month

13-18: The Importance of Being Elsewhere? -
Irish Writers

July

All month: Wales - A Land of Storytelling

August

**Aug/Sept:
The First Literature Proms**

September

Sept: Chinese Moon -
Chinese Writing from Around the World

27-30: Under the Veldt
(South African writing)

October

Early Oct: A Mouthful of Words
(gourmet writing)

Oct: Star-Crossed Lovers
(the tragedy of lovers examined from various
perspectives)

**Mid-Oct: Readers of Today, Writers of
Tomorrow**
(authors talk to young readers)

27-31: Welcome to the Nightmare -
The World of Horror Writing

End-Oct: Speaking in Tongues
(minority and majority languages, literary and
visual art forms)

November

7-12: Prose, Peace and Politics
(political writing)

17-19: The Ghost Story

25 Nov-2 Dec: Caledonian Companions

December

6-10: Out of This World
(science fiction writing)

Many other events will be taking place on themes which include scriptwriting, songwriting, sports writing, travel writing and writing from the USA.

Swansea was the birthplace of Dylan Thomas, one of Wales's greatest writers and poets – so it's appropriate that the city is playing host to this festival. Dylan's life and work will be commemorated throughout the year at events such as 'Dylan Days'.
One of 1995's highlights promises to be 'Swansea's Dylan Thomas' in June, a month-long celebration of the poet's genius.

The word is out!

Swansea will be on everyone's lips during 1995. For further details please contact the
Festival Bureau, which handles Box Office and accommodation bookings.

Tel (01792) 652211

1995 promises to be the biggest celebration of arts and culture that Britain has ever seen.

Llangollen's International Musical Eisteddfod

Festival of Arts and Culture

All parts of the country will be participating in an exciting festival which embraces a huge programme of events, performances, exhibitions and entertainment – and Wales, with its thriving arts scene, is scheduled to play a major part.
Here, we have listed just some of the events you'll enjoy, beginning with the main activities.

All year
UK Festival of Literature and Writing –
Swansea
(see pages 4/5)

6 May-31 December
Mid Wales Festival of the
Countryside

A festival which brings together over 500 events taking place throughout beautiful Mid Wales – birdwatching, guided walks, arts and crafts, sheepdog trials, farm and garden visits. David Bellamy, a keen supporter, has called it 'the role model for sustainable tourism'. Tel (01686) 625384

24 May-4 June
Hay Festival of Literature

Hay-on-Wye, the borderland 'town of books', provides an ideal setting for this literary festival which has quickly established an international reputation. Attracts leading writers, poets and celebrities. Tel (01497) 821299

4-9 July
Llangollen International Musical
Eisteddfod

A colourful, cosmopolitan gathering of singers and dancers from all over the world perform in the beautiful little town of Llangollen. A unique festival first held in 1947 to help heal the wounds of war by bringing the peoples of the world together. A special appearance this year by Luciano Pavarotti. Tel (01978) 860236

24-27 July
Royal Welsh Agricultural Show (illustrated)

Four days of fascination – and a show that attracts a wide audience to Builth Wells, not just from the farming community but from all walks of life. One of Wales's premier events, held in the heart of the country, covering all aspects of agriculture – and a lot more besides. Tel (01982) 553683

An Eventful Year

Jazz at Brecon

11-13 August
Brecon Jazz International Festival

The streets of Brecon come alive with the sounds of summer jazz. A great three-day international festival with a wonderful atmosphere, which attracts the top names from the world of jazz. Over 80 concerts by bands and solo artists held throughout the town, both indoors and in the open air. Tel (01874) 625557

5-12 August
Royal National Eisteddfod

Wales's most important cultural gathering, dating back to 1176, and held at a different venue each year. A festival dedicated to Welsh, Britain's oldest living language, with competitions, choirs, concerts, stands and exhibitions. Translation facilities available. This year's event will be held at Abergele in the Borough of Colwyn. Tel (01222) 763777

19-27 August
Llandrindod Wells Victorian Festival

The Mid Wales spa town of Llandrindod Wells celebrates its Victorian past. The festival includes street theatre, walks, talks, drama, exhibitions and music – all with a Victorian flavour. Tel (01597) 823441

Events for everyone

18 February
Wales v England
International Rugby Union
Cardiff Arms Park

1 March
St David's Day Concert
St David's Hall, Cardiff

10-12 March
Folk Weekend
Llanwrtyd Wells

18 March
Wales v Ireland
International Rugby Union
Cardiff Arms Park

29 April-6 May
Landsker Walking Festival
Narberth

6 May
Dee and Clwyd Festival of Music
Choral Concert
Corwen

6-8 May
All Our Yesterdays Steam Gala
Ffestiniog Railway, Porthmadog

Llandudno Extravaganza

6-27 May
Wrexham Maelor Arts Festival
Wrexham

12-14 May
Mid Wales May Festival
Newtown

19-21 May
Llangollen International Jazz Festival

25-28 May
Llantilio Crossenny Festival of
Music and Drama
Llantilio Crossenny, nr Abergavenny

26-29 May
Llanfair Folk Fayre
Llanfair Clydogau, nr Lampeter

27-28 May
Crafts in Action Festival
St Donat's Castle, nr Llantwit Major

27 May-3 June
St David's Cathedral Festival

27 May-4 June
Gŵyl Beaumaris Festival

29 May-3 June
Urdd National Eisteddfod
Crymych, nr Cardigan

11-17 June
1995 Cardiff Singer of the World
Competition
St David's Hall, Cardiff

12-24 June
Passion Play 'Behold the Man'
Margam Park, nr Port Talbot

17 June
Man versus Horse Marathon
Llanwrtyd Wells

Three Peaks Yacht Race
(Barmouth to Fort William)
Barmouth

17-26 June
Criccieth Festival of Music
and the Arts

23-25 June
Gŵyl Ifan – Festival of Welsh Folk
Dancing
Cardiff

24 June
RAF St Athan At Home Day
and Air Show
St Athan, nr Barry

26 June-4 July (provisional)
Gregynog Festival
Nr Newtown

27 June-2 July
Lower Machen Festival
Machen, nr Newport (Gwent)

29 June-16 July (provisional)
Dyffryn Festival of Music and Drama
Dyffryn Gardens, St Nicholas, nr Cardiff

30 June-2 July
Beyond the Border – The Welsh
International Festival of Storytelling
St Donat's Castle, nr Llantwit Major

Morris in the Forest
(Morris dancing, forest walks, etc)
Llanwrtyd Wells

8-9 July
Mid Wales Festival of Transport
Powis Castle, Welshpool

13-21 July (provisional)
Welsh Proms '95
St David's Hall, Cardiff

14-16 July
5th International Potters' Festival
Aberystwyth

17-30 July
Gower Festival

22 July-4 August
Musicfest – Aberystwyth International
Music Festival and Summer School

22-29 July
Fishguard Music Festival

23-30 July
Ian Rush International Soccer
Tournament
Aberystwyth

24-30 July
Conwy Festival

2-5 August
West Wales Children's Festival
Narberth

9-10 August
Walker Cup Golf Championships
Royal Porthcawl Golf Club

10-11 August
United Counties Show
Carmarthen

10-13 August
Mountain Bike Festival
Llanwrtyd Wells

21-27 August
Vale of Glamorgan Festival
Vale of Glamorgan and Cardiff

26 August-2 September
Presteigne Festival of Music
and the Arts

28 August
World Bog-Snorkelling Championships
Llanwrtyd Wells

7-15 September
Barmouth Arts Festival

9 September-7 October
Cardiff Festival
(Fun, fable and fantasy)

14-16 September
1995 International Sheepdog Trials
Whitford, Holywell

15-23 September
Tenby Arts Festival

19-22 September
Welsh International Four Days
of Walks
Llanwrtyd Wells

27-30 September
Booktide Children's Art Festival
Aberystwyth

October (dates to be confirmed)
Swansea Festival

14-22 October
Llandudno October Festival

19-22 October
Welsh International Four Days of Cycle
Races
Llanwrtyd Wells

17-26 November
Mid Wales Beer Festival
Llanwrtyd Wells

More details are contained within the 1995 Wales Arts Season brochure. A general 'What's happening in Wales' events list is also available. For copies of these free publications, please write to Wales Tourist Board, Davis Street, Cardiff CF1 2FU, stating your requirements.

*When you travel through Wales
you take a journey through time.*

Caerphilly Castle, a stirring medieval monument

A Glimpse into the Past

In Wales, you'll come across prehistoric and Roman remains, mighty medieval castles,
manor houses and mansions, and memories of Britain's Industrial Revolution.

Cromlechs and castles

Powis Castle, Welshpool

Skeletal Pentre Ifan Cromlech in Pembrokeshire's Preseli Hills is one of many prehistoric monuments scattered throughout Wales. Thousands of years later, the Romans left camps, roadways, an extraordinary amphitheatre and bath-house at Caerleon and unique gold mine at Pumsaint. But more than anything else, Wales is famous for its castles – mighty medieval monuments such as Caernarfon, Conwy and Caerphilly, as well as dramatic ruins like Carreg Cennen, Llandeilo and remote Castell-y-Bere hidden beneath Cader Idris.

Historic houses

History also lives on at Llancaiach Fawr, a restored Tudor manor house in the Rhymney Valley which recreates the times of the Civil War. You can glimpse into grand country houses at National Trust properties such as Plas Newydd on Anglesey, Welshpool's Powis Castle and Erddig near Wrexham (an unusual 'upstairs, downstairs' house). Dignified Tredegar House at Newport (Gwent) is another mansion with two sides to its personality – a glittering interior and preserved servants' quarters.

Industrial heritage

Llechwedd Slate Caverns

In Wales, you'll also discover gripping monuments to the era of coal, slate, iron and steel. 'King Coal's' reign is remembered at places like the Big Pit Mining Museum, Blaenafon, and the Rhondda Heritage Park. North Wales's slate industry has a successful modern spin-off at the popular Llechwedd Slate Caverns, Blaenau Ffestiniog – and slate is again the theme at the Gloddfa Ganol Mine, also in Blaenau Ffestiniog, and Llanberis's Welsh Slate Museum.

8

At Your Service

Welcome Host

Service and hospitality are as important as good accommodation and good food. We attach top priority to customer care – which is why we launched our 'Welcome Host' scheme a few years ago. Open to everyone from taxi drivers to hotel staff, the scheme places the emphasis on friendliness and first-class service.

Welcome Host is part of a fine tradition in Wales – a tradition embodied in the welcoming greeting of *croeso*. Look out for the Welcome Host certificate or badge – it's a sure sign of the best in Welsh hospitality and service.

A Taste of Wales

Good food is another important ingredient of any holiday. In Wales, you're in for a treat, for there's been an explosion of talent on the cooking scene. Throughout the country – in restaurants and hotels, inns and bistros – talented chefs are making the most of fresh, local produce to create tasty, innovative dishes as well as traditional favourites.

A tempting menu

That's what Taste of Wales-*Blas ar Gymru* is all about. Around 350 establishments are members of this scheme, which seeks to promote the best in Welsh foods. More and more chefs are now taking advantage of Wales's top-quality fresh produce such as succulent Welsh lamb, superb seafoods, delicious Pembrokeshire potatoes and wonderful cheeses. These ingredients are used to make not only the old favourites such as *cawl* (a nourishing, hearty broth) and lamb served the traditional way. They also form the basis of modern, imaginative cuisine, often cooked with a lighter touch.

Look out for the Taste of Wales window sticker on your travels – it's a sign of good food.

9

Wales has excellent road and rail links with most of Britain. Travel is fast, inexpensive and hassle-free — so you'll enjoy your holiday or short break to the full.

So Accessible

By car

Travel to South-West Wales is easy on the M4 and onward dual carriageway systems. The A55 North Wales coast 'Expressway' whisks traffic past the old bottlenecks, including Conwy. Mid Wales is easily reached by the M54 which links with the M6/M5/M1. And when you arrive, you'll enjoy the increasingly rare pleasures of the open road, for most highways remain blissfully traffic free apart from a few peak summer weekends.

By rail

InterCity, British Rail's flagship service, will speed you in style and comfort from London (Paddington) to Cardiff in less than 2 hours and to Swansea in under 3 hours (there are onward Regional Railways services to South-West Wales). Fast InterCity trains also link London (Euston) with the North Wales coast, serving both Bangor and Holyhead.

Regional Railways' modern, air-conditioned trains provide a direct link to Cardiff from the South Coast, Exeter and Torbay, Birmingham, Manchester and Liverpool. North Wales is served by regular direct trains from Manchester. Aberystwyth and other Mid Wales resorts have direct services from Birmingham and Shrewsbury.

Exploring Wales by train is a delight. Take a scenic trip on the beautiful Heart of Wales line from Shrewsbury to Swansea, or on the Conwy Valley line into the mountains from Llandudno Junction to Blaenau Ffestiniog. The views are also superb on the Cambrian Coast line, which runs along the mountain-backed shoreline from Pwllheli to Machynlleth and Aberystwyth. And ask about the money-saving unlimited-travel Rover fares, some of which include the use of bus services.

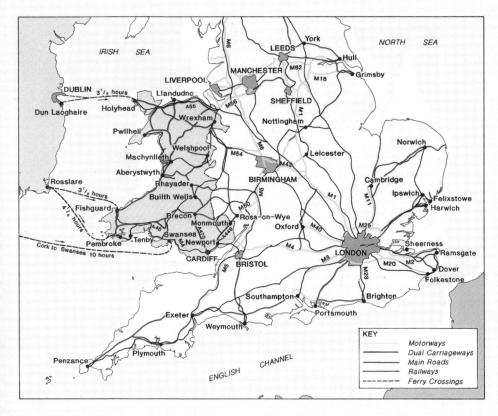

By coach

National Express provides a nationwide network of express coach services. Convenient services to Wales operate from London's Victoria Coach Station and from almost all other major towns and cities in England and Scotland.

Towns and resorts throughout Wales are, of course, connected by a whole range of local and regional services. Details from Tourist Information Centres and local bus stations. You can travel cross-country by the TrawsCambria services running between Cardiff and Bangor (via Aberystwyth) and Cardiff and Chester/Mold (via Llandrindod Wells). Within North and Mid Wales you can combine coach and rail services through unlimited-travel Rover tickets (see 'By rail' for details).

Further information

Please see 'Further Information' at the back of this guide for rail and coach travel offices, plus details of sea and air services to Wales.

The remainder of this guide is filled with a great choice of places to stay.

Where to Stay

It's not surprising that bed and breakfasting in Wales is so popular. It's friendly. It's flexible. And it's great value for money. You'll not pay more than £19 per person per night for any B&B featured in this guide – and in most cases, the price is considerably less.

The confidence factor

There's a great choice of places to stay. And you can choose in confidence, because the accommodation featured – from the remotest farmhouse to the largest hotel – has been thoroughly checked out by a visit from one of our inspectors. Not only that, but we also spell out clearly the quality and standards for you.

Making the grade

Grades are your guide to QUALITY. In determining them, our inspectors take into account standards of comfort, service, food, atmosphere and so on.

Approved – Good

Commended – Very good

Highly Commended – Excellent

De Luxe – A special accolade representing exceptional comfort and service

How well equipped is it?

You'll also want to know about the range of FACILITIES, EQUIPMENT and SERVICES on offer. Crowns have all the answers.

☐ (Listed) Clean and comfortable accommodation usually with washbasins in all bedrooms

≋ Better equipped accommodation, with a wider range of facilities including lounge area

≋≋ A more extensive range of facilities and services, including early morning tea/coffee and calls

≋≋≋ The facilities and services increase. At least 50% of bedrooms have en-suite WC and bath or shower, and evening meal must be served

≋≋≋≋ An even wider range of facilities and services. At least 90% of bedrooms en-suite, with colour TV, radio and telephone in all bedrooms

≋≋≋≋≋ An extensive range of facilities and services, including room service, night porter and laundry service. All bedrooms en-suite

Please note: Crowns are not a measure of quality. A lower Crown classification does not imply lower standards in comparison to an establishment with more Crowns. Further information on the Crown and grading schemes is available from the Visitor Services Unit, Wales Tourist Board, Davis Street, Cardiff CF1 2FU.

Accommodating wheelchair users

The Wales Tourist Board actively encourages the provision of facilities for disabled visitors. Properties are visited on request to assess their suitability.

◖ Accessible to a wheelchair user travelling independently

◖◖ Accessible to a wheelchair user travelling with assistance

◖◖◖ Accessible to a wheelchair user able to walk a few paces and up a maximum of three steps

All relevant establishments are identified by the ♿ symbol and access grade. For further details, please see 'Information for visitors with disabilities' at the back of this guide.

If you want extra-special guest house or farmhouse accommodation then choose a place which has won a Wales Tourist Board Award. Award-winning establishments are supremely comfortable and welcoming – they're as good as many a hotel

Please note: All classifications and gradings were correct at the time of going to press. Inspections are on-going and improvements made by establishments may have resulted in a revised classification or grade since publication. Please check when booking.

Making Your Booking

Book direct

Telephone or write to the place of your choice direct. It's as simple as that. If you phone, please check the prices and follow up the call with a letter of confirmation enclosing whatever deposit you've agreed with the proprietor.

TICs for travellers

If you're out and about in Wales and looking for a place to stay, then use the Bed Booking Service available through the network of Tourist Information Centres. This free service can arrange accommodation for you either locally or further afield. See the TIC list at the back of this guide for more details.

Prices

There's nothing more expensive in this guide than a per person price of £19 a night. You'll find that most rates quoted are even less.

Single rates are for ONE PERSON in a single room. Double rates are for TWO PEOPLE sharing a double or twin room. There may be supplements for single occupancy of a double/twin room and private/bath shower.

All prices quoted include VAT at the current rate (17 1/2%). Prices and other specific holiday information in this guide were supplied to the Wales Tourist Board during June-September 1994. So do check all prices and facilities before confirming your booking.

Children stay free

Many hotels, guest houses and farmhouses offer free accommodation for children if sharing their parents' room (you only pay for their meals) – look out for the places with the C symbol in this guide. Even if the symbol isn't displayed, it's worth asking about child reductions, for most operators will offer discounts for children. Family holiday hotels, especially in major resorts, also cater for one-parent families.

Deposits

Most operators will ask for a deposit when a reservation is being made. Some establishments may request payment in advance of arrival.

Cancellation and insurance

When you confirm a holiday booking, please bear in mind that you are entering a legally binding contract which entitles the proprietor to compensation if you fail to take up the accommodation. It's always wise to arrange holiday insurance to cover you for cancellation and other unforeseen eventualities. If you have to alter your travel plans, always advise the holiday operator or proprietor immediately.

Don't forget Phoneday!

On 16 April 1995, all area codes starting with 0 will change to 01. Inner London, for example, changes from 071 to 0171, Cardiff from 0222 to 01222.

Looking after your best interests

Whilst we are confident that your stay in Wales will be a success, there may be an occasion when your holiday accommodation does not meet expectations. In the unlikely event of this happening, please advise the owner or manager without delay, so that your grievances can be dealt with immediately. Proprietors welcome the chance to keep their guests happy. It is always very difficult for any problem to be resolved once the guest has left the accommodation.

Key to symbols

H	Hotel
GH	Guest House
FH	Farmhouse
⌘	Total number of bedrooms
⬥	Number of en-suite bedrooms
AWARD	Recipient of the Wales Tourist Board Guest House and Farmhouse Award
●	Welcome Host (Minimum of 50% of staff trained)
P	Private car parking/garage facilities at establishment
🐕	Dogs/pets accepted into establishment by arrangement
C	Children under 12 accommodated free if sharing parents' room (meals charged extra)
⚱	Liquor licence
⽊	Cots and high chairs provided – please check when booking
⬛	Central heating throughout
✁	Areas provided for non-smokers
✗	Totally no-smoking establishment
☕	Tea/coffee making facilities in all bedrooms
❍	Evening meals available by prior arrangement
TW	'Taste of Wales' member
⚒	Establishment is a working farm
T	Bookable through travel agents
♿	Accommodation is graded for access by wheelchair users
⇌	Railway Station

Please note: The symbols, together with the descriptive wording in the following accommodation advertisements, have been provided by the proprietors.

Using This Guide

It's easy to find your way around this guide. The rest of the book is filled with 'where to stay' information
presented as follows. First, we divide the accommodation up into three main regions –
North Wales, Mid Wales, and **South and West Wales** – which are colour coded.
Each region is then divided into smaller areas so that you can turn immediately to the specific part of
Wales that interests you (see the map and index below).

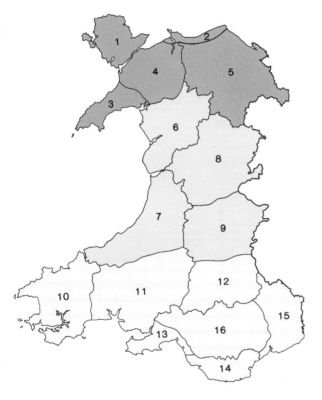

North Wales

1 Isle of Anglesey

2 North Wales Coast Resorts

3 Llŷn – Snowdon's Peninsula

4 Snowdonia Mountains and Coastline

5 Clwyd Countryside and Heritage

Mid Wales

6 Meirionnydd

7 Ceredigion

8 Montgomeryshire

9 Heart of Wales

South and West Wales

10 Pembrokeshire

11 The Coastline and Vales of Dyfed

12 Brecon and the Beacons

13 Swansea Bay, Mumbles and Gower

14 Cardiff and the South Wales Coast

15 Vale of Usk and Wye Valley

16 South Wales Valleys

Within each individual area, the resorts, towns and villages are listed alphabetically.
Each place has a map reference enabling you to pinpoint it on the detailed gridded maps
at the back of the book.

This region has it all –
colourful and calm seashores, green hills and rugged
highlands, big beaches and tiny coves.

Porthdinllaen on the Llŷn Peninsula

North Wales

Families love the North Wales coast for its string of popular resorts, superb sands and up-to-the-minute attractions. Fans of the great outdoors head for the Snowdonia National Park, a spectacular upland area formed by the highest mountains in England and Wales. Those in search of the quieter style of seaside holiday make for the beautiful Isle of Anglesey, or the cliff-backed coves of the Llŷn Peninsula.

Dominant in the landscape is the Snowdonia National Park, a highland expanse of mountains, moors, lakes and wooded valleys. Further east, bordered by the lovely Vales of Conwy and Clwyd, are the lonely, heather-clad Hiraethog Moorlands, the Clocaenog Forest and the dramatic waters of Llyn Brenig. And rising above the lush Vale of Clwyd like silent guardians are the smooth, rounded hills of the Clwydian Range, yet more magnificent walking countryside.

Much of the accommodation here is based along the coast – elegant Llandudno, in particular, has the largest selection of hotels in Wales. Other popular spots include Colwyn Bay, Rhyl and Prestatyn. Wooded Betws-y-Coed, medieval Ruthin and the mountain village of Beddgelert are amongst North Wales's many attractive inland destinations.

Ruthin

Wherever you choose to stay, coast or country, you'll find that everything's on your doorstep. You can spend the mornings in the mountains and the afternoons on the beach, go walking in the hills or fishing off the pier. North Wales is a compact region. But don't underestimate the amount of things to see and do here. The region is bursting with attractions – everything from castles to slate caverns, sea and mountain zoos to butterfly and farm parks.

17

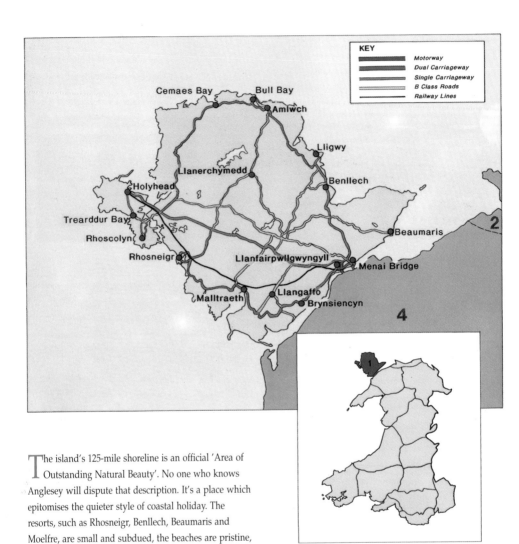

The island's 125-mile shoreline is an official 'Area of Outstanding Natural Beauty'. No one who knows Anglesey will dispute that description. It's a place which epitomises the quieter style of coastal holiday. The resorts, such as Rhosneigr, Benllech, Beaumaris and Moelfre, are small and subdued, the beaches are pristine, and the dunes and headlands are undisturbed save for the cry of seabirds.

Go to the cliffs of South Stack to see the island's coastline – and its prolific birdlife – at its most spectacular. At the opposite end of Anglesey, you'll find the spacious sands of Red Wharf Bay. Newborough is a strange area of forest, dune and sparkling sand. Cemaes Bay, the most northerly village in Wales, has the perfect sheltered harbour.

Anglesey's attractions and places to visit are as varied as its coastline. Call in at Llanfairpwllgwyngyll (this is just the abbreviated version of the world's longest placename!). And visit the National Trust's Plas Newydd, the award-winning Anglesey Sea Zoo, the Pili Palas Butterfly Farm and the island's many prehistoric sites.

Ae3 Beaumaris

Beautifully sited Anglesey coastal resort with splendid 13th-century castle. Other historic buildings along main street, Victorian Gaol, enchanting Museum of Childhood, fascinating old courthouse, and Beaumaris Marine World. Yachting centre with golf course and excellent fishing. 16th-century Penmon Priory nearby. Ideal touring centre for Snowdonia with superb views of mountains across Menai Strait.

Ad2 Benllech

Popular holiday village above a sweeping bay on Anglesey's east coast. 4 miles of good sands, swimming, sailing, bowls, walking. Nearby cliffs are rich in fossils. Visit the Rhuddlan Fawr Open Farm at nearby Brynteg

Ad4 Brynsiencyn

Anglesey hamlet near shores of Menai Strait, looking across to Snowdonia. Bodowyr Burial Chamber, Plas Newydd stately home, Anglesey Bird World, Anglesey Model Village, Foel farm Park, Bryntirion Open Farm, and award-winning Anglesey Sea Zoo all nearby.

Ac1 Cemaes Bay

Quaint unspoilt village with stone quay, boating, fishing and swimming on rugged northern shores of Anglesey. Wylfa Nuclear Power Station open to the public.

Aa2 Holyhead

Stands on Holy Island, linked by causeway to Anglesey. Port for Irish ferries. Roman remains and maritime museum in town. Sailing school. Sea angling, cliff and hill walking. Enjoy the sight of seabirds, coastal flora and the view from the cliffs to South Stack Lighthouse. RSPB centre located on cliffs. Penrhos Coastal Park on approach to the town.

Ac2 Llanerchymedd

Central Anglesey village with easy access to island's beaches. Visit Din Llugwy, prehistoric remains of fortified village, the working windmill at Llanddeusant and the Llyn Alaw Visitor Centre.

Ad3 Llanfairpwllgwyngyll

Famous for its 58-letter name of Llanfairpwllgwyngyllgogerychwyrndrobwllllantysilio-gogogoch, which means 'St Mary's church by the white aspen near the violent whirlpool and St Tysilio's church by the red cave'. Fine crafts centre with extensive choice of products. Plas Newydd stately home nearby. Marvellous views from the 90ft Marquess of Anglesey Column. Bryn Celli Ddu Burial Chamber.

Ac4 Llangaffo

On an Anglesey crossroads in the south-western corner of the island. Good birdwatching along Malltraeth Sands and Marsh, excellent, spacious beach at Newborough (drive through the forest), award-winning Anglesey Sea Zoo at Brynsiencyn.

Ad3 Menai Bridge

The first town motorists enter on Anglesey after crossing Telford's graceful Suspension Bridge (built in 1826) over the Menai Strait. Grand views of Snowdonia on mainland. Tegfryn Gallery has works by contemporary Welsh artists; Pili Palas Butterfly Farm and Anglesey Column nearby.

Aa3 Trearddur Bay

Most attractive holiday spot set amongst low cliffs on Holy Island near Holyhead. Golden sands, golf, sailing, fishing, swimming.

Benllech Bay, Isle of Anglesey

Beaumaris Benllech Brynsiencyn Cemaes Bay Holyhead

FH Plas Cichle

Beaumaris,
Isle of Anglesey,
Gwynedd LL58 8PS
Tel: (01248) 810488

AWARD · HIGHLY COMMENDED

This period farmhouse , on a 200 acre farm, offers accommodation in spacious double or family rooms, with private facilities, TV, clock/radio, hair-dryer and hospitality tray. Close to historic Beaumaris and many attractions. Only 30 minutes from Snowdonia. Enjoy the freedom of the farm and the tasty home-cooking. Relax in the friendly atmosphere of Plas Cichle. Brochure available.

P ⚡ 🍴	SINGLE PER PERSON B&B		DOUBLE FOR 2 PERSONS B&B		🛏 3 🛁 3
	MIN £ -	MAX £ -	MIN £ 36.00	MAX £ 38.00	OPEN 2-11

FH Tyddyn Goblet

Brynsiencyn,
Isle of Anglesey,
Gwynedd LL61 6TZ
Tel: (01248) 430 296

AWARD · HIGHLY COMMENDED

Character farmhouse set back 200 yards from A4080 road. Ground floor en-suite bedrooms with colour television and tea making facilities. Evening dinner optional. Attractive lounge and pleasant dining room with separate tables. Close to many of Anglesey's main attractions. Less than half an hour's drive from Snowdonia and the North Wales coast.. Brochure from Mrs M. Williams.

P 🐾	SINGLE PER PERSON B&B		DOUBLE FOR 2 PERSONS B&B		🛏 2 🛁 2
	MIN £ 14.00	MAX £ 16.00	MIN £ 28.00	MAX £ 32.00	OPEN 1-12

GH Grenville

2 Plashyfryd Mews,
Plas Road,
Holyhead,
Isle of Anglesey,
Gwynedd LL65 2AA
Tel: (01407) 762361
Fax: (01407) 762361

L

Situated 5 minutes from railway and ferry terminal. We will collect all late arrivals from railway or ferry terminal. All rooms TV, wash hand basin, tea/coffee facilities. Private off road car parking.

P 🐾	SINGLE PER PERSON B&B		DOUBLE FOR 2 PERSONS B&B		🛏 3 🛁 -
	MIN £ 15.00	MAX £ 18.00	MIN £ 25.00	MAX £ 30.00	OPEN 1-12

GH Woodlands Guest House

Bangor Road,
Benllech,
Isle of Anglesey,
Gwynedd LL74 8PU
Tel: (01248) 852735

HIGHLY COMMENDED

An Edwardian house furnished in period style. Warm and welcoming, your room is individually decorated and has a private bathroom, tea-making facilities and remote control TV. Guests are requested not to smoke in bedrooms. There is a licensed bar, with a good bar menu. Large garden and car park. Open all year.

P ⚡	SINGLE PER PERSON B&B		DOUBLE FOR 2 PERSONS B&B		🛏 6 🛁 6
	MIN £ -	MAX £ -	MIN £ 34.00	MAX £ 38.00	OPEN 1-12

H Woburn Hill Hotel

High Street,
Cemaes Bay,
Isle of Anglesey,
Gwynedd LL67 0HU
Tel: (01407) 711388

Small friendly hotel 5 minutes from beaches and old fishing harbour. Home cooked meals. En-suite rooms with colour television, centrally heated. Beverage facilities, licensed bar and restaurant. Good bar menu with local fish dishes. Ideal for fishing and water sports, golf, bird watching, walking or just relaxing. Parking for cars and boat. Open all year round.

P ⚡	SINGLE PER PERSON B&B		DOUBLE FOR 2 PERSONS B&B		🛏 5 🛁 5
	MIN £ -	MAX £ -	MIN £ 32.00	MAX £ 35.00	OPEN 1-12

GH Oaklands

12 London Road,
Holyhead,
Isle of Anglesey,
Gwynedd LL65 2NW
Tel: (01407) 769348

L APPROVED

Mid terrace Georgian style house two minutes from ferry terminal and Holyhead station. Good food, pleasant accommodation, friendly relaxed atmosphere. Open twenty four hours. Vegetarians welcome. Parking spaces available. Tea/coffee facilities, wash hand basin, television and central heating in all rooms. A warm welcome awaits you.

🐾	SINGLE PER PERSON B&B		DOUBLE FOR 2 PERSONS B&B		🛏 4 🛁 -
	MIN £ 12.50	MAX £ 12.50	MIN £ 25.00	MAX £ 25.00	OPEN 1-12

GH Fron Guest House

Brynsiencyn,
Isle of Anglesey,
Gwynedd LL61 6TX
Tel: (01248) 430310

HIGHLY COMMENDED

Comfortable traditional B&B in centrally heated farmhouse. Peaceful off road situation with magnificent views. Ideal location for both Anglesey and Snowdonia. Many tourist attractions, beaches, golf and fishing nearby. Tea/coffee, TV's in all rooms. Sunlounge; patio with outdoor heated swimming pool in summer. Ample safe parking. Several pubs and restaurants nearby for evening meals.

P	SINGLE PER PERSON B&B		DOUBLE FOR 2 PERSONS B&B		🛏 a 🛁 1
	MIN £ 14.00	MAX £ 14.00	MIN £ 27.00	MAX £ 30.00	OPEN 3-11

GH Bryn Awel

Edmund Street,
Holyhead,
Isle of Anglesey,
Gwynedd LL65 1SA
Tel: 01407 762948

L

Friendly comfortable family run guest house centrally situated, five minutes walk car ferry, five minutes shops. TV lounge, hot and cold water, tea making facilities in all rooms. Sandy beaches nearby, golf course one mile, day trips Ireland. Good home cooking, pleasant family atmosphere, hospitality guaranteed, children welcome. Ideal for journey break en-route to Ireland.

P 🍴	SINGLE PER PERSON B&B		DOUBLE FOR 2 PERSONS B&B		🛏 3 🛁 -
	MIN £ 12.00	MAX £ 14.00	MIN £ 24.00	MAX £ 26.00	OPEN 1-12

GH Roselea

26 Holborn Road,
Holyhead,
Isle of Anglesey,
Gwynedd LL65 2AT
Tel: (01407) 764391

L

Homely guest house five minutes from ferry, station, beaches and golf course. Walking distance town centre. Good home cooking. Hot and cold water, tea/coffee facilities and TV in bedrooms. Guest lounge. Also catering for early and late ferry travellers. Packed lunches available. All rooms furnished to a high standard. Proprietor Mrs S. Foxley.

🍴	SINGLE PER PERSON B&B		DOUBLE FOR 2 PERSONS B&B		🛏 3 🛁 -
	MIN £ 16.00	MAX £ 16.00	MIN £ 24.00	MAX £ 30.00	OPEN 1-12

Holyhead Llanerchymedd Llanfairpwllgwyngyll Llangaffo Menai Bridge Trearddur Bay

---

GH | Tan-y-Cytiau Country Guest House

South Stack Road,
Holyhead,
Isle of Anglesey,
Gwynedd LL65 1YH
Tel: (01407) 762763

HIGHLY COMMENDED

Country house peacefully situated in 3 acres of lovely gardens on slopes of Holyhead mountain, with magnificent views from all rooms. Ideal for walking and bird watching. Adjacent to RSPB reserve. Good sailing facilities in large sheltered harbour. Excellent 18 hole golf course nearby. Convenient for ferry to Ireland. Write or telephone for brochure.

P ⚲ 〠 🛏 🍴 🍽	SINGLE PER PERSON B&B		DOUBLE FOR 2 PERSONS B&B		🛏 7
	MIN £	MAX £	MIN £	MAX £	OPEN
	17.00	19.00	34.00	38.00	3-9

FH | Trer'ddol Farm

Llanerchymedd,
Isle of Anglesey,
Gwynedd LL71 7AR
Tel: (01248) 470278
Fax: (01248) 470276

AWARD   HIGHLY COMMENDED

Welcome to peace and paradise at this historic 17th century former manor house. A 200 acre working farm where guests' comfort is a priority and food a speciality. Spacious en-suite rooms with TV, beverage facilities and heating. Cosy lounge. Dinner optional. Free pony rides. Centrally situated 6 miles from Llangefni on the B5109 to Holyhead. Irish ferry 20 minutes. Stamp for brochure.

P 🐕 ⚲ 🛏 T	SINGLE PER PERSON B&B		DOUBLE FOR 2 PERSONS B&B		🛏 3
	MIN £	MAX £	MIN £	MAX £	OPEN
	19.00	19.00	36.00	38.00	1-11

GH | Bryn Aethwy

Menai Bridge,
Isle of Anglesey,
Gwynedd LL59 5HS
Tel: (01248) 712228
Fax: (01248) 716844

Bryn Aethwy is the perfect venue for a holiday or break, being so perfectly situated. The house is charming, friendly and every aspect is taken to a high level of quality. Visitors come back year after year to sample our hospitality and wonderful breakfasts. All rooms en-suite, tea/coffee making facilities. Non-smoking please. Car park.

P 〠 🛏 🍴 TW	SINGLE PER PERSON B&B		DOUBLE FOR 2 PERSONS B&B		🛏 3
	MIN £	MAX £	MIN £	MAX £	OPEN
	19.00	19.00	34.00	38.00	1-12

GH | Wavecrest

93 Newry Street,
Holyhead,
Isle of Anglesey,
Gwynedd LL65 1HU
Tel: (01407) 763637

COMMENDED

Situated in a quiet location yet only two minutes from ferry terminal, town centre and yards from beach. Ideal for break journey en-route to or from Ireland. Late arrivals, early departures welcome. All rooms furnished to high standard with tea making facilities, colour satellite TV, radio alarms. Large family en-suite available, children welcome. AA Recommended.

P 🐕 〠 🛏 🍴 T	SINGLE PER PERSON B&B		DOUBLE FOR 2 PERSONS B&B		🛏 4
					🛏 2
	MIN £	MAX £	MIN £	MAX £	OPEN
	13.00	16.00	25.00	32.00	1-12

GH | Carreg Goch

Llanedwen,
Llanfairpwllgwyngyll,
Isle of Anglesey,
Gwynedd LL61 6EZ
Tel: (01248) 430315

Carreg Goch, adjacent National Trust property of Plas Newydd, stands back from A4080 and is surrounded by 4 acres of gardens. 2 ground floor bedrooms have tea-making facilities, hot and cold and separate toilets. Both have central heating, share a private patio and have glorious views to Snowdonia. There is a guest bath/shower room and TV lounge. Convenient beaches and mountains. Brochure: Mrs Kirkland.

P 🐕 〠 🛏 ⚲ 🍴	SINGLE PER PERSON B&B		DOUBLE FOR 2 PERSONS B&B		🛏 2
	MIN £	MAX £	MIN £	MAX £	OPEN
	-	-	28.00	28.00	4-10

GH | Bwthyn

Brynafon,
Menai Bridge,
Isle of Anglesey,
Gwynedd LL59 5HA
Tel: (01248) 713119

HIGHLY COMMENDED

Just two warm, welcoming, beautifully fitted en-suite double rooms in century-old terrace close to Menai Strait, and Snowdonia and 1 mile from A5/A55 Expressway, 2 miles rail / coaches. Full, varied traditional breakfasts or delicious healthy alternative - fresh fruit, whole grain bread, cereals, yoghurt, luscious Welsh preserves, with real coffee. Come as guests - leave as friends. Positively non-smoking.

〠 ⚲ 🍴	SINGLE PER PERSON B&B		DOUBLE FOR 2 PERSONS B&B		🛏 2
					🛏 2
	MIN £	MAX £	MIN £	MAX £	OPEN
	-	-	24.00	30.00	1-12

FH | Drws y Coed

Llanerchymedd,
Isle of Anglesey,
Gwynedd LL71 8AD
Tel: (01248) 470473

AWARD   HIGHLY COMMENDED

With wonderful panoramic views of Snowdonia, this beautifully appointed farmhouse on a 550 acre working farm (beef, sheep, arable), is situated in peaceful wooded countryside in the centre of Anglesey. Comfortable en-suite bedrooms with TV, clock-radio, hair-dryer and beverage facilities. Central heating, log fire. Delicious meals, games room. Lovely private walks. Visitors return year after year.

P 〠 ⚲ 🍴 TW 🐕	SINGLE PER PERSON B&B		DOUBLE FOR 2 PERSONS B&B		🛏 3
					🛏 3
	MIN £	MAX £	MIN £	MAX £	OPEN
	19.00	19.00	34.00	38.00	1-11

FH | Plas Llangaffo

Llangaffo,
Isle of Anglesey,
Gwynedd LL60 6LR
Tel: (01248) 440452

L

Peaceful location situated near Newborough forest and Llanddwyn Bay with its miles of golden sand. Dinner, bed and breakfast per person £130.00 per week. Children under 10 half price. Horse riding available. Free range eggs and home-made marmalade for breakfast. "Taste of Wales" member. Use us as a base to visit Ireland. Phone David or Ann for brochure.

P 🐕 〠 🍴 T ⚲	SINGLE PER PERSON B&B		DOUBLE FOR 2 PERSONS B&B		🛏 5
	MIN £	MAX £	MIN £	MAX £	OPEN
	14.00	14.00	28.00	28.00	1-12

GH | Moranedd Guest House

Trearddur Road,
Trearddur Bay,
Isle of Anglesey,
Gwynedd LL65 2UE
Tel: (01407) 860324

Moranedd is a lovely house with a sun patio overlooking the 3/4 acre garden. Only five minutes stroll to the beach, shops, restaurants, sailing and golf clubs. The bedrooms are large, with wash basins and tea-making facilities. Residents' lounge with colour TV. AA, RAC Listed.

P 〠 ⚲ 🍴	SINGLE PER PERSON B&B		DOUBLE FOR 2 PERSONS B&B		🛏 6
	MIN £	MAX £	MIN £	MAX £	OPEN
	14.00	15.00	28.00	30.00	1-12

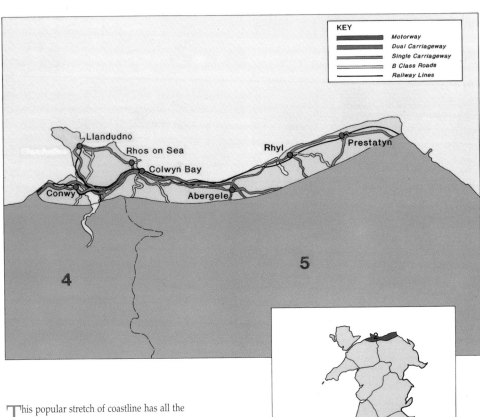

This popular stretch of coastline has all the ingredients for entertainment-packed or relaxing seaside holidays. Llandudno, the dignified 'Queen' of the Welsh resorts, preserves a period charm now rarely found at the seaside. Its wide promenade, pier, wealth of Victorian architecture and magnificent setting between two headlands give it a unique personality. But don't think that the resort is stuck in the 19th century – its many attractions include a cabin lift, copper mines and ski slope.

On the other hand, we could say that neighbouring Conwy is essentially a 13th-century town (especially since it is now by-passed by through traffic). Dominated by its mighty castle and ring of ancient walls, Conwy is undoubtedly one of Britain's best-preserved medieval towns.

The sands, which begin at Llandudno, stretch all the way to Prestatyn. Colwyn Bay and Rhyl are perennially popular family resorts. Overlooking Colwyn Bay's superb beach is the famous Welsh Mountain Zoo. Rhyl's colourful seafront is bursting with attractions – its Sun Centre and lofty Skytower to name but two. And there's a similar family appeal at Prestatyn, where attractions include the Nova Centre.

Bd4 Abergele

Convenient centre, located between Colwyn Bay and Rhyl, for exploring the popular coastal resorts. Wooded walks nearby, 18-hole golf course, livestock market. Miles of sand at nearby Pensarn.

Bc4 Colwyn Bay

Bustling seaside resort with large sandy beach. Promenade amusements. Good touring centre for Snowdonia. Leisure centre, Eirias Park, Dinosaur World, famous Mountain Zoo with Chimpanzee World. Puppet theatre. Golf, tennis, riding and other sports. Quieter Rhos on Sea at western end of bay.

Bb4 Conwy

Historic town with mighty castle and complete ring of medieval town walls. Dramatic estuary setting. Many ancient buildings including Aberconwy House. Telford Suspension Bridge, popular fish quay, spectacular wall walks. Golf, pony trekking, Butterfly House, aquarium, pleasure cruises. Tiny 'smallest house' on quay. Touring centre for Snowdonia.

Bb3 Llandudno

Premier coastal resort of North Wales with everything the holidaymaker needs. Two beaches, spacious promenade, Victorian pier, excellent shopping. Donkey rides, Punch and Judy, ski slope, Alice in Wonderland exhibition, art gallery, museum, old copper mines open to the public, splendid North Wales Theatre. Visit the Great Orme headland above the resort and ride by cabinlift or tramway. Conference centre. Many daily coach excursions.

Be3 Prestatyn

Family seaside resort on popular North Wales coast. Entertainment galore at superb Nova Centre including heated swimming pools and aquashute. Sailing, swimming on long, sandy coastline. Close to pastoral Vale of Clwyd and Clwydian Range.

Bb3 Rhos on Sea

Attractive seaside village linking Llandudno and Colwyn Bay with promenade, beach, golf, water-skiing, puppet theatre. Colwyn Bay Mountain Zoo nearby.

View of Llandudno from Little Orme

Abergele   Colwyn Bay   Conwy

GH | The Haven Guest House

Towyn Road,
Belgrano,
Abergele,
Clwyd LL22 9AB
Tel: (01745) 823534

Cliff and Barbara Pilley welcome you to the Haven, a friendly guest house with single, double and family rooms, central heating, hot and cold water, shaver points and tea and coffee making facilities (all ingredients supplied). Lounge with colour TV. Dining room has separate tables. Access to rooms and lounge at all reasonable times.

P, ▯, T, 🐕		SINGLE PER PERSON B&B		DOUBLE FOR 2 PERSONS B&B		🛏 4 -
		MIN £ 13.00	MAX £ 13.00	MIN £ 24.00	MAX £ 24.00	OPEN 1-12

GH | Crossroads Guest House

15 Coed Pella Road,
Colwyn Bay,
Clwyd LL29 7AT
Tel: (01492) 530736

Crossroads guest house is in the centre of all the wonders of North Wales. Mountains, lakes, fast flowing rivers, forests and a stunning coastline with castles, stately homes, narrow gauge railways, and the underground world of slate mines to explore and be thrilled by, in this land of myths and legends. AA QQ.

▯, 🐕		SINGLE PER PERSON B&B		DOUBLE FOR 2 PERSONS B&B		🛏 5 2
		MIN £ 12.00	MAX £ 16.00	MIN £ 24.00	MAX £ 32.00	OPEN 1-12

GH | Church House

HIGHLY COMMENDED

Llanbedr-y-Cennin,
Conwy Valley,
Gwynedd LL32 8JB
Tel: (01492) 660 521

Lovely 16th century listed building with oak beams and inglenook fireplaces. Central heating, TV, hot and cold water and tea trays in its two double bedrooms. Situated in a small village complete with 16th century inn in the Snowdonia foothills just off the B5106 between Conwy and Betws-y-Coed. Ideal for Bodnant Garden, sightseeing, walking, coast etc.

P, ▯🔥, 🍴		SINGLE PER PERSON B&B		DOUBLE FOR 2 PERSONS B&B		🛏 2
		MIN £ -	MAX £ 19.00	MIN £ -	MAX £ 34.00	OPEN 1-12

H | Grosvenor Hotel

🅛

106-108 Abergele Road,
Colwyn Bay,
Clwyd LL29 7PS
Tel: (01492) 531586

Centrally situated close to leisure centre and park, only a delightful short walk to the beach. Licensed dining room and olde worlde bar, games room and TV lounge. All bedrooms have TV, radio, intercom, tea and coffee facilities, hot and cold water and shaver points. Large private car park in front of hotel.

P, 🏆, 👤, 🍴, T		SINGLE PER PERSON B&B		DOUBLE FOR 2 PERSONS B&B		🛏 18 2
		MIN £ 16.90	MAX £ 17.90	MIN £ 33.80	MAX £ 35.80	OPEN 1-12

FH | Bryn Car Farm

COMMENDED

Betws-yn-Rhos,
Abergele,
Clwyd LL22 8DB
Tel: (01492) 680605

17th century farmhouse in peaceful surroundings ³⁄₄ mile from village, four miles from coast at Colwyn Bay and Abergele. Easy reach of Conwy, Llandudno. Ideal for touring. All bedrooms have wash basin, tea and coffee making facilities. Separate toilet and shower room. Oak beamed lounge with inglenook fireplace. Separate tables in dining room. Central heating. Pony trekking and golf nearby.

P, ▯, 🚜, T		SINGLE PER PERSON B&B		DOUBLE FOR 2 PERSONS B&B		🛏 3 -
		MIN £ -	MAX £ -	MIN £ 30.00	MAX £ 32.00	OPEN 4-10

GH | Glan Heulog Guest House

Llanrwst Road,
Conwy,
Gwynedd LL32 8LT
Tel: (01492) 593845

Close to Conwy Castle and historic walled town. An ideal centre for touring Snowdonia, North Wales coast, and Bodnant Garden. Colour TV in all bedrooms. Traditional home cooking. Our guests say "wonderful meals, great rooms", "excellent service", "charming hosts", "lovely warm welcome", "we will be back". Ask about our winter breaks and romantic weekends. Welsh spoken.

P, ▯, ✂, 🍴		SINGLE PER PERSON B&B		DOUBLE FOR 2 PERSONS B&B		🛏 7 4
		MIN £ 13.00	MAX £ 16.00	MIN £ 26.00	MAX £ 30.00	OPEN 1-12

H | Whitehall Hotel

HIGHLY COMMENDED

Cayley Promenade,
Rhos on Sea,
Colwyn Bay,
Clwyd LL28 4EP
Tel: (01492) 547296

*Small select family run hotel on lovely Cayley Promenade. Ideal location to tour North Wales. Renowned for our excellent cuisine and friendliness. Lovely sea view patio. Sandy beach only yards away. Llandudno, Betws-y-Coed, Conwy, all within easy reach. Car park. Packed lunches available, licensed bar, sea view lounge. A55 Expressway very close. AA** RAC Merit Award.*

P, 🏆, ✂, 🍴, ▯, 👤		SINGLE PER PERSON B&B		DOUBLE FOR 2 PERSONS B&B		🛏 13 7
		MIN £ 16.50	MAX £ 19.00	MIN £ 33.00	MAX £ 38.00	OPEN 3-11

GH | Bryn Derwen

Woodlands,
Conwy,
Gwynedd LL32 8LT
Tel: (01492) 596134

Your host and hostess offer a friendly welcome to their spacious Victorian home. Good beds, good food, good views and a comfortable environment make an excellent base for exploring Snowdonia. Your hosts will be happy to supply some local knowledge of history and legends and exciting routes. Bryn Derwen is on the B5106 approximately 800 yards from Conwy's castle.

P, ▯, ✂, 🍴, T		SINGLE PER PERSON B&B		DOUBLE FOR 2 PERSONS B&B		🛏 5 1
		MIN £ 14.00	MAX £ 18.00	MIN £ 28.00	MAX £ 33.00	OPEN 2-11

GH | Pen-y-Bryn Tearooms

🅛
HIGHLY COMMENDED

Lancaster Square,
Conwy,
Gwynedd LL32 8DE
Tel: (01492) 596445

Guests are once again invited to sample Pen-y-Bryn's own brand of hospitality and comfort, on offer above their unique 16th century tea rooms, Egon Ronay Recommended. All bedrooms have central heating, colour TV, hair dryer and beverage facilities. Two rooms have en-suite shower and WC. Non smoking throughout. Private car parking available nearby.

P, ▯, 🐕, 👤		SINGLE PER PERSON B&B		DOUBLE FOR 2 PERSONS B&B		🛏 3 2
		MIN £ 15.00	MAX £ 19.00	MIN £ 30.00	MAX £ 38.00	OPEN 1-12

North Wales Coast Resorts

Conwy   Llandudno

FH | Henllys Farm

Llechwedd,
Conwy,
Gwynedd LL32 8DJ
Tel: (01492) 593269

HIGHLY COMMENDED

In the heart of beautiful countryside ideally placed for touring Snowdonia, North Wales coast, Bodnant Garden, and Anglesey. 1¹/₂ miles from Conwy. Twin/double, family bedrooms with en-suite, tea/coffee making facilities. TV lounge, good home cooking from fresh local produce. A warm welcome awaits you from Mrs Ceinwen Roberts.

P IIII ¶OI T	🐾 👤 🏍	SINGLE PER PERSON B&B	DOUBLE FOR 2 PERSONS B&B	🛏 2 🛁 2
		MIN £ 18.00	MAX £ 19.00	MIN £ 30.00	MAX £ 36.00	OPEN 2-11

H | Carmel Private Hotel

17 Craig-y-Don Parade,
Promenade,
Llandudno,
Gwynedd LL30 1BG
Tel: (01492) 877643

COMMENDED

Carmel welcomes you to a family run hotel situated in a prime position on the main promenade. Twin bedded ground floor en-suite bedroom, all other rooms on two floors only. Six en-suite rooms plus three standard rooms. Colour TV, tea/coffee making facilities in all rooms. Excellent home cooking, separate tables in dining room.

P IIII 👤 ¶OI	🐾 👤	SINGLE PER PERSON B&B	DOUBLE FOR 2 PERSONS B&B	🛏 9 🛁 6
		MIN £ 13.50	MAX £ 18.50	MIN £ 27.00	MAX £ 32.00	OPEN 4-10

H | Lynton House Hotel

80 Church Walks,
Llandudno,
Gwynedd LL30 2HD
Tel: (01492) 875057

HIGHLY COMMENDED

A small homely hotel fifty yards from the pier. Close to shops, ski-ing and all amenities. All rooms are decorated to a high standard with en-suite bathroom, colour TV, tea/coffee tray and telephone. Highly recommended home cooking with choice of menu. Vegetarian and special diets catered for. Four poster room available. Car park.

P C IIII ¶OI	🐾 👤 👤	SINGLE PER PERSON B&B	DOUBLE FOR 2 PERSONS B&B	🛏 11 🛁 11
		MIN £ 19.00	MAX £ 19.00	MIN £ 38.00	MAX £ 38.00	OPEN 1-12

H | Ashby

31 Church Walks,
Llandudno,
Gwynedd LL30 2HL
Tel: (01492) 875608
Fax: (01492) 875608

HIGHLY COMMENDED

Attractive Victorian detatched house now a comfortable family run licensed hotel. Located between both shores in quiet tree-lined road close to Great Orme and amenities. Excellent home cooked food, varied menu. Spacious rooms with en-suite facilities, colour TV, beverage makers. All bedrooms no smoking. Centrally heated. A warm welcome awaits you at the Ashby.

P IIII 👤 ¶OI T	¶ 👤	SINGLE PER PERSON B&B	DOUBLE FOR 2 PERSONS B&B	🛏 7 🛁 7
		MIN £ 16.50	MAX £ 18.50	MIN £ 33.00	MAX £ 37.00	OPEN 4-9

H | Cliffbury Hotel

34 St Davids Road,
Llandudno,
Gwynedd LL30 2UH
Tel: (01492) 877224

HIGHLY COMMENDED

Non-smoking, quietly situated in garden area. En-suites available. Colour TV, tea/coffee facilities, car parking, family rooms, good food, special diets, separate tables in dining room. Close to beaches, shops, mountains, castles. Central heating in winter. Access to rooms all day. High repeat clientele. Perfect for touring, walking, climbing. Personal attention at all times.

P IIII ¶OI T	🐾 👤	SINGLE PER PERSON B&B	DOUBLE FOR 2 PERSONS B&B	🛏 9 🛁 5
		MIN £ 13.00	MAX £ 19.00	MIN £ 26.00	MAX £ 38.00	OPEN 1-12

H | Plas Madoc Private Hotel

60 Church Walks,
Llandudno,
Gwynedd LL30 2HL
Tel: (01492) 876514

A homely "no smoking" hotel run by Kathy and Nigel Lawrence. With the number of guests limited to twelve adults, a high standard of service and comfort is assured. All rooms are fully en-suite and have colour TV and beverage facilities. Superbly situated within easy walking distance of town, promenade and other attractions. Car park.

P IIII 👤 ¶OI T	¶ 👤	SINGLE PER PERSON B&B	DOUBLE FOR 2 PERSONS B&B	🛏 6 🛁 6
		MIN £ 18.00	MAX £ 18.00	MIN £ 36.00	MAX £ 36.00	OPEN 3-10

H | Beach House Hotel

82 Church Walks,
Llandudno,
Gwynedd LL30 2HD
Tel: (01492) 877933
Fax: (01492) 877277

A family run hotel giving personal service. Colour TV with video and satellite channels in all rooms. Car parking. Residential licence. Close to pier, shopping centre, ski slope, Great Orme tram and most of Llandudno's major attractions. South facing with sunny aspect for a really warm welcome in Wales. Phone Sue for more details.

P 👤 IIII ¶OI	🐾 👤	SINGLE PER PERSON B&B	DOUBLE FOR 2 PERSONS B&B	🛏 9 🛁 9
		MIN £ 16.00	MAX £ 18.00	MIN £ 32.00	MAX £ 36.00	OPEN 1-12

H | Karden House Hotel

16 Charlton Street,
Llandudno,
Gwynedd LL30 2AA
Tel: (01492) 879347/879990

COMMENDED

Conveniently situated for beach, shops and station. Vera and Des Steward provide friendly caring service, fresh home cooking, vegetarian/allergy diets catered for. Tea/coffee, central heating, en-suite available. Licensed bar. Separate lounge. Open Christmas. Reductions OAP's, children. Ideally situated for visiting scenic beauty spots and activities on Great Orme. Ski-ing, toboggan run, cable car, tram.

👤 IIII ¶OI T	🐾 👤	SINGLE PER PERSON B&B	DOUBLE FOR 2 PERSONS B&B	🛏 10 🛁 3
		MIN £ 12.00	MAX £ 13.50	MIN £ 24.00	MAX £ 27.00	OPEN 1-12

H | Seaclyffe Hotel

11 Church Walks,
Llandudno,
Gwynedd LL30 2HG
Tel: (01492) 876803

A family run hotel with a warm and friendly atmosphere. Close to all amenities. 27 bedrooms all en-suite with colour TV and tea/coffee makers. Sun lounge. Pleasant garden. Licensed bar. Dance floor. Entertainment 3 nights. Heating in all rooms. Excellent home cooking with a varied choice of menu.

👤 C IIII ¶OI	🐾 👤	SINGLE PER PERSON B&B	DOUBLE FOR 2 PERSONS B&B	🛏 27 🛁 27
		MIN £ 17.25	MAX £ 18.50	MIN £ 34.50	MAX £ 37.00	OPEN 2-12

Llandudno Prestatyn Rhos on Sea

H | Sunnycroft Private Hotel

4 Claremont Road,
Llandudno,
Gwynedd LL30 2UF
Tel: (01492) 876802

HIGHLY COMMENDED

Delightfully situated, friendly family run licensed hotel, located in a flat area, near all amenities, beaches and promenade. Traditional home cooking, special diets catered for. All rooms have remote control colour TV, radio alarm and hair dryer. En-suite facilities include ground floor accommodation. We have been highly commended by Wales Tourist Board for our excellent food and service.

SINGLE PER PERSON B&B		DOUBLE FOR 2 PERSONS B&B		🛏 9
				9
MIN £	MAX £	MIN £	MAX £	OPEN
14.00	18.00	28.00	36.00	1-12

GH | Tŷ Glandŵr

42 St Marys Road,
Llandudno,
Gwynedd LL30 2UE
Tel: (01492) 871802

HIGHLY COMMENDED

Elegant Edwardian house within easy level walking distance of shops, beaches and public transport. Close to several fine golf courses. Warm friendly welcome throughout the year. Colour TV, central heating and tea/coffee making facilities in all rooms. For further information please contact Mrs Cynthia Beesley.

SINGLE PER PERSON B&B		DOUBLE FOR 2 PERSONS B&B		🛏 3
				-
MIN £	MAX £	MIN £	MAX £	OPEN
14.00	15.00	25.00	28.00	1-12

H | Cabin Hill Hotel

College Avenue,
Rhos on Sea,
Clwyd LL28 4NT
Tel: (01492) 544568

COMMENDED

We would like to welcome you to our friendly hotel. Situated on level ground, 150 yards from promenade in a quiet residential area. Licensed. Most rooms en-suite, colour television, tea/coffee facilities, cental heating. Breakfast, six course evening dinner. Write or phone for brochure. Mr and Mrs Edwards proprietors since 1970.

SINGLE PER PERSON B&B		DOUBLE FOR 2 PERSONS B&B		🛏 10
				7
MIN £	MAX £	MIN £	MAX £	OPEN
16.50	19.00	33.00	38.00	4-9

GH | Dolwen Guest House

7 St Marys Road,
Llandudno,
Gwynedd LL30 2UB
Tel: (01492) 877757

HIGHLY COMMENDED

Situated within easy reach of beach, shops and new North Wales Theatre, Dolwen is a family run guest house highly recommended by guests. All bedrooms are en-suite with colour TV, clock radio, tea/coffee making facilities. Home comforts with lounge with colour TV. Special diets catered for. Write or phone for colour brochure.

SINGLE PER PERSON B&B		DOUBLE FOR 2 PERSONS B&B		🛏 3
				3
MIN £	MAX £	MIN £	MAX £	OPEN
-	-	-	30.00	4-10

GH | Winston Guest House

5 Church Walks,
Llandudno,
Gwynedd LL30 2HD
Tel: (01492) 876144

COMMENDED

Family run for the past 23 years. 80 yards from the pier. Close to ski slope and shopping centre. Colour TV, tea/coffee facilities in all bedrooms. Full central heating. Evening meal provided, choice of menu. Different diets catered for. Comfortable lounge with colour television. No restrictions. AA Listed.

SINGLE PER PERSON B&B		DOUBLE FOR 2 PERSONS B&B		🛏 7
				7
MIN £	MAX £	MIN £	MAX £	OPEN
17.00	18.00	32.00	35.00	1-12

GH | The Cedar Tree

27 Whitehall Road,
Rhos on Sea, Colwyn Bay,
Clwyd LL28 4HW
Tel (01492) 545867

COMMENDED

Comfortable friendly guest house, 300 yards promenade, convenient Snowdonia, Conwy, Llandudno, Caernarfon, Bodnant Garden. Rail and coach stations one mile. All bedrooms en-suite, centrally heated, tea/coffee facilities, family rooms, reduction children sharing parents' room. Private parking. Separate tables. Attractive lounge with colour television. Fire certificate. Weekly terms available. Non-smoking throughout. Excellent breakfast. Sorry no evening meals.

SINGLE PER PERSON B&B		DOUBLE FOR 2 PERSONS B&B		🛏 7
				7
MIN £	MAX £	MIN £	MAX £	OPEN
15.00	18.00	30.00	36.00	1-12

GH | Stoneleigh Guest House

10 St Davids Road,
Llandudno,
Gwynedd LL30 2UL
Tel: (01492) 875056

COMMENDED

Family run homely guest house situated in residential area on level close to all amenities. All bedrooms with Sky TV and tea/coffee facilities. Central heating throughout. High standard of cuisine, separate tables in dining room. Established sixteen years. Ample parking. Ideal centre for touring Snowdonia.

SINGLE PER PERSON B&B		DOUBLE FOR 2 PERSONS B&B		🛏 7
				1
MIN £	MAX £	MIN £	MAX £	OPEN
-	17.00	-	30.00	1-12

GH | Roughsedge Guest House

26/28 Marine Road,
Prestatyn,
Clwyd LL19 7HD
Tel: (01745) 887359
Fax: (01745) 887359

COMMENDED

Family run establishment, close to beaches, Pontins Presthaven Sands, Nova complex, golf, bowls and Offa's Dyke. Pleasant rooms, some en-suite, all with colour TV, tea/coffee facilities and clock radios. Home cooking, choice of menu, special diets, residential licence. Centrally heated, open lounge fire. Handy for rail and bus services and town centre. Children welcome. Credit cards accepted. AA.

SINGLE PER PERSON B&B		DOUBLE FOR 2 PERSONS B&B		🛏 10
				3
MIN £	MAX £	MIN £	MAX £	OPEN
14.00	-	28.00	36.00	1-12

GH | Sunnyside

146 Dinerth Road,
Rhos on Sea,
Colwyn Bay,
Clwyd LL28 4YF
Tel: (01492) 544048

L

A warm Welsh welcome awaits you at our comfortable home situated in Rhos on Sea adjacent to Colwyn Bay and Llandudno offering ample shopping facilities, miles of excellent coastline and within easy driving distance of the mountains of Snowdonia. Lovely country views from our home with good home cooked breakfast to start off your day and excellent value accommodation.

SINGLE PER PERSON B&B		DOUBLE FOR 2 PERSONS B&B		🛏 2
				-
MIN £	MAX £	MIN £	MAX £	OPEN
12.50	12.50	25.00	25.00	1-12

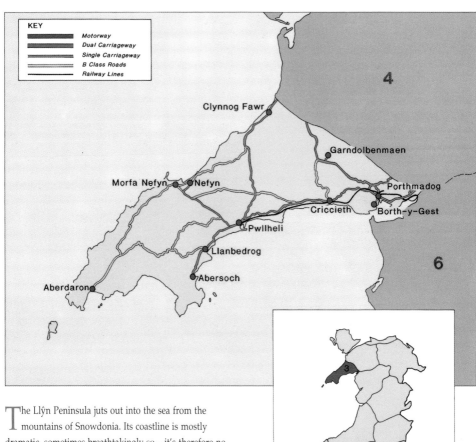

The Llŷn Peninsula juts out into the sea from the mountains of Snowdonia. Its coastline is mostly dramatic, sometimes breathtakingly so – it's therefore no surprise to discover that Llŷn's shores have been declared an 'Area of Outstanding Natural Beauty'.

Llŷn's narrow finger of land points towards Ireland. And it's to the west that Llŷn sets its sights, for the peninsula retains a traditional, almost Celtic atmosphere. You sense it when exploring the wildly beautiful coastline, or when gazing across patchwork fields studded with old farmsteads.

It's a place where the culture is in tune with the landscape. Llŷn clings firmly to its Welsh ways, but it also has a long tradition of welcoming visitors. Criccieth, for example, is a charming little castle-crowned resort which has been popular since Victorian times. Further

along the south coast there's Pwllheli, another well-established resort close to the exciting Starcoast World leisure complex. Abersoch, further south again, is a popular sailing centre, Aberdaron stands at the spectacular 'Land's End' of North Wales, and Nefyn, on the north coast, boasts an excellent choice of sandy beaches.

Ac5   Abersoch

Dinghy sailing and windsurfing centre with sandy beaches. Superb coastal scenery with easy walks. Pony trekking, golf, fishing and sea trips. Llanengan's historic church nearby.

Ab6   Morfa Nefyn

Popular north Llŷn seaside village, with extensive sandy beaches, between little harbour of Porthdinllaen and resort of Nefyn. Set against mountainous backdrop of Garn Boduan. Historical and Maritime Museum at Nefyn.

Ad7   Criccieth

Ideal family resort with good beach. Romantic ruined castle on headland overlooking sea. Salmon and trout in nearby rivers and lakes. Festival of Music and the Arts in June. Village of Llanystumdwy with Lloyd George Museum nearby.

Ae7   Porthmadog

Harbour town and shopping centre named after William Madocks, who built mile-long Cob embankment. Steam narrow-gauge Ffestiniog Railway runs to Blaenau Ffestiniog, with its slate caverns. Also Welsh Highland Railway. Pottery, maritime museum, car museum. Portmeirion Italianate village and good beaches nearby.

Ad6   Garndolbenmaen

Small hillside village high above the sea, 4 miles from Criccieth. Nearby woollen mill to visit and excellent walking. Good base for touring Llŷn Peninsula and Snowdonia.

Porthdinllaen, on the Llŷn Peninsula

Abersoch Criccieth Garndolbenmaen Morfa Nefyn Porthmadog

GH | Llysfor Guest House

Abersoch,
Near Pwllheli,
Gwynedd LL53 7AL
Tel: (01758) 712248

COMMENDED

A well established family run guest house, our aim is to please and make your stay enjoyable. Hot and cold water, shaver points, tea/coffee facilities in all bedrooms. Some en-suite rooms. Comfortable dining room, separate lounge with TV, licensed. One minute to beach, overlooking harbour. Private parking, own grounds. Fire certificate. Reduced rates for children. Enquiries Mr A. Hiorns.

	SINGLE PER PERSON B&B	DOUBLE FOR 2 PERSONS B&B		8
	MIN £	MAX £	MIN £	MAX £	OPEN
	13.50	17.50	27.00	35.00	4-10

(icons: P, dog, knife/fork, bed, T; open 4-10; 8 / 2)

H | Min y Gaer Hotel

Porthmadog Road,
Criccieth,
Gwynedd LL52 0HP
Tel: (01766) 522151
Fax: (01766) 522151

COMMENDED

A pleasant licensed hotel, conveniently situated near the beach with delightful views of Criccieth Castle and the Cardigan Bay coastline. Ten comfortable, centrally heated rooms, all with colour TV and tea/coffee making facilities. An ideal base for touring Snowdonia and the Llŷn Peninsula. Reduced rates for children. Car parking on premises. RAC Acclaimed. AA Recommended.

	SINGLE PER PERSON B&B	DOUBLE FOR 2 PERSONS B&B		10
	MIN £	MAX £	MIN £	MAX £	OPEN
	17.00	-	34.00	-	3-10

(icons: P, C, knife/fork, bed; open 3-10; 10 / 9)

GH | Llys Olwen

Morfa Nefyn,
Gwynedd LL53 6BT
Tel: (01758) 720493

Small family owned guest house established for 23 years. Situated along quiet country lane. Lovely beaches, shooting, fishing, golf, watersports nearby. Home cooking, special diets catered for with pleasure. Licensed to serve wine only.

	SINGLE PER PERSON B&B	DOUBLE FOR 2 PERSONS B&B		8
	MIN £	MAX £	MIN £	MAX £	OPEN
	16.00	16.00	32.00	32.00	4-10

(icons: P, bed, plate; open 4-10; 8)

H | Abereistedd Hotel

West Parade,
Criccieth,
Gwynedd LL53 0EN
Tel: (01766) 522710

COMMENDED

Family run hotel on the quiet west front of Criccieth, with beautiful sea and mountain views. We are within easy reach of Snowdonia and the Ffestiniog and Welsh Highland Railways, local golf course and fishing. En-suite bedrooms with TV, tea-trays and sea views. Comfortable lounge, cosy bar and licensed dining room. AA/RAC.

	SINGLE PER PERSON B&B	DOUBLE FOR 2 PERSONS B&B		12
	MIN £	MAX £	MIN £	MAX £	OPEN
	17.50	19.00	35.00	38.00	3-10

(icons: P, dog, knife/fork, bed, plate; open 3-10; 12 / 7)

H | Neptune Hotel

Min y Mor,
Criccieth,
Gwynedd LL52 0EF
Tel: (01766) 522794/522878/522802

Large sea front bedrooms overlooking Cardigan Bay and 100 miles of coastline. All rooms en-suite with hospitality trays and colour TV. Established over 20 years by Williams family and noted for good food and friendliness. Warm Welsh welcome. Croeso cynnes Cymraeg.

	SINGLE PER PERSON B&B	DOUBLE FOR 2 PERSONS B&B		6
	MIN £	MAX £	MIN £	MAX £	OPEN
	17.00	-	-	-	1-12

(icons: dog, C, bed, TW, T, plate; open 1-12; 6 / 6)

GH | The Oakleys Guest House

The Harbour,
Porthmadog,
Gwynedd LL49 9AS
Tel: (01766) 512482

L

Situated on the harbour in Porthmadog. An excellent base for visiting Snowdonia, Portmeirion and the beaches of the Llŷn Peninsula, taking in Pwllheli, Abersoch and Criccieth. Fishing sea trout, salmon, golf course nearby. Spacious free car park. Comfortable lounge, informal holiday atmosphere, 2 bedrooms with showers, one en-suite bedroom. Electric blankets. Contact Mr & Mrs H. A. Biddle.

	SINGLE PER PERSON B&B	DOUBLE FOR 2 PERSONS B&B		8
	MIN £	MAX £	MIN £	MAX £	OPEN
	14.00	15.00	26.00	30.00	3-10

(icons: P, dog, bed; open 3-10; 8 / 1)

H | Glyn y Coed Hotel

Portmadog Road,
Criccieth,
Gwynedd LL52 0HL
Tel: (01766) 522870
Fax: (01766) 523341

HIGHLY COMMENDED

Lovely Victorian house overlooking sea, mountains, castle. Cosy bar, highly recommended home cooking catering for most diets. En-suite bedrooms with colour TV, tea-making facilities. Ground floor bedroom in annexe. Private parking. Children and seniors rates available. AA/RAC Acclaimed. Credit cards. Self-catering bungalow sleeps 8 plus cot. Brochure with pleasure, SAE please.

	SINGLE PER PERSON B&B	DOUBLE FOR 2 PERSONS B&B		10
	MIN £	MAX £	MIN £	MAX £	OPEN
	19.00	-	38.00	-	1-12

(icons: dog, C, knife/fork, bed, plate, T; open 1-12; 10 / 10)

FH | Bryn Efail Uchaf Farm

Bryn Efail Uchaf,
Garndolbenmaen,
Gwynedd LL51 9LQ
Tel: (01766) 530232

Traditional stone built farmhouse on working beef and sheep farm. En-suite family room, home with private bathroom. Shaver points, hospitality tray. Lounge with colour television. Enjoy a taste of farm life with excellent food and comfortable accommodation. An ideal base for exploring the Llŷn Peninsula or Snowdonia. Criccieth 5 miles, Porthmadog 6 miles, Caernarfon 12 miles.

	SINGLE PER PERSON B&B	DOUBLE FOR 2 PERSONS B&B		2
	MIN £	MAX £	MIN £	MAX £	OPEN
	13.00	15.00	26.00	30.00	4-10

(icons: P, bed, plate; open 4-10; 2 / 2)

Porthmadog

GH	Skellerns

35 Madoc Street,
Porthmadog,
Gwynedd LL49 9BU
Tel: (01766) 512843

Friendly welcome for all. Good home cooking, heating in all rooms. Colour TV and tea/coffee making facilities in all bedrooms. Keys supplied. Special rates for children. Shops, buses, trains, cinema nearby. Ideally situated for visiting Portmeirion Italianate Village, the mountains of Snowdonia and the Ffestiniog Railway. Sandy beaches nearby. Open all year. Proprietor Mrs. R. Skellern.

	SINGLE PER PERSON B&B		DOUBLE FOR 2 PERSONS B&B		4
	MIN £ 12.00	MAX £ 13.00	MIN £ 24.00	MAX £ 26.00	OPEN 1-12

GH	Ty-Newydd Guest House

30 Dublin Street,
Tremadog,
Porthmadog,
Gwynedd LL49 9RH
Tel: (01766) 512553

Family bedroom, two double, one twin. Private car park. All facilities. Tremadog is one mile from Porthmadog and is central to all parts of North Wales. Ample sea and river fishing. Golf, pony trekking, rock exploration, miles of sandy beaches and Ffestiniog and Snowdon railways.

	SINGLE PER PERSON B&B		DOUBLE FOR 2 PERSONS B&B		3
	MIN £ 14.00	MAX £ -	MIN £ 28.00	MAX £ -	OPEN 1-12

Porthmadog harbour

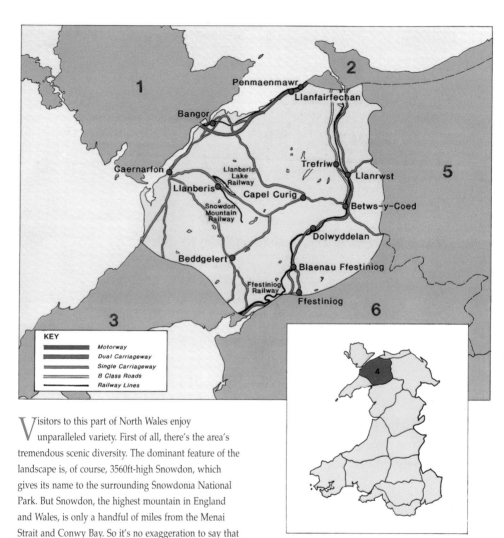

Visitors to this part of North Wales enjoy unparalleled variety. First of all, there's the area's tremendous scenic diversity. The dominant feature of the landscape is, of course, 3560ft-high Snowdon, which gives its name to the surrounding Snowdonia National Park. But Snowdon, the highest mountain in England and Wales, is only a handful of miles from the Menai Strait and Conwy Bay. So it's no exaggeration to say that you can be standing on Snowdon's summit in the morning, and in the afternoon enjoy a view of the sea from Bangor's beautifully renovated Victorian pier.

There's also a huge choice of places to visit. The list – a long one – includes Caernarfon Castle, the National Trust's Penrhyn Castle, Llanberis's narrow-gauge railways and museums, Beddgelert's Sygun Copper Mine, and two popular attractions at Blaenau Ffestiniog, the Llechwedd Slate Caverns and the Gloddfa Ganol Slate Mine.

Variety is again the keynote when deciding where to stay. Choose the mountain resorts of Betws-y-Coed, Llanberis or Beddgelert. Or stay along the coast at Penmaenmawr, Llanfairfechan, Bangor or Caernarfon.

31

Ae3   Bangor

Compact cathedral city of character overlooking the Menai Strait; gateway to Anglesey and Snowdonia's Ogwen Valley, with university college and 6th-century cathedral. Attractions include Theatr Gwynedd, Penrhyn Castle, museum and art gallery and an exquisitely renovated pier. Heated swimming pool, yachting and fishing.

Ba7   Blaenau Ffestiniog

One-time centre of the Welsh slate industry, now a tourist town with two cavernous slate quarries - Llechwedd and Gloddfa Ganol - open to visitors. Narrow-gauge Ffestiniog Railway runs from Porthmadog. Nearby Stwlan Dam, part of hydro-electric scheme, reached through marvellous mountain scenery. Visitor centre explains how electricity is generated.

Ae6   Beddgelert

Village romantically set amid glorious mountain scenery, with Nant Gwynant Valley to the east and rocky Aberglaslyn Pass to the south. Snowdonia's grandeur all around; Wordsworth made a famous dawn ascent of Mount Snowdon from here. Marvellous walks; links with legendary dog named Gelert. Visit Sygun Copper Mine and Cae Du Farm Park, two nearby attractions.

Caernarfon Castle

Bb6   Betws-y-Coed

Wooded village and popular mountain resort in picturesque setting where three rivers meet. Good touring centre, close to best mountain area of Snowdonia. Tumbling rivers and waterfalls emerge from a tangle of treetops. Trout fishing, craft shops, golf course, railway and motor museums, Snowdonia National Park Visitor Centre. Nature trails very popular with hikers. Swallow Falls a 'must'.

Ad4   Caernarfon

Dominated by magnificent 13th-century castle, most famous of Wales's medieval fortress. Many museums in castle, maritime museum in town. Caernarfon Air World at Dinas Dinlle, Segontium Roman Fort and Museum on hill above town. Popular sailing centre, old harbour, market square, Lloyd George statue. Holiday centre at gateway of Snowdonia. Parc Glynllifon nearby.

Nant Gwynant near Beddgelert

Snowdon Mountain Railway

Ba6   Capel Curig

Village ringed by Snowdonia's highest mountains. Great favourite with climbers. Good walking and fishing. Craft shops.

Ae4   Llanberis

Popular centre for walkers and climbers, least difficult (5 miles) walk to Snowdon summit starts here. For easy ride up take Snowdon Mountain Railway. Many things to see and do in this lively mountain town - Llanberis Lake Railway, slate industry museum. Power of Wales interpretive centre with unforgettable trip into the awesome tunnels of the Dinorwig Hydro-Electric Scheme, activity-packed Padarn Country Park, ancient Dolbadarn Castle, Bryn Brâs Castle at nearby Llanrug.

Bb6   Llanrwst   🚆

Attractive town where the crystal-clear River Conwy runs through lush meadows; chief shopping centre of upper Conwy Valley. Handsome bridge designed by Inigo Jones in 1636. Gwydir Park has bowling, putting and children's playground. Charming Gwydir Uchaf chapel and scenic Llyn Geirionydd in woodlands above town. Gwydir Castle open to the public. Bodnant Garden 8 miles away.

Bb5   Trefriw

Woollen mill village on western side of Conwy Valley, with Trefriw Wells Spa. Lakes at Llyn Geirionydd and Llyn Crafnant, both local beauty spots. Good walking country.

Bangor   Beddgelert

H   The British Hotel

High Street,
Bangor,
Gwynedd LL57 1NP
Tel: (01248) 364911
Fax: (01248) 370569

COMMENDED

Bangor's largest hotel within easy reach of Anglesey, Snowdonia and Holyhead sea link to Ireland. Golf, sailing, swimming pool available nearby. The hotel has comfortable lounge, cocktail bar, buttery bar, carvery. Car park, night porter, lift to en-suite bedrooms, all with colour television, trouser press and hospitality tray. Conference facilities. Special Christmas programme.

P C ▥ T ⚲	SINGLE PER PERSON B&B		DOUBLE FOR 2 PERSONS B&B		🛏 49 ⚲ 49
	MIN £ 13.00	MAX £ 19.00	MIN £ 26.00	MAX £ 38.00	OPEN 1-12

GH   Rainbow Court

Pentir Square,
Pentir,
Near Bangor,
Gwynedd LL57 4UY
Tel: (01248) 353099

Delightful village just off B4366 close A5/A55. Close to golf, riding, walking, castles, seaside. Llanberis 5 miles, Caernarfon 6 miles, Bangor 5¹/₂ miles. Converted village store with attractive restaurant serving traditional and vegetarian food, diets catered for if advised. Potted village history available. Many lovely walks. Double/family room en-suite, twin with private facilities.

▥ C ▥ ⚲ ⛄	SINGLE PER PERSON B&B		DOUBLE FOR 2 PERSONS B&B		🛏 2 ⚲ 2
	MIN £ 13.00	MAX £ 18.00	MIN £ -	MAX £ -	OPEN 1-12

GH   Ael-y-Bryn

Caernarfon Road,
Beddgelert,
Gwynedd LL55 4YB
Tel: (01766) 890310

A detached house with beautiful views across the River Colwyn and Moel Hebog mountain. All rooms have vanity units with shaver point and tea/coffee making facilities. Packed lunches and good home cooked evening meals available. Vegetarians welcome. Ample free parking. A well situated family run house, ideal for holidays in the Snowdonia National Park.

P ▥ ⚲ ⛄ ⛄	SINGLE PER PERSON B&B		DOUBLE FOR 2 PERSONS B&B		🛏 3 ⚲ -
	MIN £ 17.00	MAX £ -	MIN £ 29.00	MAX £ 36.00	OPEN 1-12

GH   Nant y Fedw

Tre Felin,
Llandygai,
Near Bangor,
Gwynedd LL57 4LH
Tel: (01248) 351683

Bed and breakfast in charming beamed country cottage situated in countryside between mountains of Snowdonia and the sea. All rooms are of very high standard, en-suite with tea and coffee making facilities, radio alarm clock, hair dryer and keys. Use of sitting room with colour TV.

P ▥ ▥ ⚲ ⛄ T	SINGLE PER PERSON B&B		DOUBLE FOR 2 PERSONS B&B		🛏 2 ⚲ 2
	MIN £ 18.00	MAX £ 18.00	MIN £ 26.00	MAX £ 32.00	OPEN 1-12

FH   Goetre Isaf Farmhouse

Caernarfon Road,
Bangor,
Gwynedd LL57 4DB
Tel: (01248) 364541
Fax: (01248) 364541

COMMENDED

Superb country situation with magnificent views. Although isolated, Goetre Isaf is only 2 miles (3km) from Bangor mainline station. Ideal touring centre for the mountains of Snowdonia, Isle of Anglesey and the beaches of the Llŷn Peninsula. Imaginative farmhouse cooking, special diets accommodated and vegetarians welcome. "Taste of Wales" member. All bedrooms with dial phone facilities. Stabling by arrangement.

P ▥ ▥ ⚲ ⛄ T	SINGLE PER PERSON B&B		DOUBLE FOR 2 PERSONS B&B		🛏 3 ⚲ 1
	MIN £ 15.00	MAX £ -	MIN £ 26.00	MAX £ 36.00	OPEN 1-12

GH   Colwyn

Beddgelert,
Gwynedd LL55
Tel: (01766) 890276

Peaceful old riverside cottage-guest house in the centre of a beautiful and unspoilt village right at the foot of Snowdon. Surrounded by wooded mountains, lakes and streams. Warm and friendly, with an open stone hearth in the low-beamed lounge and small, pretty en-suite bedrooms. Walkers, muddy boots and exhausted dogs welcome. Mon-Fri four nights DB&B low season £112. B&B from £17. Booking usually advisable. Also tiny cottage, sleeps two, £150.

P ▥ ⚲ ⛄ ⛄	SINGLE PER PERSON B&B		DOUBLE FOR 2 PERSONS B&B		🛏 3 ⚲ 3
	MIN £ -	MAX £ -	MIN £ 34.00	MAX £ -	OPEN 1-12

GH   The Old Drovers Inn

Treborth Road,
Bangor,
Gwynedd LL57 2RZ
Tel: (01248) 362327

L

Situated on the outskirts of the university city of Bangor. Formerly old droving inn, within walking distance of Menai Strait and Telford's Menai Bridge. Central for Anglesey, castles, Snowdonia and ideal stop-over to/from Ireland. Friendly comfortable bed and breakfast. Wash hand basin, tea facility each room. Lounge with TV and log fire.

P C ▥ T	SINGLE PER PERSON B&B		DOUBLE FOR 2 PERSONS B&B		🛏 3 ⚲ -
	MIN £ 15.00	MAX £ 17.00	MIN £ 27.00	MAX £ 30.00	OPEN 1-12

GH   Plas Colwyn Guest House

Beddgelert,
Gwynedd LL55 4UY
Tel: (01766) 890458
Fax: (01766) 890514

Enjoy a warm welcome, whilst exploring Snowdonia's beauty. Delicious fresh home cooked meals served in our intimate licensed restaurant. Special diets and vegetarians welcome. Guests' private lounge with log fire, and non-smoking throughout. Families, walkers and pets welcome. Private parking. All rooms with refreshment facilities. Some en-suite rooms. Northern Section Organiser for Cambrian Way Walkers Association.

P C ▥ ⚲ ⛄	SINGLE PER PERSON B&B		DOUBLE FOR 2 PERSONS B&B		🛏 6 ⚲ 3
	MIN £ 15.00	MAX £ -	MIN £ 30.00	MAX £ 38.00	OPEN 1-12

34

Betws-y-Coed

H   Cross Keys Inn & Restaurant

Betws-y-Coed
Gwynedd LL23 0HJ
Tel: (01690) 710334

Charming well run family hotel dating back to the 14th century. Golf, fishing and pony trekking nearby. Most bedrooms en-suite. All have colour TV, central heating, tea/coffee facilities. Our restaurant is renowned for excellent food and value for money. Only fresh produce used throughout. Excellent bar food also available.

P ▮ ⊞ ⚲ ☕ ⦿	SINGLE PER PERSON B&B	DOUBLE FOR 2 PERSONS B&B	🛏 16 / 🛁 12
	MIN £ -	MAX £ -	MIN £ 27.00 MAX £ 37.00 OPEN 1-12

H   Princes Arms Hotel

Near Betws-y-Coed,
Trefriw,
Gwynedd LL27 0JP
Tel: (01492) 640592
Fax: (01492) 640592

Quiet location with easy access to all of Snowdonia's attractions. En-suite rooms. Private lounge. Beautiful views, full facilities including TV, beverages and telephone. Drying room, central heating. Enviable reputation for restaurant and bar meals. Real ales, packed lunches, attentive friendly service. Special break packages available. A rather nice place to find.

P 🐾 ▮ ⊞ ⦿ ⊤	SINGLE PER PERSON B&B	DOUBLE FOR 2 PERSONS B&B	🛏 14 / 🛁 12
	MIN £ 18.00 MAX £ 19.00	MIN £ 36.00 MAX £ 38.00	OPEN 1-12

GH   Bron Eirian

Town Hill,
Llanrwst,
Gwynedd `LL26 0NF
Tel: (01492) 641741

HIGHLY COMMENDED

An attractive Victorian country house in a peaceful elevated position overlooking the Conwy Valley and Snowdonia Mountains. Bron Eirian offers warm, comfy rooms, all en-suite and tastefully furnished with tea making facilities and TV. Hearty breakfast, dinner on request. Convenient for Bodnant Garden, Betws-y-Coed, Gwydyr Forest and coast. Station nearby. Be assured of a warm welcome.

P ⊞ ⚲ ⦿	SINGLE PER PERSON B&B	DOUBLE FOR 2 PERSONS B&B	🛏 3 / 🛁 3
	MIN £ -	MAX £ -	MIN £ 32.00 MAX £ 38.00 OPEN 1-12

H   Meadowsweet Hotel

Station Road,
Llanrwst,
Nr Betws-y-Coed,
Gwynedd LL26 0DF
Tel: (01492) 642111

Newly refurbished family run hotel and restaurant in the historic market town of Llanrwst, near Betws-y-Coed. 12 rooms all with full facilities. Ideally situated for touring. On the edge of beautiful Snowdonia and opposite the spectacular 20,000 acre Gwydir Forest Park with its countless lakes and endless walks in glorious scenery.

P 🐾 ▮ ⊞ ⚲ ⦿ ⊤	SINGLE PER PERSON B&B	DOUBLE FOR 2 PERSONS B&B	🛏 12 / 🛁 12
	MIN £ 19.00 MAX £ 19.00	MIN £ 35.00 MAX £ 38.00	OPEN 1-12

H   Swallow Falls Hotel

Betws-y-Coed,
Gwynedd LL24 0DW
Tel: (01690) 710796
Fax: (01690) 710796

COMMENDED

Situated just outside the picturesque village of Betws-y-Coed in the beautiful Snowdonia National Park nestling between the mountains and the sea. The hotel has 12 en-suite bedrooms with two licensed bars offering delicious home cooked food. Ideal base for walking and climbing! Don't miss our unique Welsh fudge pantry, see demonstrations and enjoy free tasting.

P 🐾 ▮ ⊞ ⚲ ⦿	SINGLE PER PERSON B&B	DOUBLE FOR 2 PERSONS B&B	🛏 12 / 🛁 12
	MIN £ -	MAX £ -	MIN £ 30.00 MAX £ 38.00 OPEN 1-12

GH   Bryn Llewelyn

Holyhead Road,
Betws-y-Coed,
Gwynedd LL24 0BN
Tel: (01690) 710601

COMMENDED

Welcome to Betws-y-Coed. Bryn Llewelyn is an attractive stone house near the centre of this beautiful Snowdonia National Park village. Restaurants, shops, riverside and forest walks close to our doorstep. Within easy reach of mountains, castles, slate mines, beaches etc. Comfortable rooms with central heating, tea/coffee, television on request. Guests' lounge. Ample car park. AA/RAC.

P 🐾 ⊞ ▮ ⚲ ⦿	SINGLE PER PERSON B&B	DOUBLE FOR 2 PERSONS B&B	🛏 7 / 🛁 2
	MIN £ 13.50 MAX £ 17.50	MIN £ 27.00 MAX £ 37.00	OPEN 1-12

H   Mount Garmon Hotel

Betws-y-Coed,
Gwynedd LL24 0AN
Tel: (01690) 710335

Small Victorian residential licensed hotel. Tastefully furnished. All rooms en-suite with colour TV and beverage facilities. Located on A5 in centre of village. An extensive breakfast is available. Floodlit private car park. The hotel is able to offer its own salmon and sea trout fishing on the famous River Conwy. Bird watching and photographic hide available

P 🐾 ▮ ⊞ ⚲ ⦿ ⊤	SINGLE PER PERSON B&B	DOUBLE FOR 2 PERSONS B&B	🛏 5 / 🛁 5
	MIN £ -	MAX £ -	MIN £ 30.00 MAX £ 36.00 OPEN 1-12

GH   Bron Celyn Guest House

Llanrwst Road,
Betws-y-Coed,
Gwynedd LL24 0HD
Tel: (01690) 710333

HIGHLY COMMENDED

Enjoy traditional comfort and good food in a relaxed atmosphere. Situated within Snowdonia National Park overlooking picturesque village of Betws-y-Coed. We provide the ideal base for walking, touring and exploring this interesting area. All rooms have colour TV and a beverage tray. Most rooms en-suite. Hearty breakfasts. Packed lunches, snacks, evening meals. Special diets by arrangement. Welcome!

P 🐾 ▮ ⚲ ⦿ ⊤	SINGLE PER PERSON B&B	DOUBLE FOR 2 PERSONS B&B	🛏 5 / 🛁 3
	MIN £ 16.00 MAX £ 16.00	MIN £ 36.00 MAX £ 38.00	OPEN 1-12

GH   Coed-y-Fron

Vicarage Road,
Betws-y-Coed,
Gwynedd LL24 0AD
Tel: (01690) 710365

A lovely Victorian building in middle of village in quiet elevated position, superb outlook over Betws-y-Coed which is the premier touring centre for Snowdonia. Dining room, lounge, 7 bedrooms, 2 en-suite plus 2 extra bathrooms. All have hot and cold water, central heating, tea and coffee, colour TV. Parking. Fire certificate held. Warm welcome awaits you.

🐾 ▮ ⚲ ⦿	SINGLE PER PERSON B&B	DOUBLE FOR 2 PERSONS B&B	🛏 7 / 🛁 2
	MIN £ 15.00 MAX £ 17.00	MIN £ 30.00 MAX £ 35.00	OPEN 1-12

Betws-y-Coed

GH | Eirianfa Guest House

15-16 Castle Road,
Dolwyddelan,
Gwynedd LL25 0NX
Tel: (01690) 6360

APPROVED

Homely guest house in Snowdonia National Park between Betws-y-Coed and Blaenau Ffestiniog. Relaxing guest lounge. Double or twin-bedded rooms. All en-suite, remote controlled satellite colour television, tea making facilities. Excellent home cooked meals, laundry/drying services. Central for touring Snowdonia, coastal resorts, slate mines etc. Ideal for trekking, hiking, climbing, fishing. Reductions: short breaks, weekly stay. Brochure awaiting.

		SINGLE PER PERSON B&B		DOUBLE FOR 2 PERSONS B&B			3
							3
		MIN £	MAX £	MIN £	MAX £	OPEN	
		-	-	24.00	28.00	1-12	

GH | Glan Llugwy

Holyhead Road,
Betws-y-Coed,
Gwynedd LL24 0BN
Tel: (01690) 710592

COMMENDED

Small friendly guest house overlooking River Llugwy and Gwydir Forest. Beautiful walking country all around. Central for Snowdonia Mountains and coast. All rooms have central heating, hot and cold water, tea/coffee making facilities, colour TV. Guests' lounge. Private parking. Fire certificate held. Family/double / twin rooms available. Showers. A warm welcome awaits you.

		SINGLE PER PERSON B&B		DOUBLE FOR 2 PERSONS B&B			5
							-
		MIN £	MAX £	MIN £	MAX £	OPEN	
		14.00	16.00	25.00	28.00	1-12	

GH | Ty'n-y-Celyn House

Llanrwst Road,
Betws-y-Coed,
Gwynedd LL24 0HD
Tel: (01690) 710202
Fax: (01690) 710800

HIGHLY COMMENDED

Ty'n-y-Celyn House is situated in a quiet position overlooking the popular and picturesque village. It is superbly and tastefully re-furnished with all facilities for comfort and relaxation. There are beautiful views of the Llugwy Valley, surrounding mountains and the Conwy and Llugwy rivers. Robust breakfast and warm welcome awaiting from Ann and Clive Muskus.

		SINGLE PER PERSON B&B		DOUBLE FOR 2 PERSONS B&B			8
							8
		MIN £	MAX £	MIN £	MAX £	OPEN	
		-	-	38.00	-	1-12	

GH | The Ferns Guest House

Holyhead Road,
Betws-y-Coed,
Gwynedd LL24 0AN
Tel: (01690) 710587

HIGHLY COMMENDED

Keith and Teresa Roobottom welcome you to their delightful Victorian non-smoking guest house in the heart of Snowdonia. There are eight bedrooms each tastefully furnished. Each one has colour TV, beverage tray, central heating and en-suite facilities. A delightful breakfast room where a varied menu awaits you. Car park a great asset in this popular village. AA qqq Recommended. RAC Acclaimed.

		SINGLE PER PERSON B&B		DOUBLE FOR 2 PERSONS B&B			9
							7
		MIN £	MAX £	MIN £	MAX £	OPEN	
		18.00	19.00	32.00	-	1-12	

GH | Riverside Restaurant & Guest House

Holyhead Road,
Betws-y-Coed,
Gwynedd LL24 0BN
Tel: (01690) 710650
Fax: (01690) 710650

L

We offer exceptional value for money accommodation. All rooms are centrally heated, clean and comfortable with television, tea and coffee making facilities. Our location is central for the whole of North Wales especially Snowdonia and Anglesey. Easy access by bus, rail and road. Credit cards accepted

		SINGLE PER PERSON B&B		DOUBLE FOR 2 PERSONS B&B			4
							1
		MIN £	MAX £	MIN £	MAX £	OPEN	
		11.00	16.00	18.00	26.00	1-12	

FH | The Cottage

Royal Oak Farm,
Betws-y-Coed,
Gwynedd LL24 0AH
Tel: (01690) 710760

An attractive stone farm cottage and buildings set in a sunny courtyard on the banks of the River Llugwy. The house is very close to the centre of Betws-y-Coed, yet quiet and secluded.

		SINGLE PER PERSON B&B		DOUBLE FOR 2 PERSONS B&B			3
							3
		MIN £	MAX £	MIN £	MAX £	OPEN	
		15.00	18.00	30.00	36.00	1-12	

GH | Fron Heulog Country House

Betws-y-Coed,
Gwynedd LL24 0BL
Tel: (01690) 710736

AWARD
HIGHLY COMMENDED

"The Country House in the Village!". Friendly welcome from Jean and Peter Whittingham to their elegant Victorian stone-built house in peaceful wooded riverside scenery. Snowdonia's ideal centre - tour, walk, relax. Excellent modern accommodation - comfort, warmth, style. Premium bedrooms have full en-suite bathrooms. "More home than hotel!" Croeso! Welcome!

		SINGLE PER PERSON B&B		DOUBLE FOR 2 PERSONS B&B			5
							5
		MIN £	MAX £	MIN £	MAX £	OPEN	
		19.00	-	28.00	38.00	1-12	

GH | Tan y Cyrau Guest House

Betws-y-Coed,
Gwynedd LL24 0BL
Tel: (01690) 710653

HIGHLY COMMENDED

Peace, quiet and glorious views are what to expect at Tan y Cryau. An elevated unique alpine style house situated on a private forestry road, only 5 minutes walk from village. Superb walks from house. Delightful rooms, two have own WC, all have colour TV, heating, washbasin, tea/coffee facilities. Lovely secluded garden. Non smokers only. Good parking.

		SINGLE PER PERSON B&B		DOUBLE FOR 2 PERSONS B&B			3
							1
		MIN £	MAX £	MIN £	MAX £	OPEN	
		15.00	15.00	26.00	35.00	1-12	

FH | Maes Gwyn Farmhouse

Pentrefoelas
Betws-y-Coed,
Gwynedd LL24 0LR
Tel: (01690) 770668

L
HIGHLY COMMENDED

Maes Gwyn is a 17th century farmhouse with oak beams and panelling. Separate lounge and dining room, both with coal and log fires. Situated in quiet countryside six miles from Betws-y-Coed, within easy reach of coast, Snowdonia, pony-trekking, slate mines, woollen mills etc. One double and one family room both with tea/coffee and hot and cold water.

		SINGLE PER PERSON B&B		DOUBLE FOR 2 PERSONS B&B			2
							-
		MIN £	MAX £	MIN £	MAX £	OPEN	
		13.00	14.50	26.00	29.00	3-11	

36

Betws-y-Coed   Blaenau Ffestiniog   Caernarfon

Wales: Castles and Historic Places

Beautifully produced full-colour guide to more than 140 historic sites

- Castles, abbeys, country houses, prehistoric and Roman remains
- Detailed maps

£7 inc. p&p

(see "Guide Books" page).

FH   Tyddyn Gethin Farm

Penmachno,
Betws-y-Coed,
Gwynedd LL24 0PS
Tel: (01690) 760392

Tyddyn Gethin farm is 200 yards off B406, 3¹/₂ miles from Betws-y-Coed and ¹/₂ mile from Penmachno. Lovely views from farmhouse. Clean and comfortable, good home cooking. Ideal for touring, very central. Dining room, separate tables, 2 sitting rooms, colour TV in one room. Bathroom with shower, hot and cold in bedrooms, shaver points, shower room. Ample parking. Always a warm welcome here.

SINGLE PER PERSON B&B		DOUBLE FOR 2 PERSONS B&B		3
MIN £	MAX £	MIN £	MAX £	OPEN
13.00	14.00	25.00	28.00	1-12

H   Bryn Eisteddfod Hotel

Clynnog Fawr,
Caernarfon,
Gwynedd LL54 5DA
Tel: (01286) 660431

HIGHLY COMMENDED

Situated 10 miles south of Caernarfon (A499) on the outskirts of Clynnog Fawr. All rooms have colour TV, tea/coffee facilities and afford beautiful sea or mountain views. Quiet location, one acre garden. Vegetarian meals available. Real ale. Family rooms, children welcome. 2 night breaks available D,B&B from £46 pp. Single room supplement £5 per person per night. Prices quoted relate to 2 rooms only.

SINGLE PER PERSON B&B		DOUBLE FOR 2 PERSONS B&B		10
				8
MIN £	MAX £	MIN £	MAX £	OPEN
-	-	34.00	38.00	1-12

FH   Maes y Garnedd Farm

Capel Garmon,
Llanrwst,
Gwynedd LL26 0RR
Tel: (01690) 710428

L APPROVED

A 140 acre mixed farm situated in Capel Garmon (2 miles off A5). Beautiful scenery and excellent walks. An ideal centre for touring Snowdonia and within easy reach of beaches. One double and one family bedroom. Children welcome. A warm and friendly welcome awaits you. Washbasins in bedrooms. Evening meal optional. AA Listed. SAE for brochure.

SINGLE PER PERSON B&B		DOUBLE FOR 2 PERSONS B&B		2
				1
MIN £	MAX £	MIN £	MAX £	OPEN
14.00	16.00	26.00	28.00	1-12

GH   Afallon

Manod Road,
Blaenau Ffestiniog,
Gwynedd LL41 4AE
Tel: (01766) 830468

HIGHLY COMMENDED

Family run guest house situated in Snowdonia National Park. Good food, clean homely accommodation. Washbasins, shaver point, colour TV, tea/coffee facilities, central heating all rooms. Separate shower, bathroom, toilet. Slate mines, narrow gauge railway, beaches within easy reach. Dinner by arrangement. Children reduced rates. A Welsh welcome awaits all guests. Mrs Griffiths.

SINGLE PER PERSON B&B		DOUBLE FOR 2 PERSONS B&B		3
				-
MIN £	MAX £	MIN £	MAX £	OPEN
12.00	14.00	24.00	28.00	1-12

H   Menai Bank Hotel

North Road,
Caernarfon,
Gwynedd LL55 1BD
Tel: (01286) 673297
Fax: (01286) 673297

HIGHLY COMMENDED

*Family owned period hotel with original features. Extensive sea views. Close to castle and Snowdonia. Tastefully decorated, comfortable bedrooms with colour television, tea maker, clock radio. Ground floor bedroom, attractive restaurant, varied menu, bar, residents' lounge, pool table. Car park, lawned flower gardens. Access, Visa, Amex. Short breaks, en-suite supplement. AA/RAC**. Colour brochure.*

SINGLE PER PERSON B&B		DOUBLE FOR 2 PERSONS B&B		15
				10
MIN £	MAX £	MIN £	MAX £	OPEN
-	-	29.00	36.00	1-11

FH   Ty Coch Farm and Trekking Centre

Penmachno,
Betws-y-Coed,
Gwynedd LL25 0HJ
Tel: (01690) 760248

COMMENDED

Set in lovely valley in hills six miles from Betws-y-Coed. Good centre for touring, walking, fishing, Snowdon, castles, narrow gauge railways, woollen mills, waterfalls. Trekking available. Short drive to coast. Many recommendations and return visits. Guests made very welcome. Good food and excellent accommodation. Full fire certificate.

SINGLE PER PERSON B&B		DOUBLE FOR 2 PERSONS B&B		4
				4
MIN £	MAX £	MIN £	MAX £	OPEN
15.00	16.00	30.00	32.00	1-12

GH   Gwynfryn

Gellilydan,
Blaenau Ffestiniog,
Gwynedd LL41 4EA
Tel: (01766) 85225

Situated in Snowdonia National Park. Friendly welcome assured. Family run guest house in quiet situation between Ffestiniog and Porthmadog off A470 in village of Gellilydan. Slate mines, Ffestiniog Railway, castles, walks, beaches within easy reach. Many recommendations and return visits. All bedrooms with washbasin, shaver point, tea/coffee facilities, central heating. TV lounge. Good food, homely welcome.

SINGLE PER PERSON B&B		DOUBLE FOR 2 PERSONS B&B		2
				-
MIN £	MAX £	MIN £	MAX £	OPEN
12.50	13.50	25.00	27.00	1-11

GH   The Menai View Hotel

North Road,
Caernarfon,
Gwynedd LL55 1BD
Tel: (01286) 674602

COMMENDED

Victorian town house overlooking beautiful Menai Strait. All rooms have central heating, colour TV, tea/coffee facilities. Some rooms sea views, some en-suite. Ground floor en-suite bedroom. Close to town centre. Excellent base for castles, mountains, lakes and railways of Snowdonia, local beaches, Llŷn Peninsula and Anglesey. Many attractions. Open all year. Sporting activities nearby. AA/RAC.

SINGLE PER PERSON B&B		DOUBLE FOR 2 PERSONS B&B		8
				3
MIN £	MAX £	MIN £	MAX £	OPEN
16.00	19.00	25.00	35.00	1-12

Caernarfon   Capel Curig   Llanberis

GH Caer Siddi

Llanddeiniolen,
Caernarfon,
Gwynedd LL55 3AD
Tel: (01248) 670462

AWARD — HIGHLY COMMENDED

Former Georgian vicarage in a peaceful rural setting with glorious views to Snowdon, Caernarfon Bay and the Rivals. Ideally situated for Gwynedd attractions, being 4 miles from Caernarfon town on the B4366. Fully modernised, warm spacious accommodation. TV lounge. Children price reduction. Farmhouse breakfast, 3 course evening meals, home baking. Tea/coffee making facilities. Fire certificate. Private parking, walled garden.

	SINGLE PER PERSON B&B	DOUBLE FOR 2 PERSONS B&B	🛏 2 / -
MIN £ 14.00	MAX £ 14.00	MIN £ 28.00 / MAX £ 28.00	OPEN 4-10

GH Tyn Llwyn Cottage

Llanllyfni,
Caernarfon,
Gwynedd LL54 6RP
Tel: (01286) 881526

Situated on a quiet country road, half a mile off the A487 Caernarfon to Porthmadog road, beautiful Welsh stone cottage with exposed beams and attractive garden. Ideal for walking, castles, beach, bird watching. We have two en-suite bedrooms, one on ground floor, one bedroom with private bathroom, all with colour TV. Tea/coffee made when requested.

	SINGLE PER PERSON B&B	DOUBLE FOR 2 PERSONS B&B	🛏 3 / 2
MIN £ -	MAX £ -	MIN £ 37.00 / MAX £ 38.00	OPEN 3-10

GH Llugwy Guest House

Capel Curig,
Betws-y-Coed,
Gwynedd LL24 0ES
Tel: (016904) 218
From May 1995 Tel: (01690) 720218

COMMENDED

Established over 100 years, located in centre of village, five miles from Snowdon. Ideal for walking, climbing, fishing, boating, beaches, small trains, castles, ski slope. Two public lounges, one with TV, beamed dining room, central heating. Tea/coffee facilities in bedrooms. Superb mountain views. Private car park. Friendly advice on the local area if required.

	SINGLE PER PERSON B&B	DOUBLE FOR 2 PERSONS B&B	🛏 6 / -
MIN £ 15.50	MAX £ 18.00	MIN £ 27.00 / MAX £ 30.00	OPEN 1-12

GH Chatham Farmhouse

Llandwrog,
Caernarfon,
Gwynedd LL54 5TG
Tel: (01286) 831257

AWARD — HIGHLY COMMENDED

Croeso, welcome to our quiet, friendly guest house on the fringe of Snowdonia. Enjoy a lazy breakfast and a relaxing dinner cooked with home-grown organic vegetables and free-range eggs. Beach two miles. Good birdwatching area. Within easy reach of Anglesey, Llŷn Peninsula, Caernarfon four miles. Family room available.

	SINGLE PER PERSON B&B	DOUBLE FOR 2 PERSONS B&B	🛏 4 / 2
MIN £ 16.00	MAX £ 16.00	MIN £ 32.00 / MAX £ 32.00	OPEN 4-9

GH The White House

Llanfaglan,
Caernarfon,
Gwynedd LL54 5RA
Tel: (01286) 673003

HIGHLY COMMENDED

Large, quietly situated country house in own grounds with magnificent views to sea and mountains. All rooms have either en-suite bathroom or private facilities, colour TV, tea/coffee maker. Two bedrooms ground floor. Guests welcome to use lounge, outdoor pool and gardens. Ideally situated for ornithologists, walkers, windsurfing, golf and visiting Welsh castles and Snowdonia National Park.

	SINGLE PER PERSON B&B	DOUBLE FOR 2 PERSONS B&B	🛏 5 / 3
MIN £ 16.50	MAX £ 18.50	MIN £ 33.00 / MAX £ 37.00	OPEN 1-12

H Dolafon Hotel

High Street,
Llanberis,
Gwynedd LL55 4SU
Tel: (01286) 870993

COMMENDED

A pleasant family hotel in its own grounds. Near foot route to Snowdon. Six en-suite, two family rooms with colour TV and tea/coffee all rooms. Comfortable lounge, residents' bar. Rambling, climbing groups welcome. An ideal base for touring or exploring our lakes and local amenities including lakeside and mountain railways.

	SINGLE PER PERSON B&B	DOUBLE FOR 2 PERSONS B&B	🛏 9 / 6
MIN £ 14.50	MAX £ 18.00	MIN £ 29.00 / MAX £ 36.00	OPEN 3-9

GH Old School Accommodation

Hen Ysgol,
Bwlch Derwin,
Pantglas,
Gwynedd LL51 9EQ
Tel: (01286) 660701

Old Welsh school dated 1858 retaining character with a past in rural Wales. Centrally located for mountains, valleys, beaches and numerous attractions of the Llŷn Peninsula and Snowdonia. Ground floor rooms centrally heated with ease of access, including en-suite family room. Vegetarians catered for, packed lunches and evening meals available on request.

	SINGLE PER PERSON B&B	DOUBLE FOR 2 PERSONS B&B	🛏 3 / 1
MIN £ 14.00	MAX £ 17.00	MIN £ 28.00 / MAX £ 34.00	OPEN 1-12

FH Pengwern Farm

Saron,
Llanwnda,
Caernarfon,
Gwynedd LL54 5UH
Tel: (01286) 830717

AWARD — DE LUXE

Charming spacious farmhouse of character set in 130 acres of land. Beautifully situated between mountains and sea. Well appointed bedrooms all with en-suite. Our land runs down to Foryd Bay and is noted for its bird life. Situated 3 miles from Dinas Dinlle beach. Jane Rowlands has a cookery diploma and provides all the excellent meals.

	SINGLE PER PERSON B&B	DOUBLE FOR 2 PERSONS B&B	🛏 4 / 4
MIN £ 19.00	MAX £ 19.00	MIN £ 38.00 / MAX £ 38.00	OPEN 2-11

H Glyn Afon Hotel

High Street,
Llanberis,
Gwynedd LL55 4HA
Tel: (01286) 872528
Fax: (01286) 872528

Eight bedroomed family run hotel centrally situated in Llanberis village 10 minutes from Mount Snowdon and its railway. Twin, double, family accommodation some en-suite, all with television, tea/coffee facilities, central heating. residents' lounge. Parking, table d'hôte, à la carte menu. Convenient Holyhead ferry. Central for touring all North Wales attractions.

	SINGLE PER PERSON B&B	DOUBLE FOR 2 PERSONS B&B	🛏 8 / 2
MIN £ 15.00	MAX £ 16.00	MIN £ 28.00 / MAX £ 33.00	OPEN 1-12

H	Gwynedd Hotel

High Street,
Llanberis,
Gwynedd LL55 4SU
Tel: (01286) 870203
Fax: (01286) 870203

COMMENDED

Set at the foot of Snowdon and opposite Lake Padarn with its magnificent surroundings, the Gwynedd is an ideal touring and walking base. There are eleven fully equipped en-suite guest rooms. The lounge bar provides a relaxing setting to enjoy a drink or bar meal, alternatively the elegant restaurant provides a comprehensive à la carte menu.

		SINGLE PER PERSON B&B		DOUBLE FOR 2 PERSONS B&B			11
							10
		MIN £	MAX £	MIN £	MAX £	OPEN	
		17.00	19.00	32.00	38.00	1-12	

GH	The White Cottage

Maenan,
Llanrwst,
Gwynedd LL26 0UL
Tel: (01492) 640346

Situated in the beautiful Conwy Valley 2 miles north of Llanrwst. All rooms have open views, hot and cold water and central heating. Comfortable lounge with colour TV. Bathroom with shower, separate toilet. Relax in lovely garden, or stroll in woodland dells. Two excellent hotels close by for evening meals. Bodnant Garden and many local attractions within easy reach.

		SINGLE PER PERSON B&B		DOUBLE FOR 2 PERSONS B&B			3
							-
		MIN £	MAX £	MIN £	MAX £	OPEN	
		16.00	16.00	30.00	30.00	1-12	

GH	Llys Caradog Guest House

Trefriw,
Gwynedd LL27 0RQ
Tel: (01492) 640919

A friendly welcome awaits you in our large Welsh stone guest house and tea room. Central heating, Aga cooking. Tea making, hot and cold water in all rooms. Showers. Children welcome. Many beautiful walks to nearby lakes and mountains. Coast within easy reach. Brochure available.

		SINGLE PER PERSON B&B		DOUBLE FOR 2 PERSONS B&B			4
							-
		MIN £	MAX £	MIN £	MAX £	OPEN	
		12.50	15.00	25.00	30.00	1-12	

Llyn Padarn

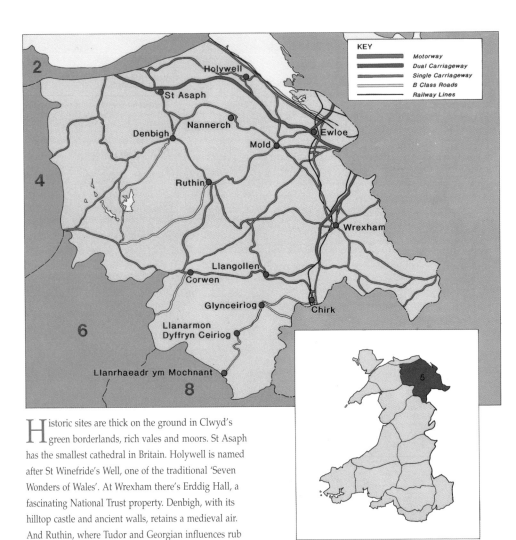

Historic sites are thick on the ground in Clwyd's green borderlands, rich vales and moors. St Asaph has the smallest cathedral in Britain. Holywell is named after St Winefride's Well, one of the traditional 'Seven Wonders of Wales'. At Wrexham there's Erddig Hall, a fascinating National Trust property. Denbigh, with its hilltop castle and ancient walls, retains a medieval air. And Ruthin, where Tudor and Georgian influences rub shoulder, is an architectural gem.

That's by no means all. Opulent Bodelwyddan Castle houses works from the National Portrait Gallery. The Clywedog Valley Heritage Park at Wrexham preserves sites of rural and industrial heritage. And Llangollen, home of the celebrated International Musical Eisteddfod, is overlooked by Castell Dinas Brân.

Part of the Offa's Dyke Footpath runs north from Llangollen to the rounded summits of the Clwydian Range, an 'Area of Outstanding Natural Beauty'. This range commands marvellous views across much of Clwyd – below into the rich farming country of the verdant Vale of Clwyd, westwards to the lakes, moors and forests of the Hiraethog Moorlands, and southwards to the Berwyn Mountains.

Be7 Corwen

Pleasant market town in Vale of Edeyrnion. Livestock market held regularly. Fishing in River Dee, swimming pool, good walks. Well-located touring centre for Snowdonia and border country.

Be5 Denbigh

Castled town in Vale of Clwyd with much historic interest. Friary and museum. Pony trekking, riding, fishing, golf, tennis and bowls. Indoor heated swimming pool. Centrally located for enjoying the rolling hills of Clwyd, a rich farming area full of small, attractive villages.

Ec1 Glynceiriog

Vale of Ceiriog village in foothills of the Berwyn Mountains. Ideal for walking, pony trekking. Ceiriog Memorial Institute an important shrine to Welsh poetry. Visitors welcome at the nearby Chwarel Wynne Slate Mine and Museum.

Cb4 Holywell

Place of pilgrimage for centuries, the 'Lourdes of Wales' with St Winefride's Holy Well. Remains of Basingwerk Abbey (1131) nearby. Leisure centre with swimming pools. Interesting and attractive Greenfield Valley Heritage Park

Ec1 Llangollen

Romantic town on River Dee, famous for its International Musical Eisteddfod; singers and dancers from all over the world come here every July. The town's many attractions include a canal museum, pottery, weavers, ECTARC European Centre for Traditional and Regional Cultures and a standard-gauge steam railway. Plas Newydd (home of 'Ladies of Llangollen' fame) is nearby. Valle Crucis Abbey is 2 miles away in a superb setting and ruined Castell Dinas Brân overlooks the town. Browse through the town's little shops; stand on its 14th-century stone bridge; cruise along the canal. Golf course and wonderful walking in surrounding countryside.

Cb5 Mold

County town of Clwyd on edge of Clwydian Range. Excellent Theatre Clwyd offers wide range of entertainment Visit Daniel Owen Centre, memorial to the 'Dickens of Wales'. Golf course. Loggerheads Country Park in wooded setting to the west.

Ca6 Ruthin

Attractive and historic market town noted for its fine architecture; curfew is still rung nightly! Many captivating old buildings. Medieval banquets in Ruthin Castle. Ancient St Peter's Church has beautiful gates and carved panels. Good range of small shops; craft centre with workshops. Ideal base for Vale of Clwyd.

Be4 St Asaph

Tiny city with the smallest cathedral in Britain, scene of the annual North Wales Music Festival. Prehistoric Cefn Caves nearby. Pleasantly situated on River Elwy in verdant Vale of Clwyd. Three important historic sites on doorstep - medieval Rhuddlan Castle, Bodelwyddan Castle (with noted art collection) and Bodrhyddan Hall.

Cc6 Wrexham

Busy industrial and commercial town, gateway to North Wales. St Giles's Church has graceful tower and altar piece given by Elihu Yale of Yale University fame (his tomb is in the churchyard). Visit Erddig Hall, an unusual country house on outskirts, and the Clywedog Valley Heritage Park. Good shopping and excellent little heritage centre. Industrial museum at neighbouring Bersham.Art gallery, swimming pool, golf

Llangollen Canal

Corwen Denbigh Glynceiriog Holywell Llangollen

H | Central Hotel

The Square,
Corwen,
Clwyd LL21 0DE
Tel: (01490) 412462

For all year round holidays and short breaks. A warm welcome and excellent cuisine await you. Situated at the foot of the Berwyn Mountains on a bend of the beautiful River Dee, it is the perfect centre for walking, sightseeing, a gateway to the "wilds of North Wales" and central to Llangollen, Ruthin and Bala. Pets by arrangement.

P ▯ ▯ ▯ ✂ ▯ T ▯		SINGLE PER PERSON B&B		DOUBLE FOR 2 PERSONS B&B		🛏 10 🛁 9
		MIN £ 14.50	MAX £ 16.50	MIN £ 29.00	MAX £ 33.00	OPEN 1-12

GH | Tyn-Llidiart

Corwen,
Clwyd LL21 9RS
Tel: (01490) 412729

👑👑
HIGHLY COMMENDED

Welcome to Tyn-Llidiart, a country house set in the Berwyn Mountains. Rooms are en-suite with colour TV, tea/coffee facilities, clock radio, trouser press and complimentary shampoos and bath gels. Guests' comfort is our main concern. We are a central base for the coast and countryside. Many sports facilities close by. Walkers and ramblers welcome.

P ▯ ▯ ✂ ▯		SINGLE PER PERSON B&B		DOUBLE FOR 2 PERSONS B&B		🛏 2 🛁 2
		MIN £ 15.00	MAX £ 15.00	MIN £ 30.00	MAX £ 30.00	OPEN 1-12

FH | Greenhill Farm

Bryn Celyn,
Holywell,
Clwyd CH8 7QF
Tel: (01352) 713270

Our 15th century timber framed farmhouse overlooks the Dee Estuary. Modernised to include one family room (en-suite), twin and double bedrooms all with tea/coffee facilities and colour TV. Comfortable oak beamed lounge and panelled dining room. Games/utility room with snooker table and washing facilities. Children are made especially welcome.

P ▯ ▯ T		SINGLE PER PERSON B&B		DOUBLE FOR 2 PERSONS B&B		🛏 3 🛁 1
		MIN £ -	MAX £ -	MIN £ 31.00	MAX £ -	OPEN 3-10

GH | Corwen Court Private Hotel

London Road,
Corwen,
Clwyd LL21 0DP
Tel: (01490) 412854

👑👑

Situated on the A5. Converted old police station and courthouse. Six prisoners' cells now single bedrooms, hot and cold water in each. Three only sharing a bathroom. Double bedrooms have en-suite bathroom. Comfortable lounge. Colour TV. Dining room with separate tables where magistrates once presided. Centrally heated. Fire certificate. Convenient base for touring North Wales. AA QQQ.

P ▯ ▯ ▯ ▯		SINGLE PER PERSON B&B		DOUBLE FOR 2 PERSONS B&B		🛏 10 🛁 4
		MIN £ 13.00	MAX £ 14.00	MIN £ 28.00	MAX £ 30.00	OPEN 3-11

GH | Cayo Guest House

74 Vale Street,
Denbigh,
Clwyd LL16 3BW
Tel: (01745) 812686

👑

Long established, centrally situated guest house. Guests have access at all times. Family room available, most rooms en-suite. Well behaved dogs welcome. Good food using local produce. Special menus on request. Centrally heated, TV lounge. Ideal for touring North Wales. Excellent area for golf, gliding, angling, walking. Riding holidays can be arranged.

▯ ▯ ▯ ▯		SINGLE PER PERSON B&B		DOUBLE FOR 2 PERSONS B&B		🛏 5 🛁 4
		MIN £ 15.00	MAX £ 16.00	MIN £ 30.00	MAX £ 32.00	OPEN 1-12

GH | Bryn Hyfryd

Llantysilio,
Llangollen,
Clwyd LL20 7YU
Tel: (01978) 860011

👑👑

Bryn Hyfryd is situated in the tiny hamlet of Llantysilio. All rooms have magnificent views over Dee Valley and are equipped with private bathroom, TV and drink making facilities. Lovely walks can be taken. Llangollen Steam Railway, Canal Museum and many attractions just two and a half miles away. Stroll to local 16th century inn.

P ▯ ▯ C ▯ ▯ ▯		SINGLE PER PERSON B&B		DOUBLE FOR 2 PERSONS B&B		🛏 3 🛁 3
		MIN £ -	MAX £ -	MIN £ -	MAX £ 30.00	OPEN 1-11

GH | Powys House Estate

Bonwm,
Corwen,
Clwyd LL21 9EG
Tel: (01490) 412367

AWARD
👑👑👑
HIGHLY COMMENDED

Country house only 9 miles from Llangollen, set in large gardens with swimming pool and tennis court. Spacious, well furnished en-suite bedrooms; all with colour TV, hairdryer, beverage making facilities. Large guest lounge with log burning stove. Friendly, relaxed atmosphere. Ideal touring base. Full brochure on request. Self-catering cottage also available.

P ▯ ▯ ✂ ▯ ▯		SINGLE PER PERSON B&B		DOUBLE FOR 2 PERSONS B&B		🛏 3 🛁 3
		MIN £ -	MAX £ -	MIN £ 32.00	MAX £ 34.00	OPEN 1-12

GH | Glyn Valley Hotel

Glynceiriog,
Nr Llangollen,
Clwyd LL20 7EU
Tel: (01691) 718896
Fax: (01691) 718896

👑👑
COMMENDED

Situated amidst glorious scenery; only six miles off A5 on B4500. Quality accommodation with a peaceful relaxing atmosphere. Five of the nine bedrooms en-suite, all with colour TV and central heating. An extensive menu in both bar and restaurant, including vegetarian dishes. Ideal centre from which to explore North Wales. A friendly and handy place to stay.

P ▯ ▯ ▯ ▯ T		SINGLE PER PERSON B&B		DOUBLE FOR 2 PERSONS B&B		🛏 9 🛁 5
		MIN £ 18.50	MAX £ -	MIN £ 34.00	MAX £ -	OPEN 1-12

GH | Dinbren House

Dinbren Road,
Llangollen,
Clwyd LL20 8TF
Tel: (01978) 860593

👑👑

Lovely country house in 2½ acre gardens. Beautiful views yet easy walking distance to Llangollen. Large comfortable "Laura Ashley" bedrooms all with tea/coffee, television, washbasin and private bath or shower. Family room available. Short drive Chester and Snowdonia. Ample parking in grounds.

P ▯ ▯ ▯ ✂ ▯ T		SINGLE PER PERSON B&B		DOUBLE FOR 2 PERSONS B&B		🛏 3 🛁 2
		MIN £ 15.00	MAX £ 16.00	MIN £ 30.00	MAX £ 32.00	OPEN 1-12

Llangollen Mold Ruthin

GH	Glanafon

Abbey Road,
Llangollen,
Clwyd LL20 8SS
Tel: (01978) 860725

Friendly family run Victorian guest house overlooking River Dee and adjacent to the Eisteddfod field. Spacious comfortable room which is a double, twin or family. Colour TV and guests' own bathroom. Children welcome at reduced rates. Ideally situated for fishing, canoeing, walking, touring. Six minute walk to town centre along the canal towpath.

SINGLE PER PERSON B&B		DOUBLE FOR 2 PERSONS B&B		1
MIN £	MAX £	MIN £	MAX £	OPEN
-	-	30.00	32.00	1-12

GH	The Old Vicarage Guest House

Bryn Howel Lane,
Llangollen,
Clwyd LL20 7YR
Tel: (01978) 823018

Attractive Georgian country house set in private grounds offering spacious, quality en-suite accommodation. The former vicarage is located beside the River Dee amidst outstanding natural beauty. Bar and restaurant meals within easy walking distance. Telford's aquaduct and the picturesque canal marina close by. Secure parking, gorgeous location for country folks, half mile off A5/A539.

SINGLE PER PERSON B&B		DOUBLE FOR 2 PERSONS B&B		3
				2
MIN £	MAX £	MIN £	MAX £	OPEN
-	-	26.00	34.00	4-11

GH	Heulwen

Maes Bodlonfa,
Mold,
Clwyd CH7 1DR
Tel: (01352) 758785
HIGHLY COMMENDED

Surrounded by parkland, 2 minutes from town centre. Superior family/double/twin/single rooms. Comfortable, well furnished with hot and cold, colour TV, tea/coffee making facilities. Private bathroom and shower room. Luxury dining room, home cooking. Garden and conservatory. Personal friendly service - ideal base for business and tourists. No smoking. Private parking.

SINGLE PER PERSON B&B		DOUBLE FOR 2 PERSONS B&B		2
				-
MIN £	MAX £	MIN £	MAX £	OPEN
16.50	16.50	33.00	33.00	1-12

GH	The Grange

Grange Road,
Llangollen,
Clwyd LL20 8AP
Tel: (01978) 860366
HIGHLY COMMENDED

An attractive country house of character situated in town within a tranquil and secluded 2 acre garden. Spacious and comfortable twin, double or family bedrooms, all en-suite with tea/coffee facilities and central heating. Child reductions and cot available. Interesting beamed lounge with TV. Parking in grounds. Vegetarians catered for.

SINGLE PER PERSON B&B		DOUBLE FOR 2 PERSONS B&B		3
				3
MIN £	MAX £	MIN £	MAX £	OPEN
-	-	35.00	35.00	1-12

GH	Dee Farm

Rhewl,
Llangollen,
Clwyd LL20 7YT
Tel: (01978) 861598
Fax: (01978) 861187
COMMENDED

Dee Farm is situated below the Horseshoe Pass beside the River Dee in the hamlet of Rhewl. Surrounded by pasture land and hills, it is ideal for walking and touring, yet is only 30 miles from Chester, Shrewsbury and Betws-y-Coed. Furnished to a high standard, very comfortable en-suite bedrooms, central heating, tea/coffee. Log fires.

SINGLE PER PERSON B&B		DOUBLE FOR 2 PERSONS B&B		2
				2
MIN £	MAX £	MIN £	MAX £	OPEN
15.00	17.00	30.00	34.00	2-11

GH	Maes Garmon Farm

Off Gwernaffield Road,
Gwernaffield,
Mold,
Clwyd CH7 5DB
Tel: (01352) 759887
HIGHLY COMMENDED

Imagine a peaceful secluded valley, a converted stable adjoining a 17th century farmhouse, a welcome of tea and scones. Accommodation of the highest standard, a wealth of beams, antiques, oak and pine furnishings. Guests' own lounge, pretty en-suite bedrooms. Two double, one twin. Beautiful three acre garden, summerhouse, pond, stream. Convenient for Chester and Snowdonia.

SINGLE PER PERSON B&B		DOUBLE FOR 2 PERSONS B&B		3
				3
MIN £	MAX £	MIN £	MAX £	OPEN
17.00	19.00	-	30.00	1-12

GH	The Nant Guest House

Nant Ucha Farm,
Tower Hill,
Garth, Llangollen,
Clwyd LL20 7YH
Tel: (01978) 823421

The comfortably furnished apartments at this farm guest house, four miles from the friendly town of Llangollen, provide an ideal base for walking, relaxing or exploring North Wales. These 17th century converted farm buildings back onto ancient woodland and a shallow trout stream. A delightful setting for a restful and refreshing break.

SINGLE PER PERSON B&B		DOUBLE FOR 2 PERSONS B&B		8
				6
MIN £	MAX £	MIN £	MAX £	OPEN
-	-	36.00	36.00	1-12

GH	Tyn Celyn Farmhouse

Tyndwr,
Llangollen,
Clwyd LL20 8AR
Tel: (01978) 861117

Spacious oak beamed farmhouse on the outskirts of Llangollen. Situated in a peaceful valley with beautiful views. All bedrooms have en-suite bathroom, beverage tray, television and central heating. Ideally situated for walking, golf, horse-riding and for visiting Snowdonia, North Wales coast and Chester. Just 1½ miles from Llangollen town centre. Ample secure parking.

SINGLE PER PERSON B&B		DOUBLE FOR 2 PERSONS B&B		3
				3
MIN £	MAX £	MIN £	MAX £	OPEN
-	-	34.00	36.00	1-12

GH	Berllan Bach

Ffordd Las,
Llandyrnog,
Clwyd LL16 4LR
Tel: (01824) 790732

18th century cottage and barn conversion in picturesque Vale of Clwyd. Stripped beams, inglenook fireplaces and olde worlde charm. All bedrooms are en-suite with TV and French windows opening onto individual patios overlooking the orchard. Ideal for walking, Offa's Dyke 1 mile. Horseriding, gliding, paragliding, golf, fishing available locally. Children and dogs warmly welcomed.

SINGLE PER PERSON B&B		DOUBLE FOR 2 PERSONS B&B		3
				3
MIN £	MAX £	MIN £	MAX £	OPEN
-	-	35.00	38.00	1-12

Ruthin St Asaph Wrexham

GH | Eyarth Station

Llanfair D.C.,
Ruthin,
Clwyd LL15 2EE
Tel: (01824) 703643
Fax: (01824) 707464

AWARD · HIGHLY COMMENDED

Former railway station, now a superbly converted country house. Six bedrooms, all en-suite with shower. TV lounge, swimming pool, car park, magnificent views. Located in beautiful countryside, only 3 minutes drive to Ruthin Castle's medieval banquets and town. Centre for Chester, Snowdonia, Llangollen, Bala and coast. Home cooking. Credit cards accepted. Listen to our local Welsh choir. BTA commended. AA Merit Awards.

		SINGLE PER PERSON B&B	DOUBLE FOR 2 PERSONS B&B	🛏 6
				6
		MIN £	MAX £	MIN £	MAX £	OPEN
		19.00	-	38.00	38.00	1-12

GH | Plas Uchaf

Graigadwywynt,
Llanfair D.C.,
Ruthin,
Clwyd LL15 2TF
Tel: (01824) 705794

HIGHLY COMMENDED

16th century manor house set in beautiful countryside and of historical interest. Wealth of beams, panelling and log fires. Tastefully decorated and furnished. All rooms with en-suite facilities, TV and tea making facilities. Centrally situated for Snowdonia, Llangollen and Chester. A warm welcome is assured with a Welsh speaking family.

		SINGLE PER PERSON B&B	DOUBLE FOR 2 PERSONS B&B	🛏 3
				3
		MIN £	MAX £	MIN £	MAX £	OPEN
		14.00	16.00	28.00	32.00	1-12

GH | Grove Guest House

36 Chester Road,
Wrexham,
Clwyd LL11 2SD
Tel: (01978) 354288

Charming Tudor style guest house five minutes walk from town centre. Ten bedrooms, some en-suite, for up to 26 people. Centrally heated, TV, tea/coffee all rooms. Large car park. Snowdonia and coast within half an hour. Swimming, riding, golf, sports centre nearby. Business travellers and tourists welcome.

		SINGLE PER PERSON B&B	DOUBLE FOR 2 PERSONS B&B	🛏 10
				4
		MIN £	MAX £	MIN £	MAX £	OPEN
		17.00	19.00	32.00	36.00	1-12

GH | Gorffwysfa

Llanfair D.C.,
Ruthin,
Clwyd LL15 2UN
Tel: (01824) 702432

Gorffwysfa - "Resting Place". Victorian country house set in its own grounds 1½ miles from medieval town of Ruthin. Ideal location for exploring North Wales and Chester. Spacious, well furnished accommodation with en-suite or private facilities. Ground floor room available. Good home cooking and warm friendly welcome awaits you. Non smoking establishment. Families welcome.

		SINGLE PER PERSON B&B	DOUBLE FOR 2 PERSONS B&B	🛏 3
				3
		MIN £	MAX £	MIN £	MAX £	OPEN
		-	18.00	-	36.00	1-12

FH | Pentre Bach

Llandyrnog,
Nr Ruthin,
Clwyd LL16 4LA
Tel: (01824) 790725

Georgian farmhouse built in 1745 and today providing a tranquil setting for a break away from it all. An ideal base to appreciate the Vale of Clwyd, but within easy touring distance of Snowdonia and the city of Chester. Comfortable guest bedrooms with all facilities. Sitting room with colour TV.

		SINGLE PER PERSON B&B	DOUBLE FOR 2 PERSONS B&B	🛏 2
				2
		MIN £	MAX £	MIN £	MAX £	OPEN
		17.50	19.00	32.00	36.00	1-12

GH | Buck Farm

Hanmer,
Clwyd SY14 7LX
Tel: (01948) 74339

COMMENDED

On the A525. A warm, welcoming and cosy Tudor farmhouse. An excellent touring base for North Wales, Cheshire, Shropshire and Staffordshire. We provide vegetarian or vegan or meat meals on request. We always make our own muesli, granola, hot cakes and wonderful vegetable soups (sans MSG). French spoken. Library, music, cycle shelter, spacious interesting garden.

		SINGLE PER PERSON B&B	DOUBLE FOR 2 PERSONS B&B	🛏 4
				-
		MIN £	MAX £	MIN £	MAX £	OPEN
		17.00	18.00	32.00	34.00	1-12

GH | The Old Rectory

Clocaenog,
Ruthin,
Clwyd LL15 2AT
Tel: (01824) 750740

A warm welcome to a comfortable Georgian house in peaceful countryside below Clocaenog Forest. near Ruthin. All bedrooms en-suite or with private bathroom. Centrally heated throughout. Lounge, colour TV and radio. Pub for evening meals nearby. Snowdonia, Llangollen, North Wales and Chester all within easy reach. Craft studio/workshop adjoining premises creating colourful traditional canalware.

		SINGLE PER PERSON B&B	DOUBLE FOR 2 PERSONS B&B	🛏 3
				3
		MIN £	MAX £	MIN £	MAX £	OPEN
		15.00	17.00	30.00	34.00	1-12

GH | Plas Penucha

Caerwys,
Mold,
Clwyd CH7 5BH
Tel: (01352) 720210

HIGHLY COMMENDED

Welcome to this 16th century farmhouse altered over succeeding generations, but retaining history and serenity in comfortable surroundings. Extensive gardens overlooking Clwydian Hills. Spacious lounge with extensive library. Four well equipped bedrooms, 2 en-suite. Full central heating, log fires. 2 miles A55 Expressway. Ideal touring centre for North Wales. Brochure from Nest Price.

		SINGLE PER PERSON B&B	DOUBLE FOR 2 PERSONS B&B	🛏 4
				2
		MIN £	MAX £	MIN £	MAX £	OPEN
		16.50	16.50	33.00	33.00	1-12

Don't forget Phoneday!

On 16 April 1995, all area codes starting with 0 will change to **01**.

Inner London, for example, changes from 071 to **0171**,

Cardiff from 0222 to **01222**.

*This is the quietest holiday region in Wales,
where country lanes wind their way tentatively through
unexplored territory, and where highlands run down
to an untouched coastline.*

The lovely
Elan Valley
lakelands

Below:
The Centre of
Alternative
Technology, near
Machynlleth

Mid Wales

Some of Wales's – and Britain's – best-kept secrets are to be found within this tranquil, timeless area of gentle hills, fresh green mountains and sweeping shores.

True to its character, the places to stay here are small and friendly. Mid Wales's 'capital' is the resort of Aberystwyth, which stands midway along Cardigan Bay, a gently curving shoreline of dunes, grassy headlands and outstandingly beautiful estuaries. Aberystwyth is a charming Victorian seaside town which doubles up as an ideally located touring centre. Other places to stay along Cardigan Bay include Barmouth, Tywyn, Aberaeron and New Quay.

Inland, there's the true 'Wild Wales' of lonely high country, remote lakes, forests and traditional stone-built farmsteads. It's a little-known fact that Mid Wales has the lion's share of the Snowdonia National Park – 500 of its 840 square miles, to be precise.

The Park extends southwards all the way to Machynlleth, and eastwards to Bala.

These two traditional towns, together with Dolgellau, are convenient centres from which to explore Mid Wales's upland wildernesses. And there's much to explore, for in addition to the Snowdonia National Park there are the Cambrian Mountains, the 'backbone' of Wales. Further east, high mountains decline to rolling, sleepy border country around Welshpool, Newtown and Llandrindod Wells.

But don't be deceived by Mid Wales's tranquillity. This is an active landscape in many ways. There's lot's going on here, including pony trekking, fishing, walking, narrow-gauge railway riding, canoeing, sailing and mountain biking.

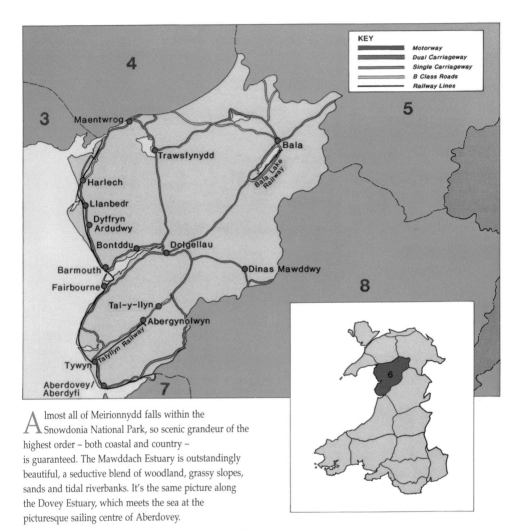

Almost all of Meirionnydd falls within the Snowdonia National Park, so scenic grandeur of the highest order – both coastal and country – is guaranteed. The Mawddach Estuary is outstandingly beautiful, a seductive blend of woodland, grassy slopes, sands and tidal riverbanks. It's the same picture along the Dovey Estuary, which meets the sea at the picturesque sailing centre of Aberdovey.

Other places to stay along the coast include the small resorts of Tywyn and Barmouth – not forgetting Harlech, home of a spectacular medieval castle. Country lovers are also spoilt for choice. Bala stands beside a lake ringed by mountains which can be explored on foot or by roads which seem to climb into the clouds. North of Dolgellau lie the remote Rhinogs, one of Britain's last true wilderness areas. And looming above the town is mighty Cader Idris, a misty, boulder-clad mountain steeped in legend.

Meirionnydd's places to visit include narrow-gauge railways, a forest visitor centre, woollen mills, craft centres, a fascinating gold mine and a unique 'village of the future' known as the Centre for Alternative Technology – attractions that complement their surroundings perfectly.

Db6 Aberdovey/Aberdyfi

Picturesque little resort and dinghy sailor's paradise on the Dovey Estuary. All watersports, thriving yacht club, good inns looking out over the bay and 18-hole golf links. Superb views towards hills and mountains.

Db5 Abergynolwyn

Attractively located former slate quarrying village surrounded by forests and the green foothills of Cader Idris. Narrow-gauge Talyllyn Railway runs almost to the village from Tywyn. Good choice of local walks. Visit Tal-y-llyn Lake, Bird Rock and atmospheric Castell-y-Bere.

De2 Bala

Traditional Welsh country town with tree-lined main street and interesting little shops. Narrow-gauge railway runs one side of Bala Lake, 4 miles long (the largest natural lake in Wales) and ringed with mountains. Golf, sailing, fishing, canoeing - a natural touring centre for Snowdonia.

Db4 Barmouth

Superbly located resort at the mouth of lovely Mawddach Estuary. Golden sands, miles of wonderful mountain and estuary walks nearby. Promenade, funfair, harbour and pony rides on the beach. Lifeboat and Shipwreck Centre museums. Good shops and inns. Excellent parking on seafront.

Dd4 Dinas Mawddwy

Mountain village famed for its salmon and trout fishing and marvellous walks. On fringes of Snowdonia National Park. Visit the extensive Meirion Woollen Mill with craft shop, tea shop. Drive over the spectacular Bwlch y Groes mountain road to Bala, the highest road in Wales.

Dc4 Dolgellau

Handsome stone-built market town which seems to have grown naturally out of the mountains. The heights of Cader Idris loom above the rooftops. Interesting shops, pubs, cafes. Museum of the Quakers in town centre. Visit a gold mine in nearby forest. Excellent base for touring the coast and countryside.

Da3 Dyffryn Ardudwy

Pleasant village near the coast on Barmouth-Harlech road, set between sea and mountains. Prehistoric burial chamber and stone circles nearby; also scenic Shell Island and Museum of Transport.

Db4 Fairbourne

Quiet resort with 2 miles of sand south of Mawddach Estuary. Railway buffs travel far to ride on its 1'3" gauge Fairbourne and Barmouth Steam Railway.

Da2 Harlech

Small, stone-built town dominated by remains of 13th-century castle - site of Owain Glyndwr's last stand. Dramatically set on a high crag, the castle commands a magnificent panorama of rolling sand dunes, sea and mountains. Home of the 18-hole Royal St David's Golf Club. Shell Island nearby. Theatre and swimming pool. Visitors can explore the chambers of the Old Llanfair Slate Caverns just south of Harlech.

Aberdovey

Dc5	Tal-y-llyn

Lakeside village in magnificent setting below Cader Idris mountain, ideally placed for fishing and walking. Narrow-gauge Talyllyn Railway, which runs to a nearby halt, connects with Tywyn.

Da6	Tywyn	⇌

Seaside resort on Cardigan Bay, with beach activities, sea and river fishing and golf among its leading attractions. Good leisure centre. Narrow-gauge Talyllyn Railway runs inland from here and St Cadfan's Stone and Llanegryn Church are important Christian monuments. In the hills stands Castell-y-Bere, a native Welsh castle, and Bird Rock, a haven for birdlife.

Harlech Castle

FH Tyddyn Rhys Farm

Aberdovey,
Gwynedd LL35 0PG
Tel: (01654) 767533

HIGHLY COMMENDED

A warm Welsh welcome awaits you at Tyddyn Rhys. A working farm of 150 acres. ¹/₂ mile from Aberdovey. With panoramic view of Cardigan Bay. All bedrooms have washbasin, tea and coffee making facilities and colour TV. One double bedroom en-suite, one double and one single. 1 bathroom, two toilets. Full central heating.

P IIII 🛁		SINGLE PER PERSON B&B		DOUBLE FOR 2 PERSONS B&B		🛏 3 🛁 1
		MIN £ 15.00	MAX £ 15.00	MIN £ 28.00	MAX £ 33.00	OPEN 2-11

FH Erw Feurig Farm Guest House

Cefnddwysarn,
Bala,
Gwynedd LL23 7LL
Tel: (01678) 530262

HIGHLY COMMENDED

Beautifully situated, this farm guest house is the perfect centre for sightseeing and walking. Double, twin and family rooms, two with private facilities. One upstairs bathroom, WC and downstairs WC and shower room. One downstairs bedroom. Excellent meals served in pleasant dining room. Separate TV lounge. Tea/coffee making facilities in all rooms. Private fishing lake.

P IIII		SINGLE PER PERSON B&B		DOUBLE FOR 2 PERSONS B&B		🛏 4 🛁 2
		MIN £ -	MAX £ -	MIN £ 26.00	MAX £ 32.00	OPEN 1-12

FH Tair Felin Farm

Frongoch,
Bala,
Gwynedd LL23 7NS
Tel: (01678) 520763

Tair Felin Farm is situated three miles north of Bala (A4212 and B4501 roads). Located in a quiet rural area within the Snowdonia National Park, an ideal base for touring. One double and one twin bedroom, both with washbasin, tea/coffee facilities. Bathroom has shower. Beamed ceiling in lounge with colour TV. Relax and enjoy a homely welcome.

P �). TW		SINGLE PER PERSON B&B		DOUBLE FOR 2 PERSONS B&B		🛏 2 🛁
		MIN £ 13.50	MAX £ 16.00	MIN £ 27.00	MAX £ 32.00	OPEN 3-10

FH Tanycoed Ucha

Tanycoed Ucha,
Abergynolwyn,
Tywyn,
Gwynedd LL36 9UP
Tel: (01654) 782228

Come and stay in the peaceful Dolgoch Valley on our mixed farm, with the Talyllyn Narrow-Gauge Railway running through our land. Modernised farmhouse with double, single, twin bedded rooms. Log fires when wet and cold. Tea/coffee in bedrooms. Perfect for bird watching. Within easy reach of Cader Idris, we also have red deer roaming our mountain.

P 🐕 IIII C IIII 🍴		SINGLE PER PERSON B&B		DOUBLE FOR 2 PERSONS B&B		🛏 3 🛁 1
		MIN £ 13.50	MAX £ 14.50	MIN £ 27.00	MAX £ 29.00	OPEN 3-11

FH Penybryn Farm Guest House

Sarnau,
Bala,
Gwynedd LL23 7LH
Tel: (01678) 230297

COMMENDED

Farm guest house accommodation B&B or B&B and evening meal. Six bedrooms, two bathrooms. Hot and cold water in all bedrooms. Colour television in lounge. Delicious food. Home cooking to high standard. Fire certificate. Own lake for fishing. Marvellous views overlooking Berwyn Mountains. Terms with SAE on request. Warm welcome guaranteed.

P IIII IIII 🍴 T		SINGLE PER PERSON B&B		DOUBLE FOR 2 PERSONS B&B		🛏 6 🛁 -
		MIN £ 13.50	MAX £ 16.00	MIN £ 27.00	MAX £ 32.00	OPEN 1-12

GH Glyn Hefin

7 Marine Road,
Barmouth,
Gwynedd LL42 1NL
Tel: (01341) 280095

COMMENDED

Glyn Hefin assures all of a warm friendly welcome. Clean fresh rooms all with colour TV, hostess tray. All rooms have washbasin vanity units, some doubles with showers, bath, WC. Ground floor double with shower, WC adjacent. 100yds to the beach. Close to all other amenities and interests. Walking, pony trekking, golf, Snowdonia, bus and rail links.

IIII IIII 🍴		SINGLE PER PERSON B&B		DOUBLE FOR 2 PERSONS B&B		🛏 8 🛁 2
		MIN £ 12.50	MAX £ 13.00	MIN £ 25.00	MAX £ 30.00	OPEN 1-10

GH Frondderw Private Hotel

Stryd-y-Fron,
Bala,
Gwynedd LL23 7YD
Tel: (01678) 520301

COMMENDED

Charming period mansion quietly situated on hillside overlooking Bala town and lake with magnificent views of the Berwyn Mountains All rooms have hot and cold, central heating, tea/coffee making facilities. Lounge, separate TV lounge with colour TV. Ample parking. Dinner optional, vegetarians catered for. Licensed. Ideal centre for touring, walking, water sports, cycling, golf.

P 🍷 IIII 🍴 🍴 TW T		SINGLE PER PERSON B&B		DOUBLE FOR 2 PERSONS B&B		🛏 8 🛁 4
		MIN £ 14.00	MAX £ 19.00	MIN £ 28.00	MAX £ 38.00	OPEN 3-11

FH Rhydydefaid Farm

Frongoch,
Bala,
Gwynedd LL23 7NT
Tel: (01678) 520456

HIGHLY COMMENDED

Traditional Welsh stone farmhouse, three miles from Bala near A4212. Oak beamed lounge with inglenook fireplace, exposed beams in family bedroom with en-suite facilities. Twin or single bedrooms. Tea/coffee facilities. Evening meals available locally. Welsh welcome awaits you within beautiful countryside. Ideal base for touring Snowdonia National Park. Near National White Water Centre. Brochure from Mrs Davies.

P 🐕 IIII C IIII 🍴		SINGLE PER PERSON B&B		DOUBLE FOR 2 PERSONS B&B		🛏 3 🛁 1
		MIN £ 15.00	MAX £ 17.00	MIN £ 28.00	MAX £ 34.00	OPEN 1-12

GH Pen Parc Guest House

Park Road,
Barmouth,
Gwynedd LL42 1PH
Tel: (01341) 280150

HIGHLY COMMENDED

A small guest house in quiet situation overlooking park yet only four minutes from sea. Hot and cold water and tea making facilities in all rooms. All bedrooms on first floor. We pride ourselves on personal service and good food with traditional and vegetarian cuisine and special diets. TV lounge. Walkers welcome. Sorry no young children or pets.

P IIII 🍴		SINGLE PER PERSON B&B		DOUBLE FOR 2 PERSONS B&B		🛏 4 🛁 -
		MIN £ 14.00	MAX £ 15.00	MIN £ 28.00	MAX £ 30.00	OPEN 3-10

Barmouth   Dinas Mawddwy   Dolgellau

GH   The Sandpiper

7 Marine Parade,
Barmouth,
Gwynedd LL42 1NA
Tel: (01341) 280318

HIGHLY COMMENDED

The Sandpiper is superbly situated on Barmouth Seafront. There is parking outside and we are a short level walk from the station. Most double rooms have en-suite facilities. Television and free tea/coffee in all rooms. Ground floor bedroom available. Brochure from Susan and John Palmer.

		SINGLE PER PERSON B&B	DOUBLE FOR 2 PERSONS B&B	🛏 11
				6
MIN £	MAX £	MIN £	MAX £	OPEN
14.00	15.00	25.00	33.00	3-10

GH   Dwy Olwyn

Coed-y-Fronallt,
Dolgellau,
Gwynedd LL40 2YG
Tel: (01341) 422822

COMMENDED

A comfortable guest house situated in an acre of landscaped gardens, boasting magnificent views of the Cader Idris mountain range in a peaceful position, yet only 10 minutes walk from the town. Within Snowdonia National Park, close to all amenities and numerous walks. Good home cooking, evening dinner if desired. Tea/coffee facilities, parking, lounge with colour TV.

P	C	SINGLE PER PERSON B&B	DOUBLE FOR 2 PERSONS B&B	🛏 3
			26.00	0
MIN £	MAX £	MIN £	MAX £	OPEN
-	-	-	-	2-11

GH   Y Goedlan

Brithdir,
Dolgellau,
Gwynedd LL40 2RN
Tel: (01341) 423131

This old vicarage with adjoining farm offers peaceful accommodation in pleasant rural surroundings. Ideally placed on B4416 road for walks, sea, mountains and touring. Spacious double, twin and family rooms all with hot and cold water, colour TV, central heating, tea/coffee facilities. Bathroom with shower. Two conveniences. Lounge. Comfort with homely atmosphere. Hearty breakfast. Reduction for children. Dolgellau 2 miles.

P		SINGLE PER PERSON B&B	DOUBLE FOR 2 PERSONS B&B	🛏 3
				-
MIN £	MAX £	MIN £	MAX £	OPEN
16.00	-	28.00	30.00	2-11

FH   Bryncelyn Farm

Dinas Mawddwy,
Machynlleth,
Powys SY20 9JG
Tel: (01650) 531289

Situated in peaceful valley of Cywarch at the foot of Aran Fawddwy, amidst some of the finest scenery. Excellent centre to enjoy walking, climbing and touring. Generous home cooked meals. Tea/coffee making facilities. Spacious en-suite bedrooms including colour TV and heating. The Edwards family offer a homely holiday in a comfortable farmhouse.

P	🐕	SINGLE PER PERSON B&B	DOUBLE FOR 2 PERSONS B&B	🛏 2
				2
MIN £	MAX £	MIN £	MAX £	OPEN
16.00	18.00	-	-	1-12

GH   Llety Nest

Brithdir,
Dolgellau,
Gwynedd LL40 2RY
Tel: (01341) 450326

HIGHLY COMMENDED

1 en-suite family room with 1 double and 2 single beds, 1 double room with private bathroom. Separate dining room and lounge. TV, video. Large garden. Parking space. Situated 3 miles from Dolgellau in the Snowdonia National Park. Bungalow in secluded position with breathtaking views. Many beautiful walks on own land (90 acres). Very peaceful, house furnished with some period pieces with patchwork covers in bedrooms. Good home cooked food provided.

P	🐕	SINGLE PER PERSON B&B	DOUBLE FOR 2 PERSONS B&B	🛏 2
				1
MIN £	MAX £	MIN £	MAX £	OPEN
-	-	28.00	30.00	3-11

FH   Arosfyr Farm

Penycefn Road,
Dolgellau,
Gwynedd LL40 2YP
Tel: (01341) 422355

APPROVED

33 acre working farm with panoramic views of Cader Idris range. Dolgellau nestles in the valley below. 3 bedrooms with heating and washbasins. Dining room with separate tables. Guests' lounge with tea/coffee making facilities. Remote control TV with teletext. Access to rooms at all times and freedom to remain indoors. Parking. Own free range eggs. Flower gardens. Homely, relaxed atmosphere and a friendly welcome.

P		SINGLE PER PERSON B&B	DOUBLE FOR 2 PERSONS B&B	🛏 3
				-
MIN £	MAX £	MIN £	MAX £	OPEN
15.00	17.50	27.00	28.00	1-12

FH   Bryn Sion Farm

Cwm Cywarch,
Dinas Mawddwy,
Machynlleth,
Powys SY20 9JG
Tel: (01650) 531251

L

A warm welcome awaits you at Bryn Sion situated in the scenic valley of Cywarch at the foot of Arran Fawddwy. Fishing, shooting on farm. Two double bedrooms with hot and cold water and tea/coffee facilities. Ample car parking. Cot and highchair available. Reductions for children. Hearty cooked farmhouse meals. Log fire in beamed sitting room with colour TV. 1 1/2 miles from Dinas Mawddwy.

P	🐕	SINGLE PER PERSON B&B	DOUBLE FOR 2 PERSONS B&B	🛏 2
				0
MIN £	MAX £	MIN £	MAX £	OPEN
12.00	14.00	24.00	28.00	1-12

GH   Tanyfron

Arran Road,
Dolgellau,
Gwynedd LL40 2AA
Tel: (01341) 422638
Fax: (01341) 422638

HIGHLY COMMENDED

Comfortable, quiet, modernised 100 year old former farmhouse with lovely views, within half a mile of Dolgellau. Tastefully furnished with matching decor for your comfort. Three bedrooms all with shower or bath en-suite. Each room has teamaker, hairdryer, central heating, colour satellite TV and clock/radio. Ample private parking in own grounds. Non smokers only please.

P		SINGLE PER PERSON B&B	DOUBLE FOR 2 PERSONS B&B	🛏 3
				3
MIN £	MAX £	MIN £	MAX £	OPEN
-	-	35.00	36.00	1-11

FH   Cyfannedd Uchaf

Arthog,
Gwynedd LL39 1LX
Tel: (01341) 250526

HIGHLY COMMENDED

Situated in the Snowdonia National Park. Comfortable non-smoking farmhouse in a superb mountain setting with coastal views. Ideal walking and touring. 3 bedrooms (one en-suite) and 1 twin. All with tea/coffee trays. Why not try our 3 day break? Ask for details. Children over 14 welcome. No pets. Grid reference SH635127. Phone Mrs Anna Tovey.

P		SINGLE PER PERSON B&B	DOUBLE FOR 2 PERSONS B&B	🛏 3
				1
MIN £	MAX £	MIN £	MAX £	OPEN
-	-	32.00	34.00	3-10

Dolgellau Dyffryn Ardudwy Fairbourne Harlech Tal-y-llyn

FH	Gwanas

Cross Foxes,
Dolgellau,
Gwynedd LL40 2SH
Tel: (01341) 422624
Fax: (01341) 422624

A charming spacious farmhouse, built in 1838 situated in a peaceful setting where Tom and Mair Evans farm sheep and cattle on 1,000 acres. Delicious breakfast, twin, double, family rooms with H&C. Two bathrooms with showers. Central heating, colour TV, tea/coffee facilities. Situated off the A470, 400 yards from the Cross Foxes Inn, about three miles from Dolgellau.

		SINGLE PER PERSON B&B		DOUBLE FOR 2 PERSONS B&B			3
		MIN £	MAX £	MIN £	MAX £	OPEN	-
		16.00	17.00	27.00	29.00	1-10	

GH	Einion House

Friog,
Fairbourne,
Gwynedd LL38 2NX
Tel: (01341) 250644

 COMMENDED

Lovely old house between mountains and sea set in beautiful scenery. Reputation for good home cooking. Vegetarians catered for. All rooms colour TV, clock radio, hairdryer, teamaker. Marvellous walking, maps available. Pony trekking, fishing and birdwatching. Good centre for narrow gauge railways. Castles easy reach. Safe sandy beach few minutes walk from house.

		SINGLE PER PERSON B&B		DOUBLE FOR 2 PERSONS B&B			6
							6
		MIN £	MAX £	MIN £	MAX £	OPEN	
		18.50	-	34.00	34.00	1-12	

GH	Godre'r Graig

Lower Harlech,
Gwynedd LL46 2UD
Tel: (01766) 780905

 COMMENDED

Warm friendly welcome guaranteed. Nestling below Harlech Castle within sight of Royal St David's Golf Club. Children's rates, occasional baby-sitting. Television lounge, home cooked evening meals by arrangement with great vegetarian choice. Vanity units, tea/coffee facilities. The beautiful Snowdonia National Park, wonderful beaches, pony trekking or trout and sea fishing. Fantasia Ceramic Weekends.

		SINGLE PER PERSON B&B		DOUBLE FOR 2 PERSONS B&B			3
		MIN £	MAX £	MIN £	MAX £	OPEN	-
		14.50	19.00	28.00	-	1-11	

FH	Tyddynmawr Farmhouse

Tyddynmawr,
Islawrdref,
Cader Road,
Dolgellau,
Gwynedd LL40 1TL
Tel: (01341) 422331

 DE LUXE

It's paradise! Honestly! A warm welcome awaits you in this lovingly restored 18th century farmhouse. Beams, log fires. All bedrooms en-suite with superb mountain views. We farm the magnificent mountain of Cader Idris and have waterfalls, slate mines, caves and fishing on mountain lake on farm. We offer peace, tranquility and seclusion.

		SINGLE PER PERSON B&B		DOUBLE FOR 2 PERSONS B&B			2
							2
		MIN £	MAX £	MIN £	MAX £	OPEN	
		-	-	-	36.00	4-11	

H	Byrdir Hotel

High Street,
Harlech,
Gwynedd LL46 2YA
Tel: (01766) 780316

Byrdir, renowned for its homely atmosphere, is in the centre of Harlech close to the castle. Standard bedrooms all have wash hand basin, tea and coffee, TV and own room key. There are six en-suite rooms with colour TV and all rooms are tastefully decorated.

		SINGLE PER PERSON B&B		DOUBLE FOR 2 PERSONS B&B			15
							6
		MIN £	MAX £	MIN £	MAX £	OPEN	
		14.00	14.00	28.00	33.00	1-12	

FH	Gwrach Ynys Country Guest House

Ynys,
Talsarnau,
Gwynedd LL47 6TS
Tel: (01766) 780742

  DE LUXE

Treat yourselves to a refreshingly peaceful break in the glorious setting of our country guest house. Many returning guests attest to our friendly welcome and imaginative home cooking. Bedrooms en-suite, with colour TV's and beverage facilities. Close to sea, mountains, swimming pool, golf and lovely estuary walks. Many interesting local attractions. Illustrated brochure sent with pleasure. Croeso Cymreig.

		SINGLE PER PERSON B&B		DOUBLE FOR 2 PERSONS B&B			7
							6
		MIN £	MAX £	MIN £	MAX £	OPEN	
		16.00	19.00	-	-	1-12	

FH	Byrdir

Dyffryn Ardudwy,
Gwynedd LL44 2EA
Tel: (01341) 247200

 HIGHLY COMMENDED

Welsh stone farmhouse in peaceful setting in Snowdonia National Park with coastline in front, mountains to rear. Woods, streams, beaches, lovely walks, golf, swimming pools, fishing, riding nearby. Double and family bedrooms, 3 en-suite, sitting room, colour TV, dining room. Children welcome at reduced rates. Enquiries to Mrs A Jones.

		SINGLE PER PERSON B&B		DOUBLE FOR 2 PERSONS B&B			4
							3
		MIN £	MAX £	MIN £	MAX £	OPEN	
		17.00	19.00	34.00	38.00	3-9	

GH	Glan y Gors Guest House

Glan y Gors,
Llandanwg,
Harlech,
Gwynedd LL46 2SD
Tel: (01341) 241410

Small friendly guest house with 2 acres of land, situated 400 yards from sandy beach. All rooms have washbasin, TV, tea/coffee making facilities, electric blanket and central heating. Beautiful views from all windows. Good home cooking. Near train station. Private access to beach. Ample parking. Golf, rambling, birdwatching, sailing, fishing all to be found in the area. Warm welcome.

		SINGLE PER PERSON B&B		DOUBLE FOR 2 PERSONS B&B			3
		MIN £	MAX £	MIN £	MAX £	OPEN	-
		13.00	-	26.00	26.00	1-12	

FH	Dolffanog Fach

Tal-y-llyn,
Tywyn,
Gwynedd LL36 9AJ
Tel: (01654) 761235
Fax: (01654) 761235

Dolffanog is situated near Tal-y-llyn Lake at the foot of Cader Idris. En-suite bedroom available or bedroom with washbasin, shaver-point, central heating, colour TV, tea/coffee facilities. Lounge with colour TV. Good home cooking. Ideal touring centre, walking, fishing, trekking. Games room with full size snooker table. Large garden and car park. Contact Mrs Meirwen Pugh.

		SINGLE PER PERSON B&B		DOUBLE FOR 2 PERSONS B&B			3
		MIN £	MAX £	MIN £	MAX £	OPEN	1
		15.00	18.00	-	-	1-11	

Tywyn

GH	Glenfield

10 Idris Villas,
Tywyn,
Gwynedd LL36 9AW
Tel: (01654) 710707

Homely accommodation near shops, railway and bus stations. Five minutes walk from beach. Overlooking Cader Idris range with beautiful mountain scenery. 5 minutes walk from the famous Talyllyn Railway. Ideal centre for walking, fishing, sailing and golf. Personal supervision.

🐕 IIII. 🍴 🍷 T TW	SINGLE PER PERSON B&B	DOUBLE FOR 2 PERSONS B&B	🛏 2 🛏 -
	MIN £ 13.00	MAX £ 15.00	MIN £ 26.00	MAX £ 30.00	OPEN 3-10

GH	Glenydd Guest House

Maesnewydd,
Pier Road, Tywyn,
Gwynedd LL36 0AN
Tel: (01654) 711373
Fax: (01654) 711373

Glenydd, a beautiful modernised Edwardian house in private road. Wonderful views of Cader Idris mountain range. Lovely relaxed family atmosphere. Enjoy scrumptious home cooking. Famous Talyllyn Steam Railway, leisure centre, tennis, bowls, putting all within 5 minutes walk. 200m from beach and surfing. Fantastic area for walking, climbing, cycling, bird watching, fishing and boating.

P 🐕 IIII. 🍷 🍽 T	SINGLE PER PERSON B&B	DOUBLE FOR 2 PERSONS B&B	🛏 3 🛏 -
	MIN £ 12.50	MAX £ 15.00	MIN £ 25.00	MAX £ 30.00	OPEN 1-12

FH	Pant y Neuadd

Aberdovey Road,
Tywyn,
Gwynedd LL36 9HW
Tel: (01654) 711393

Enjoy a peaceful break within a quiet holiday environment. Town is only a 15 minute stroll away, along lover's lane with its magnificent views. Uncommercialised area, but all amenities, sports and beaches close by. Ours is a house of character. Three en-suite rooms, colour TV and teamakers. Safe parking. A warm welcome awaits you.

P 🐕 🍷 T	SINGLE PER PERSON B&B	DOUBLE FOR 2 PERSONS B&B	🛏 3 🛏 3
	MIN £ 15.00	MAX £ 19.00	MIN £ 30.00	MAX £ 30.00	OPEN 4-9

Talyllyn Narrow Gauge Railway

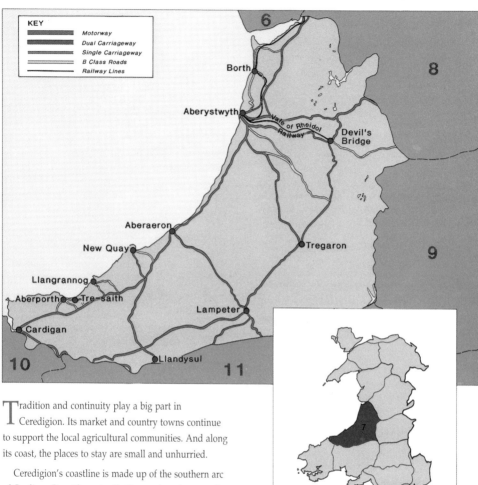

Tradition and continuity play a big part in Ceredigion. Its market and country towns continue to support the local agricultural communities. And along its coast, the places to stay are small and unhurried.

Ceredigion's coastline is made up of the southern arc of Cardigan Bay. Aberystwyth, the area's main resort, is by no means large or loud, preferring instead to stick to its genteel Victorian roots. Its convincing period atmosphere is further enhanced by a cliff railway, camera obscura, 'museum in a music hall' and steam-powered narrow-gauge trains.

Further south there's a string of charming little centres – Aberaeron, New Quay, Llangrannog and Aberporth – ideal for a relaxing seaside holiday. The pace of life can hardly be described as hectic inland – except perhaps during market days, when farmers invade places like Tregaron and Lampeter for busy buying and selling. From Tregaron, you can follow in the footsteps of the drovers by driving across the Abergwesyn Pass, one of Wales's most spectacular roads. And for a spectacular train ride, take the Vale of Rheidol Railway from Aberystwyth to Devil's Bridge.

53

Fc4 Aberaeron

Most attractive little town on Cardigan Bay, with distinctive, Georgian-style architecture. Pleasant harbour, marine aquarium, coastal centre, re-creation of Aeron Express, an extraordinary aerial ferry across harbour first built in 1885. Sailing popular, good touring centre for coast and inland.

Fe5 Lampeter

Farmers and students mingle in the distinctive small central Dyfed town in the picturesque Teifi Valley. Concerts are often held in St David's University College, and visitors are welcome. Golf and angling, range of small shops and some old inns. Visit the landscaped Cae Hir Gardens, Cribyn.

Fe2 Aberystwyth ⇌

Premier resort on the Cardigan Bay coastline. Fine promenade, cliff railway, camera obscura, harbour and many other seaside attractions. Excellent museum in restored Edwardian theatre. University town, lively arts centre with theatre and concert hall. National Library of Wales stands commandingly on hillside. Good shopping. Vale of Rheidol narrow-gauge steam line runs to Devil's Bridge falls.

Fc6 Llanydsul

Pleasant Teifiside village in a historic textile-producing area where woollen mills still work - and welcome visitors. Salmon fishing very popular; canoeing at certain times of year.

Fc4 New Quay

Picturesque little resort with old harbour on Cardigan Bay. Lovely beaches and coves around and about. Good for sailing and fishing. Resort sheltered by protective headland.

Fa5 Cardigan

Market town on mouth of River Teifi close to beaches and resorts. Good shopping facilities, accommodation, inns. Golf and fishing. Base for exploring inland along wooded Teifi Valley and west to the Pembrokeshire Coast National Park. Y Felin Corn Mill and ruined abbey at neighbouring St Dogmael's. Welsh Wildlife Centre nearby.

Cwm Tudu, near Quay

Ga2 Devil's Bridge

The spectacular Mynach Falls and Punchbowl make a glorious sight in a wooded gorge. A narrow-gauge steam railway runs here from Aberystwyth along the lovely Vale of Rheidol. Beautiful walks, nature trails, picnic sites abound.

Ga3 Tregaron

Small traditional market town with good pony trekking. Anglers and naturalists delight in this area: the great bog nearby is a nature reserve with rare flowers and birds. Wildlife centre at nearby Penuwch. On the doorstep of remote uplands - follow old drovers' road across the spectacular Abergwesyn Pass.

Devil's Bridge Falls

Aberaeron Aberystwyth Cardigan

GH | Arosfa

8 Cadwgan Place,
Aberaeron,
Dyfed SA46 0BU
Tel: (01545) 570120

COMMENDED

Real Welsh hospitality. Georgian guest house and cottage overlooking pretty yachting harbour. Central but quiet. Free parking at adjacent car park. Tea making, en-suite rooms with TV. Family suite. Ground floor bedroom. Seasonal restaurant serving imaginative home cuisine. A la carte or table d'hôte. Wine licence. No smoking. Excellent choice of breakfast. Croeso Cynnes.

		SINGLE PER PERSON B&B		DOUBLE FOR 2 PERSONS B&B		🛏 6
						🛁 3
		MIN £	MAX £	MIN £	MAX £	OPEN
		-	-	28.00	38.00	1-12

H | Southgate Hotel

Antaron Avenue,
Penparcau,
Aberystwyth,
Dyfed SY23 1SF
Tel: (01970) 611550

Small family run licensed hotel approximately one mile from town centre. On the A487 Cardigan road. Double, family, twin rooms. En-suite, with TV and tea and coffee facility. Cot available. Dinner optional. Parking in own grounds. Two ground floor bedrooms, others on first floor.

P		SINGLE PER PERSON B&B		DOUBLE FOR 2 PERSONS B&B		🛏 10
C						🛁 9
		MIN £	MAX £	MIN £	MAX £	OPEN
	T	-	19.00	-	36.00	2-12

FH | Lletty Spence Farm

Cwmerfyn,
Nr Aberystwyth,
Dyfed SY23 3JD
Tel: (01970) 828867

OS Grid 700/828. Peacefully situated traditional stone farmhouse in historic scenic valley. 8 miles Aberystwyth and Devil's Bridge. Family room, double and 2 single beds. Private bathroom. Spectacular walking. Relax by fires in 2 lounges. Bring wellies, help on farm, learn to spin, milk etc. Children most welcome. The Thomas family welcomes you. SAE or phone for brochure.

P		SINGLE PER PERSON B&B		DOUBLE FOR 2 PERSONS B&B		🛏 1
						🛁 -
		MIN £	MAX £	MIN £	MAX £	OPEN
	T	15.00	15.00	30.00	30.00	1-12

FH | Hendre Farm

Llangrannog,
Llandysul,
Dyfed SA44 6AP
Tel: (01239) 654342

HIGHLY COMMENDED

Daffodils line the drive. A buzzard soars above the valley. What better welcome to our lovely Georgian farmhouse set in tranquil countryside, 5 minutes from Cardigan Bay's notable coastline. Attractive and comfortable bedrooms, 1 en-suite. Delightful lounge. Excellent food, with our own honey for breakfast. Well located for wandering and exploring. Golf and crafts nearby. Brochure from Bethan Williams.

P		SINGLE PER PERSON B&B		DOUBLE FOR 2 PERSONS B&B		🛏 2
						🛁 1
	T	MIN £	MAX £	MIN £	MAX £	OPEN
		17.00	18.00	34.00	36.00	1-12

GH | Glynwern Guest House

Llanilar,
Aberystwyth,
Dyfed SY23 4NY
Tel: (01974) 7203

L
COMMENDED

Glynwern is an attractive house set in its own extensive grounds, with own gardens fronting the River Ystwyth, with free private fishing for guests. Two double bedrooms with washbasins, one twin and two single rooms. Comfortable lounge and pleasant dining room. Central heating. Open all year. Ideal base for peaceful, restful or exploring holiday. No dogs allowed. SAE.

P		SINGLE PER PERSON B&B		DOUBLE FOR 2 PERSONS B&B		🛏 2
						🛁 -
		MIN £	MAX £	MIN £	MAX £	OPEN
		19.00	19.00	38.00	38.00	1-12

FH | Tycam Farm

Capel-Bangor,
Aberystwyth,
Dyfed SY23 3NA
Tel: (01970) 880662

Peaceful dairy and sheep farm in glorious Rheidol Valley. $7^1/_2$ miles Aberystwyth, $2^1/_2$ miles off A44. Real home comfort and farmhouse cooking is offered in traditional Cardiganshire farmhouse. Lounge, dining room, separate tables, colour TV. Perfect walking, birdwatching, sightseeing $^1/_2$ mile. Superb salmon, sewin, trout fishing on farm plus nearby lakes. Golf.

P		SINGLE PER PERSON B&B		DOUBLE FOR 2 PERSONS B&B		🛏 2
						🛁 2
	T	MIN £	MAX £	MIN £	MAX £	OPEN
		16.00	18.00	-	-	4-9

H | The Halfway Inn

Devil's Bridge Road,
Pisgah,
Aberystwyth,
Dyfed SY23 4NE
Tel: (01970) 880631
Fax: (01970) 880631

COMMENDED

Halfway between Aberystwyth and Devil's Bridge, 700 feet up on the A4120. This traditional hostelry is world famous for real ales and fine food. Relax in old fashioned ambience of flagstone floors, log fires and candles. Extensive grounds with magnificent views of the Rheidol Valley. Outdoor pursuits in the heart of Red Kite country.

P		SINGLE PER PERSON B&B		DOUBLE FOR 2 PERSONS B&B		🛏 2
						🛁 2
	T	MIN £	MAX £	MIN £	MAX £	OPEN
		-	-	38.00	38.00	1-12

GH | Pantgwyn

Llanfarian,
Aberystwyth,
Dyfed SY23 4DE
Tel: (01970) 612031

This family run guest house is quietly situated in rural countryside in its own five acres of grounds on the A487, just outside the village of Llanfarian. Private parking. All rooms have hot and cold, colour TV, tea/coffee making facilities, central heating. Some rooms en-suite. Ideal for a touring or relaxing holiday.

P		SINGLE PER PERSON B&B		DOUBLE FOR 2 PERSONS B&B		🛏 3
						🛁 2
		MIN £	MAX £	MIN £	MAX £	OPEN
		14.00	19.00	28.00	38.00	1-12

GH | Brynhyfryd Guest House

Gwbert Road,
Cardigan,
Dyfed SA43 1AE
Tel: (01239) 612861

AWARD
HIGHLY COMMENDED

One of Cardigan's longest established guest houses, where a high standard of comfort, cleanliness and good food is always assured. Situated in a pleasant area of the town, within two miles of the coast. All bedrooms have colour television and tea/coffee making facilities, en-suites available. Guests' lounge, evening meals, easy parking. Fire Certificate. AA QQQ. RAC Acclaimed.

		SINGLE PER PERSON B&B		DOUBLE FOR 2 PERSONS B&B		🛏 7
						🛁 2
		MIN £	MAX £	MIN £	MAX £	OPEN
		14.50	15.00	28.00	34.00	1-12

Ceredigion

Cardigan Devil's Bridge Lampeter Llandysul New Quay Tregaron

GH | Berwyn

St Dogmaels,
Cardigan,
Dyfed SA43 3HS
Tel: (01239) 613555

HIGHLY COMMENDED

Privately situated in 2 acres of delightful grounds with magnificent views overlooking Teifi River, central to beautiful beaches, historic places, golf, fishing. Enjoy breakfast with gorgeous views. En-suite with private entrance from grounds. All bedrooms have vanity suites, tea/coffee facilities, colour TV. Guests' lounge. Payphone. Private parking. Warm Welsh welcome. Croeso Cynnes i Berwyn.

P 🛏 ✗ ♨		SINGLE PER PERSON B&B		DOUBLE FOR 2 PERSONS B&B		🛏 3 🛁 2
		MIN £ -	MAX £ -	MIN £ 29.00	MAX £ 38.00	OPEN 1-12

FH | Bryncastell Farm House

Llanfair Road,
Lampeter,
Dyfed SA48 8JY
Tel: (01570) 422447

HIGHLY COMMENDED
AWARD

Bilingual Welsh family on 140 acre riverside farm. Panoramic views of Teifi Valley. Excellent cuisine featuring authentic Welsh recipes and home-made wines. Combine traditional Welsh hospitality with comfort of modern conveniences. One mile from Lampeter town centre. Half mile from Pioneer Co-op store. Signposted Llanfair Clydogau. Opposite WD Lewis Agricultural Merchants. "Taste of Wales" member.

P 🛏 ✗ ♨ 🍴 ♿ T		SINGLE PER PERSON B&B		DOUBLE FOR 2 PERSONS B&B		🛏 3 🛁 2
		MIN £ 17.00	MAX £ 18.00	MIN £ 33.00	MAX £ 33.00	OPEN 1-12

FH | Gelli Aur

Pontsian,
Llandysul,
Dyfed SA44 4UD
Tel: (01545) 55359
From June 1995 Tel: (01545) 590359

Old stone farmhouse in the Clettwr Valley on B4459. Furnished with antiques. Lampeter 9 miles, New Quay and Aberaeron 12 miles. No smoking please.

P 🛏 ♨ 🍴		SINGLE PER PERSON B&B		DOUBLE FOR 2 PERSONS B&B		🛏 1 🛁 1
		MIN £ -	MAX £ 18.00	MIN £ -	MAX £ 30.00	OPEN 4-10

FH | Croft Farm Guest House

Llantood,
Cardigan,
Dyfed SA43 3NT
Tel: (01239) 615179
Fax: (01239) 615179

HIGHLY COMMENDED

Welcome to Croft, a smallholding with animals to help feed. Each attractive room has en-suite, tea/coffee facilities and colour TV, giving home from home atmosphere. Home cooked evening meals are served. There's a fully equipped kitchen and sitting room with fireplace for guests. We are situated amidst beautiful countryside close to Pembrokeshire coast. Lovely garden.

P 🛏 🛏 ✗ 🍴 ♨		SINGLE PER PERSON B&B		DOUBLE FOR 2 PERSONS B&B		🛏 3 🛁 3
		MIN £ 14.00	MAX £ 17.00	MIN £ 28.00	MAX £ 34.00	OPEN 1-12

FH | Brynog Mansion

Felinfach,
Lampeter,
Dyfed SA48 8AQ
Tel: (01570) 470266

HIGHLY COMMENDED

Spacious 250 year old mansion. Situated in the beautiful Vale of Aeron, midway between Lampeter university town and unique Aberaeron seaside resort 15 minutes by car. Approached by ³/₄ mile rhododendron lined drive off the A482 main road and village of Felinfach. 2 spacious en-suite bedrooms, other near bathroom, tea making facilities, central heating. Full breakfast served in the grand old furnished dining room.

P 🛏 ♨		SINGLE PER PERSON B&B		DOUBLE FOR 2 PERSONS B&B		🛏 3 🛁 2
		MIN £ 16.00	MAX £ 18.00	MIN £ 36.00	MAX £ 38.00	OPEN 1-12

GH | Neuadd Wen Guest House

Neuadd Wen,
Llanarth,
Dyfed SA47 0NH
Tel: (01545) 580316

Luxurious peaceful bungalow with superb views. No passing traffic. Lovely woodland/riverside walks. New Quay two miles. Spacious comfortable rooms, bathrooms en-suite, remote control colour TV, no limit free tea/coffee facilities. Safe for children. Breakfast fit for royalty. Happy welcoming atmosphere. Satisfaction guaranteed. Highly recommended.

P 🛏 🛏 🛏 ✗ ♨ 🍴		SINGLE PER PERSON B&B		DOUBLE FOR 2 PERSONS B&B		🛏 2 🛁 2
		MIN £ 16.50	MAX £ 16.50	MIN £ 30.00	MAX £ 30.00	OPEN 1-12

GH | Mount Pleasant

Devil's Bridge,
Nr Aberystwyth,
Dyfed SY23 4QY
Tel: (01970) 890219

HIGHLY COMMENDED

Family run guest house set amid beautiful scenic countryside close to famous waterfalls, Rheidol Steam Railway and Elan Valley. Ideally situated for walking, bird watching, touring. Centrally heated, comfortable, shower en-suite, bedrooms with colour TV's, drinks facilities, radio clock alarms, and many other extras. Enquiries to Janet and Dave Sherlock.

P 🛏 🍸 ♨ 🍴 T		SINGLE PER PERSON B&B		DOUBLE FOR 2 PERSONS B&B		🛏 4 🛁 2
		MIN £ 19.00	MAX £ 19.00	MIN £ 35.00	MAX £ 38.00	OPEN 1-12

GH | Pellorwel

Bwlch y Groes,
Ffostrasol,
Llandysul,
Dyfed SA44 5JU
Tel: (01239) 851226

L

HIGHLY COMMENDED

A friendly welcome awaits our guests. Comfortable accommodation, hot and cold water in all rooms, double four-poster bed. Charming Victorian style house, conveniently situated for touring. 10 miles Cardigan Bay resorts.. Meals freshly cooked using available garden and local produce. Special diets by prior arrangement. Reduced rates for three nights. Only one house rule: "please close the gate".

P 🛏 ✗ 🍴 TW		SINGLE PER PERSON B&B		DOUBLE FOR 2 PERSONS B&B		🛏 3 🛁 -
		MIN £ 12.50	MAX £ 12.50	MIN £ 25.00	MAX £ 25.00	OPEN 1-12

GH | Glanrhyd Isaf

Stags Head,
Llangeitho,
Nr Tregaron,
Dyfed SY25 6QU
Tel: (01974) 298762

HIGHLY COMMENDED

A modern bungalow situated on an elevated site surrounded by beautiful countryside. Comfortably furnished. Centrally heated. Double room en-suite, twin room, bathroom. Both rooms have colour TV and tea/coffee facilities. Ideal walking, touring, bird watching country. Pony- trekking, golf, fishing in area. 10 miles from coast, OS. sheet 146 ref. 637-591. Mrs W R Owen.

P 🛏 🛏 ✗ ♨ 🍴 C		SINGLE PER PERSON B&B		DOUBLE FOR 2 PERSONS B&B		🛏 2 🛁 1
		MIN £ 14.50	MAX £ 15.00	MIN £ 30.00	MAX £ 34.00	OPEN 1-12

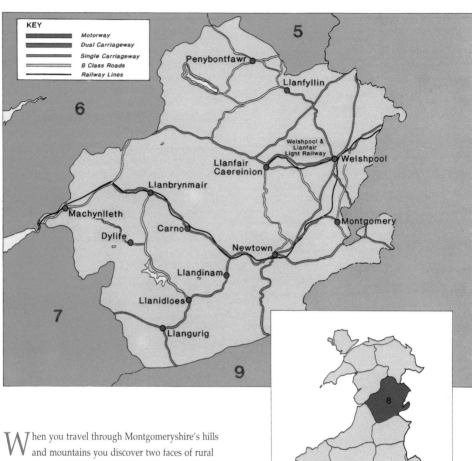

When you travel through Montgomeryshire's hills and mountains you discover two faces of rural Wales. Along the Wales/England border there's an undulating landscape of fresh green fields and broad river valleys, dotted with black-and-white half-timbered farmsteads that might have been transplanted from Shakespeare Country. But head further west, into Montgomeryshire's untamed highlands, and the scene changes dramatically. These mountains and moors, with their thin scattering of sturdy, stone-built dwellings, are the home of the hardy hill-sheep farmer.

Montgomeryshire is also home to some of Wales's most scenic lakes – remote Lake Vyrnwy, almost lost in thickly wooded uplands, and Llyn Clywedog, surrounded by rolling hills and forests.

Explore the area from market towns and country villages. Stay, for example, at Welshpool, Llanidloes or Machynlleth, three handsome historic towns. Or choose somewhere smaller, such as Montgomery with its pretty Georgian buildings and ruined castle. Nearby Powis Castle is anything but a ruin. Don't miss this sumptuous National Trust house, which stands in magnificent grounds on the outskirts of Welshpool.

De6   Carno

Located in the middle of Mid Wales - an excellent touring base for exploring southern Snowdonia, the Cardigan Bay coast, Cambrian Mountains and border country. Only a small village, but famous as the base for Laura Ashley fabrics and fashions.

Dd6   Dylife

Remote hamlet high in the Cambrian Mountains on exhilarating mountain road to Machynlleth. Remains of old lead mine workings stand amongst wonderfully wild countryside. Waterfall, good walking countryside. Llyn Clywedog and Hafren Forest nearby.

De5   Llanbrynmair

Scattered mountain-ringed village on Afon (River) Twymyn, a tributary of the Dovey. Travel south from here on the B4518 to the huge man-made lake of Llyn Clywedog - an inspiring mountain route.

Eb5   Llanfair Caereinion

Pleasant town set amid rolling hills and forests in lovely Vale of Banwy. Best known as terminus for narrow-gauge Welshpool and Llanfair Light Railway.

Eb3   Llanfyllin

Historic small country town, in rolling peaceful Powys farmlands. Lake Vyrnwy and 240ft Pistyll Rhaeadr waterfall are popular beauty spots nearby. Visit the Bird and Butterfly World, an attraction with birds from all over the world.

Market Hall, Llanidloes

Gc1   Llangurig

First village on fledgling River Wye, nearly 1000ft up in the mountains. A craft centre and a monastic 14th-century church. Good touring centre for lakes and mountains of central Wales. Ideal walking countryside.

Gd1   Llanidloes

Historic and attractive market town at confluence of Severn and Clywedog rivers; excellent touring centre. Noted for its 16th-century market hall, now a museum, and other fine half-timbered buildings. Interesting shops. Massive Clywedog dam and lake 3 miles away on B4518. Take the scenic drive around lakeside and visit the Bryn Tail Lead Mine beneath the dam.

Lake Vyrnwy

Dc5   Machynlleth   ≋

Historic market town near beautiful Dovey Estuary. Owain Glyndŵr's Parliament House in the wide handsome main street is now a museum and brass rubbing centre. Superbly equipped Bro Dyfi Leisure Centre offers wide range of activities. Celtica centre tells the story of Celtic myth and legend. Ancient and modern meet here; the inventive Centre for Alternative Technology is 3 miles away, just off the A487 to Dolgellau. Felin Crewi Flour Mill is off the A489 2 miles to the east.

Ec6	Montgomery

Hilltop market town of distinctive Georgian architecture beneath the ruins of a 13th-century castle. Offa's Dyke, which once marked the border, runs nearby. Not far from Welshpool and Powis Castle.

Eb3	Penybontfawr

Secluded village amid forests and lakes, near the spectacular 240ft Pistyll Rhaeadr waterfalls. Pony trekking and walking country, with hills and woods all around. Lake Vyrnwy Visitor Centre nearby.

Eb6	Newtown

Busy Severn Valley market town and one-time home of Welsh flannel industry. Textile history recalled in small museum; another museum based around Robert Owen, pioneer socialist, who lived here. Town also has interesting W H Smith Museum, solid old buildings, river promenade, street market and the lively Theatr Hafren.

Ec5	Welshpool

Old market town of the borderlands, full of character, with half-timbered buildings and welcoming inns. Attractive canalside museum. Good shopping centre; golf and angling. Powis Castle is an impressive stately home with a Clive of India Museum and outstanding gardens. Ride the narrow-gauge Welshpool and Llanfair Light Railway, visit the Moors Wildlife Collection.

Powysland Museum and Montgomery Canal Centre

59

Carno Dylife Llanbrynmair Llanfair Caereinion Llanfyllin Llangurig Llanidloes

---

FH Pentre Uchaf

Carno,
Powys SY17 5JP
Tel: (01686) 420663

A warm welcome awaits you at this family run farm set amidst glorious countryside situated half mile off A470 coast road. Traditional farmhouse, beams, inglenook fireplace. Colour TV lounge, dining room. Bedroom en-suite, colour TV, drinks tray. Baby facilities. Ideal base for walking, touring, golf, trekking, fishing, clay pigeon shooting. Sea 30 miles. Brochure available.

P 〽 🛏️ 🚜 T		SINGLE PER PERSON B&B	DOUBLE FOR 2 PERSONS B&B	🛁 1 🛁 1
		MIN £ 14.00	MAX £ 16.00	MIN £ 28.00	MAX £ 30.00	OPEN 1-12

FH Madog's Wells

Llanfair Caereinion,
Welshpool,
Powys SY21 0DE
Tel: (01938) 810446

Small hill farm in secluded valley. Ideal for touring Mid Wales. Washbasins in rooms. Visitors' bathroom. Reduced rates for under 12's. TV, games room. Also two fully equipped 6/8 berth caravans maximum £160pw. Bungalow sleeps 5, disabled criteria 2 max. £220. Astrological observatory with superb 16" Dobsonian telescope with NGC Max computer..

P 〽 🏠 🍽️		SINGLE PER PERSON B&B	DOUBLE FOR 2 PERSONS B&B	🛏️ 3 🛁 -
		MIN £ 14.00	MAX £ 14.00	MIN £ 28.00	MAX £ 28.00	OPEN 1-12

GH The Old Vicarage

Llangurig,
Powys SY18 6RN
Tel: (01686) 440280
Fax: (01686) 440280

AWARD HIGHLY COMMENDED

Charming Victorian vicarage in superb country setting, close to Elan Valley and Plynlimon Hills. Ideal base for walking, touring the lakes and mountains of Mid Wales. Peaceful location. All rooms tastefully decorated with en-suite facilities, colour TV, tea/coffee making tray. Residential licence. Pets welcome. WTB award for comfort and service. Two lounges with log fires.

P 🛏️ 🍽️		SINGLE PER PERSON B&B	DOUBLE FOR 2 PERSONS B&B	🛏️ 4 🛁 4
		MIN £ -	MAX £ -	MIN £ 36.00	MAX £ 38.00	OPEN 3-10

H Star Inn

Dylife,
Nr Staylittle,
Llanbrynmair,
Powys SY19 7BW
Tel: (01650) 521345

Set in some of Britain's most delightful scenery, the Star Inn offers pony trekking from the inn's own stables. Fishing, golfing, walking, cycling nearby. The inn dates back to 1640 and offers the finest home made food. Curries a speciality. The oak panelled bar and log fire add to the wonderful ambience. Guests' TV lounge. Full central heating.

P C 🏠 🍽️		SINGLE PER PERSON B&B	DOUBLE FOR 2 PERSONS B&B	🛏️ 7 🛁 2
		MIN £ 18.00	MAX £ 19.00	MIN £ 36.00	MAX £ 38.00	OPEN 1-12

FH Cwm Alan

Llanfyllin,
Powys SY22 5HX
Tel: (01691) 648301

HIGHLY COMMENDED

Magnificent views surround Cwmalan, a large, Victorian farmhouse which stands in a elevated position in the peaceful Alan Valley. Situated close to lakes Vyrnwy, Bala and Pistyll Rhaeader falls. Full central heating and tea/coffee making facilities. Spacious quality accommodation with open log fires. Open all year. Evening meals by arrangement. A warm welcome awaits.

P 🏠 🛏️ 🍽️ 🚜		SINGLE PER PERSON B&B	DOUBLE FOR 2 PERSONS B&B	🛏️ 2 🛁 2
		MIN £ 17.00	MAX £ 19.00	MIN £ 34.00	MAX £ 38.00	OPEN 1-12

H Lloyds

Cambrian Place,
Llanidloes,
Powys SY18 6BX
Tel: (01686) 412284
Fax: (01686) 412666

Combining the qualities of the best guest house with the style of a small hotel. Enjoy the informal, friendly and peaceful atmosphere, or come and go as you please. Proprietors Tom and Roy give the personal service to meet your needs - for a leisurely breakfast with fresh coffee and complimentary newspapers, or a very early start.

C 🛏️ 🍽️		SINGLE PER PERSON B&B	DOUBLE FOR 2 PERSONS B&B	🛏️ 10 🛁 2
		MIN £ 15.00	MAX £ 17.50	MIN £ 30.00	MAX £ 35.00	OPEN 1-12

GH Cyfeiliog Guest house

Bont Dolgadfan,
Llanbrynmair,
Powys SY19 7BB
Tel: (01650) 521231

COMMENDED

Licensed guest house in pretty hamlet beside River Twymyn. Centrally heated throughout. Open fire, beamed lounge. Relaxed friendly atmosphere. TV, books, information maps. Wonderful holiday centre. Walking, birdwatching, castles, lakes, touring, golf. Sea 25 miles, Machynlleth, Centre for Alternative Technology 15 miles. Evening meal, packed lunches, vegetarians welcome. Ideal cosy winter breaks.

P 🏠 🍽️ T		SINGLE PER PERSON B&B	DOUBLE FOR 2 PERSONS B&B	🛏️ 3 🛁 1
		MIN £ 14.00	MAX £ 15.50	MIN £ 28.00	MAX £ 31.00	OPEN 1-12

H Black Lion Hotel

Llangurig,
Powys SY18 6SG
Tel: (015515) 223

On the A44 Aberystwyth Road 25 miles from the coast. Llangurig is the highest village in Wales. Fully centrally heated with log fires in bar, radios and tea/coffee in all rooms. Home cooked food, lunch and evening meals available. Friendly relaxed atmosphere situated in beautiful walking country close to the Elan Valley. Pets.are very welcome.

P 🛏️ 🍽️ T		SINGLE PER PERSON B&B	DOUBLE FOR 2 PERSONS B&D	🛏️ 8 🛁 5
		MIN £ 17.00	MAX £ 17.00	MIN £ 30.00	MAX £ 34.00	OPEN 1-12

FH Esgairmaen

Fan,
Llanidloes,
Powys SY18 6UT
Tel: (01686) 430272

Esgairmaen is a farmhouse situated 1 mile from the Clywedog Reservoir, where fishing and sailing can be enjoyed. An ideal base for walking, bird watching and exploring nearby forests. The farmhouse commands magnificent views and the atmosphere is peaceful. Guests can be sure of a warm welcome.

P C 🏠 🍽️		SINGLE PER PERSON B&B	DOUBLE FOR 2 PERSONS B&B	🛏️ 2 🛁 1
		MIN £ 14.00	MAX £ 16.00	MIN £ -	MAX £ -	OPEN 3-10

Machynlleth   Montgomery

H	Braich Goch Hotel

Corris,
Powys SY20 9RD
Tel: (01654) 761229

Set in beautiful surroundings at the head of the Dulas Valley, most rooms en-suite. Family room available. Bar meals or restaurant. The Centre for Alternative Technology and the new King Arthur's Labyrinth are nearby. Beach is within easy reach. Rich in mountain walks. Steam trains, golf, fishing close by. Activity holidays arranged. Pets welcome.

	SINGLE PER PERSON B&B		DOUBLE FOR 2 PERSONS B&B		6
					4
	MIN £	MAX £	MIN £	MAX £	OPEN
	-	-	33.00	38.00	1-12

GH	Pendre Guest House

Maengwyn Street,
Machynlleth,
Powys SY20 8EF
Tel: (01654) 702088
COMMENDED

Looking for somewhere interesting to stay within Machynlleth? Pendre is a Georgian style house with some en-suite facilities. Ideal base for touring Mid Wales. Homely atmosphere, TV in all rooms. A warm and friendly welcome awaits you. Plenty to do: golf, walking, fishing, leisure centre, Celtica, Centre for Alternative Technology all nearby. Beautiful coast, beautiful breakfasts.

	SINGLE PER PERSON B&B		DOUBLE FOR 2 PERSONS B&B		3
					2
	MIN £	MAX £	MIN £	MAX £	OPEN
	17.00	19.00	30.00	34.00	1-12

FH	Mathafarn

Llanwrin,
Machynlleth,
Powys SY20 8QJ
Tel: (01650) 511226
HIGHLY COMMENDED

Henry VII is reputed to have stayed here en-route to the Battle of Bosworth. Now this 16th century elegant country house is part of a working farm. Inglenook fire, central heating, television lounge. One twin, private bathroom, double en-suite, one single. Tea/coffee making facilities. Close to Machynlleth, Centre for Alternative Technology, beautiful coastline of Aberdyfi. Contact Susan Hughes..

	SINGLE PER PERSON B&B		DOUBLE FOR 2 PERSONS B&B		2
					2
	MIN £	MAX £	MIN £	MAX £	OPEN
	17.00	17.00	34.00	34.00	1-12

GH	Maenllwyd

Newtown Road,
Machynlleth,
Powys SY20 8EY
Tel: (01654) 702928
Fax: (01654) 702928
AWARD   HIGHLY COMMENDED

Friendly guest house in historic market town. All rooms have central heating, tea/coffee making facilities and TV. We are noted for our breakfasts. Secure off road parking. Lounge with books, videos. Convenient for golf, hill walking, bird watching, leisure centre, beaches, Centre for Alternative Technology. For further information telephone Nigel or Margaret Vince.

	SINGLE PER PERSON B&B		DOUBLE FOR 2 PERSONS B&B		8
					6
	MIN £	MAX £	MIN £	MAX £	OPEN
	-	-	28.00	36.00	1-12

FH	Bacheiddon

Aberhosan,
Machynlleth,
Powys SY20 8SG
Tel: (01654) 702229

850 acre beef and sheep farm six miles from the market town of Machynlleth and within easy reach of the sea and Snowdonia National Park. Ideal centre for walking, bird watching and touring. Three double en-suite bedrooms with tea/coffee facilities. Separate dining room, lounge with colour TV and reading material. Brochure from Mrs A Lewis..

	SINGLE PER PERSON B&B		DOUBLE FOR 2 PERSONS B&B		3
					3
	MIN £	MAX £	MIN £	MAX £	OPEN
	17.00	18.00	34.00	36.00	5-10

FH	The Drewin Farm

Churchstoke,
Montgomery,
Powys SY15 6TW
Tel: (01588) 620325
AWARD   HIGHLY COMMENDED

This friendly, family run farmhouse was featured on BBC Travel Show 1993. With panoramic views, bedrooms have TV, hairdryer and drinks facilities. En-suite available. Games room with snooker table. Good home cooking is served in the oak beamed dining room, vegetarian by request. Offa's Dyke Path runs through farm. A warm welcome awaits. AA Selected.

	SINGLE PER PERSON B&B		DOUBLE FOR 2 PERSONS B&B		2
					1
	MIN £	MAX £	MIN £	MAX £	OPEN
	16.00	18.00	30.00	36.00	3-11

GH	Melin-y-Wig Guest House

Aberystwyth Road,
Machynlleth,
Powys SY20 8ET   Ⓛ
Tel: (01654) 703933

Comfortable guest house in market town. Convenient for walking, touring and golf. Leisure Centre nearby. Coast, nature reserves and Centre for Alternative Technology in easy travelling distance. Washbasin, TV, central heating and tea/coffee making facilities in all rooms. Ample car parking facilities. Contact Pat or Peter Eley.

	SINGLE PER PERSON B&B		DOUBLE FOR 2 PERSONS B&B		2
					-
	MIN £	MAX £	MIN £	MAX £	OPEN
	-	-	28.00	30.00	1-11

Visitor's Guide to Mid Wales

In full colour and packed with information – a must for all visitors to Mid Wales

- •Where to go and what to see
- •Descriptions of towns, villages and resorts •Hundreds of attractions to visit •Detailed maps and plans
- •Scenic drives, beaches, narrow-gauge railways, what to do on a rainy day **£3.55 inc. p&p**
(see "Guide Books" page).

FH	Little Brompton Farm

Montgomery,
Powys SY15 6HY
Tel: (01686) 668371
AWARD   HIGHLY COMMENDED

Charming 17th century farmhouse on working farm situated on B4385 road 2 miles east of Montgomery, 1/2 mile west off A489. Traditionally furnished. En-suite rooms available. Delicious home cooking. Central heating. Pretty rooms enhanced by quality furnishing and antiques. Offa's Dyke Path runs through farm. Offering friendly and relaxing atmosphere. Open all year. AA ๐๐๐๐ Selected. Mrs G Bright.

	SINGLE PER PERSON B&B		DOUBLE FOR 2 PERSONS B&B		3
					3
	MIN £	MAX £	MIN £	MAX £	OPEN
	17.00	19.00	32.00	38.00	1-12

Newtown   Penybontfawr

GH	Greenfields

Kerry,
Newtown,
Powys SY16 4LH
Tel: (01686) 670596
Fax: (01686) 670354

A warm welcome awaits you at our home situated on A489 1/4 mile east of Kerry. Our rooms have picturesque views of the rolling countryside. Lounge has colour TV and open log fire. Excellent stopping place for one night stops, weekends or longer breaks while exploring beautiful Mid Wales and the Borders. Your contact Mrs Vi Madeley.

P	⚬	SINGLE PER PERSON B&B	DOUBLE FOR 2 PERSONS B&B	⚬ 3
⚬	⚬			-
⚬	⚬	MIN £	MAX £	MIN £	MAX £	OPEN
⚬	⚬	13.00	15.00	26.00	30.00	1-12

FH	Llettyderyn

Mochdre,
Newtown,
Powys SY16 4JY
Tel: (01686) 626131

AWARD HIGHLY COMMENDED

Restored farmhouse with exposed beams, inglenook fireplace, traditional parlour. Rooms all en-suite with TV and drinks tray. Vegetarians catered for. Excellent farmhouse cooking including home baked bread. Just 2 miles from Newtown off A489/A470. Superb views from our working farm rearing sheep and beef. Enquiries from Margaret and John Jandrell.

P	⚬	SINGLE PER PERSON B&B	DOUBLE FOR 2 PERSONS B&B	⚬ 3
⚬	⚬			3
⚬	T	MIN £	MAX £	MIN £	MAX £	OPEN
		19.00	19.00	32.00	32.00	1-12

FH	Glanhafon

Penybontfawr,
Nr Oswestry,
Powys SY10 0EW
Tel: (01691) 74377

COMMENDED

Secluded farmhouse in the upper Tanant Valley close to Lake Vyrnwy and Pistyll Falls. A working sheep farm with hill walking on farm, ideal for a peaceful holiday. One twin with private bathroom. Double and family en-suite. Own sitting room with log fire, central heating. Children welcome. Ample car parking. Enquiries to Anne Evans.

P	⚬	SINGLE PER PERSON B&B	DOUBLE FOR 2 PERSONS B&B	⚬ 3
⚬	⚬			2
⚬	⚬	MIN £	MAX £	MIN £	MAX £	OPEN
		14.00	18.00	28.00	30.00	4-10

FH	Lower Gwestydd

Llanllwchairn,
Newtown,
Powys SY16 3AY
Tel: (01686) 626718

AWARD HIGHLY COMMENDED

Beautiful half-timbered 17th century listed farmhouse set just off the B4568 1 1/2 miles north of Newtown. 2 rooms en-suite. All centrally heated with tea/coffee making facilities. Separate dining room. Lounge with colour TV. Large garden providing produce for table. Lovely views from this 200 acre mixed farm. Guests are assured of a very warm welcome.

P	⚬	SINGLE PER PERSON B&B	DOUBLE FOR 2 PERSONS B&B	⚬ 3
⚬				2
⚬	⚬	MIN £	MAX £	MIN £	MAX £	OPEN
T		19.00	19.00	33.00	34.00	1-12

FH	Penyceunant

Penybontfawr,
Powys SY10 0PF
Tel: (01691) 860459

HIGHLY COMMENDED

Old farmhouse with spectacular views across the Tanat Valley. Substantial rooms with washbasin, colour TV and easy chair. Guests' garden lounge. Ideal as a secluded retreat yet well placed for touring. We specialise in walking holidays offering half board packages for week long or weekend breaks. Information service, routecard loan. Enquiries, brochures Anna Francis.

P	⚬	SINGLE PER PERSON B&B	DOUBLE FOR 2 PERSONS B&B	⚬ 2
⚬	⚬			-
⚬	⚬	MIN £	MAX £	MIN £	MAX £	OPEN
		16.50	16.50	29.00	29.00	1-11

FH	Dyffryn

Aberhafesp,
Newtown,
Powys SY16 3JD
Tel: (01686) 688817 or (0585) 206412
Fax: (01686) 688324

AWARD DE LUXE

Luxury en-suite accommodation in recently restored 17th century barn in the middle of a 200 acre sheep and beef farm. All rooms have colour TV, tea and coffee facilities and full central heating. Totally non smoking establishment. Lovely walks, lakes, birds and golf nearby. Delicious evening meals including vegetarian. Warm welcome guaranteed from Dave and Sue Jones.

P	⚬	SINGLE PER PERSON B&B	DOUBLE FOR 2 PERSONS B&B	⚬ 3
⚬	⚬			3
⚬	⚬	MIN £	MAX £	MIN £	MAX £	OPEN
⚬	⚬	19.00	19.00	38.00	38.00	1-12

GH	Blaen Hirnant Guest House

Hirnant,
Penybontfawr,
Powys SY10 0HR
Tel: (01691) 73330

HIGHLY COMMENDED

14th/15th century Welsh farmhouse peacefully situated in Montgomeryshire hills. Tastefully renovated exposing original cruck beam construction, inglenook fireplace. En-suite rooms have TV/radio, tea/coffee, central heating. Comfortable lounge, oak beamed dining room. Pre-booked dinner available. Special diets catered for. Own produce. 3 miles Lake Vyrnwy. Walking, bird watching, touring. Easy reach of many places of interest.

P	⚬	SINGLE PER PERSON B&B	DOUBLE FOR 2 PERSONS B&B	⚬ 3
⚬	⚬			3
⚬	T	MIN £	MAX £	MIN £	MAX £	OPEN
		-	28.00	30.00	1-12

FH	Wernddu Farm

Penybontfawr,
Via Oswestry,
Powys SY10 0HW
Tel: (01691) 74221

COMMENDED

One double bedroom with en-suite facilities and one twin or family bedroom with private bathroom. A friendly, homely atmosphere awaits you at Wernddu Farm, a working farm surrounded by beautiful countryside with magnificent views, an ideal centre from which to tour the area's many attractions. Gardens, walking, fishing, bird watching, waterfalls and lakes. Enquiries Enid Roberts.

P	⚬	SINGLE PER PERSON B&B	DOUBLE FOR 2 PERSONS B&B	⚬ 2
⚬	⚬			1
⚬		MIN £	MAX £	MIN £	MAX £	OPEN
		-	15.00	22.00	24.00	1-11

Welshpool

GH	Tresi-Aur
Brookfield Road, Welshpool, Powys SY21 7PZ Tel: (01938) 552430	

Family or double room with own bathroom and shower. Twin or single room. Car parking. Children under 14 reduction. Central heating. TV, tea or coffee and telephone available. Open January until November. No smoking. Shaver points. Warm friendly welcome awaits. Golf, fishing, pony trekking, walking facilities in area.

P 🛏️ ♿ ✕ 🚿		SINGLE PER PERSON B&B		DOUBLE FOR 2 PERSONS B&B		🛏️ 2 🛁 1
		MIN £ 15.00	MAX £ 15.00	MIN £ 27.00	MAX £ 27.00	OPEN 1-11

FH	Plasdwpa Farm
Berriew, Welshpool, Powys SY21 8PS Tel: (01686) 640298	

Dairy farm set 1 1/2 miles above the pretty black and white village of Berriew. Sensational views over the Severn Valley and Shropshire borders seen from every room. Very central for touring and local attractions. Large bathroom with bath and shower, washbasin in every room. One room has a balcony, all are nicely furnished. Children welcome.

P 🛏️ ♿		SINGLE PER PERSON B&B		DOUBLE FOR 2 PERSONS B&B		🛏️ 3 🛁 -
🍴 ⚙️ T		MIN £ 15.00	MAX £ 17.00	MIN £ 30.00	MAX £ 34.00	OPEN 3-10

FH	Tynllwyn Farm
Welshpool, Powys SY21 9BW Tel: (01938) 553175	

Tynllwyn is a family farm and farmhouse with a friendly welcome. Good farmhouse food and bar licence. All bedrooms have central heating, colour TV, tea and coffee facilities, hot and cold wash units. 1 mile from the lovely market town of Welshpool, on the A490 north. Very quiet and pleasantly situated on a hillside with beautiful views. 2 day short bargain break available October - March. Pets by arrangement. "Taste of Wales" member.

P 🛏️ ☕ ⚙️		SINGLE PER PERSON B&B		DOUBLE FOR 2 PERSONS B&B		🛏️ 5 🛁 -
🍴 T		MIN £ 14.50	MAX £ 14.50	MIN £ 29.00	MAX £ 29.00	OPEN 1-12

Powis Castle, Welshpool

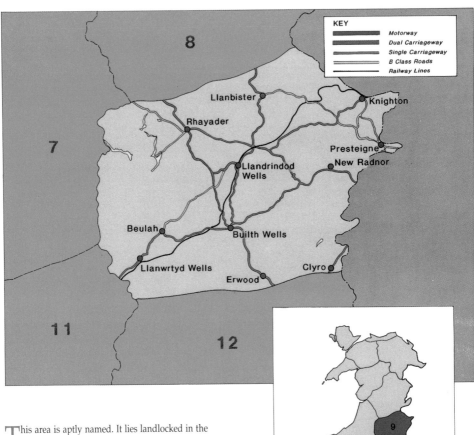

This area is aptly named. It lies landlocked in the green heart of traditional farming country. So it is entirely appropriate that Builth Wells – at the heart of the Heart of Wales! – plays host each year to the Royal Welsh Show, the premier gathering of farming folk.

Builth is one of four 'Wells' towns in the Heart of Wales. Of the others – Llandrindod, Llanwrtyd and Llangammarch – Llandrindod is the largest. All prospered during the heyday of the spa town. Llandrindod Wells, in particular, preserves memories of those fashionable times gone by – in its impressive Victorian streets, parklands and boating lake, and also during its annual Victorian Festival. Llanwrtyd Wells, Britain's smallest town, is busy again as a pony trekking, walking and mountain biking centre.

Water seems to be a dominant theme here. The Wye, a famous fishing river, flows through the middle of the area. And in the hills above Rhayader there are the Elan Valley lakes, Wales's first – and possibly most scenic – man-made reservoirs. Call in at the Elan Valley Visitor Centre for an introduction to these beautiful lakelands and their prolific wildlife.

Heart of Wales

Gc4 Beulah

Village in heart of sheep farming country west of Builth Wells. At the foot of the wild Cambrian Mountains, a wonderful landscape to explore on foot, horseback or by car. Follow the mountain road west across the spectacular Abergwesyn Pass to Tregaron, visit the lovely Welsh lakelands and Llanwrtyd Wells' Cambrian Woollen Mill.

Ge4 Builth Wells

Solidly built old country town which plays host every July to the Royal Welsh Agricultural Show, Wales's largest farming gathering. Lovely setting on River Wye amid beautiful hills. Lively sheep and cattle markets. Good shopping for local products, touring centre for Mid Wales and border country. River walk, Wyeside Arts Centre.

Ha5 Erwood

Small village on banks of the River Wye south-east of Builth Wells. Good base for fishing and walking - village is close to Brecon Beacons National Park, hills of central Wales and rolling border country.

Hb2 Knighton

Tref y Clawdd, 'the town on the dyke', stands in a deep wooded valley where the 8th-century Offa's Dyke defines the ancient border between Wales and England. Some of the best-preserved stretches of the earthen dyke can be found in the undisturbed hills near the town's Offa's Dyke Centre.

Ha2 Llanbister

Peaceful village on winding A483 Llandrindod Wells-Newtown road. St Cynllo's Church originally served as a stronghold as well as a place of worship. Nearby is the delightful little church at Llananno with its famous rood screen.

Ge3 Llandrindod Wells

Victorian spa town with spacious street and impressive architecture. Victorian-style visitor centre and excellent museum tracing the history of spa. Magic Lantern Theatre. A popular inland resort with golf, fishing, bowling, boating and tennis available. Excellent touring centre for Mid Wales hills and lakes. Annual Victorian Festival in August.

Gc5 Llanwrtyd Wells

One-time spa encircled by wild and beautiful countryside, now a centre for pony trekking, walking, fishing and mountain biking. Cambrian Woollen Mill a popular attraction. For spectacular views explore nearby Abergwesyn Pass/Llyn Brianne area. Diverse programme of events throughout the year.

Hb3 New Radnor

Historic village in sleepy border country close to Offa's Dyke Footpath. Remnants of a medieval castle. Interesting old church at nearby Old Radnor. Radnor Forest to the north, Hay-on-Wye, the 'town of books', to the south.

Gd2 Rhayader

Country market town full of character, with inviting inns and Welsh craft products in the shops. Excellent base for exploring mountains and lakes (Elan Valley and Claerwen), with opportunities for pony trekking, mountain biking and fishing. Small museum. An interesting walk through the country on the nearby Gigrin Farm Trail.

Craig-goch reservoir, Elan Valley

Beulah   Builth Wells   Erwood

FH	Cefn Hafdre Farm

Cefn Hafdre,
Beulah,
Llanwrtyd Wells,
Powys LD5 4UE
Tel: (01591) 620634

Real farmhouse home cooking. Peaceful, red kite country. Lovely walks. Bring your own horse and ride. Centrally situated to travel to both west and south coasts. Attractions in the area include woollen mills, craft shops, glorious mountain lakes. Away from it all breaks in the lush greenery of Mid Wales.

🐴 🛏️ 🍴 🐕 ♨️ 📺 🏕️	C TW T	SINGLE PER PERSON B&B	DOUBLE FOR 2 PERSONS B&B	🛁 2 🛁 -		
		MIN £ 12.00	MAX £ 15.00	MIN £ 24.00	MAX £ 30.00	OPEN 4-10

FH	Caepandy Farm

Garth Road,
Builth Wells,
Powys LD2 3NS
Tel: (01982) 3793

A welcome awaits you at Caepandy. Modernised 17th century house 1 mile from Builth Wells with magnificent views of Irfon Valley and surrounding countryside. Guests' TV lounge. Tea/coffee all rooms. Within easy reach of Black Mountains, Brecon Beacons, Hay-on-Wye, Elan Valley, Cambrian Mountains. Pony trekking, swimming pool, golf, cricket, sports hall etc nearby.

P 🛏️ 🍴 🐕	🐴	SINGLE PER PERSON B&B	DOUBLE FOR 2 PERSONS B&B	🛁 3 🛁 -		
		MIN £ 13.00	MAX £ 14.00	MIN £ 26.00	MAX £ 28.00	OPEN 1-12

FH	Ty-Isaf Farm

Erwood,
Builth Wells,
Powys LD2 3SZ
Tel: (01982) 560607

Ty-Isaf is just off the A470 near Erwood village, a 340 acre mixed farm. Ideally placed for touring Mid Wales. Guests are welcome to stroll around the farm. Hot and cold, tea/coffee making all rooms. TV lounge, dining room. Good home cooking. Bath with shower and toilet. Separate toilet. Children welcome. RAC Listed.

P 🛏️ 🐕 🍴	🐴 🍽️ TW	SINGLE PER PERSON B&B	DOUBLE FOR 2 PERSONS B&B	🛁 3 🛁 -		
		MIN £ 13.00	MAX £ -	MIN £ 26.00	MAX £ -	OPEN 1-12

H	Griffin Inn

Cwm Owen,
Builth Wells,
Powys LD2 3HY
Tel: (01982) 552778
COMMENDED

Step back in time on an adventure into the past, enjoy a meal in our gas lit restaurant, or a draught ale in the stone flagged gas lit bar. All rooms en-suite, tea/coffee facilities and TV. Nigel and Lana look forward to meeting you at the beginning of your adventure.

P 🏆 🐕 🛏️ 🍽️ T	SINGLE PER PERSON B&B	DOUBLE FOR 2 PERSONS B&B	🛁 3 🛁 3		
	MIN £ -	MAX £ -	MIN £ 38.00	MAX £ 38.00	OPEN 1-12

FH	Disserth Mill

Builth Wells,
Powys LD2 3TN
Tel: (01982) 553217

Disserth Mill is down a quiet road just 200 yards off A483 north of Builth Wells, 2 miles from Royal Welsh Showground, 4 miles from Llandrindod Wells. A beautiful garden to relax in. Firm comfortable beds. TV, coffee/tea and washbasin in all rooms. Good Welsh breakfast. Pleasant area for walking, golf, swimming and sports centre 4 miles away.

P C 🛏️ 🐕 🍽️ T	SINGLE PER PERSON B&B	DOUBLE FOR 2 PERSONS B&B	🛁 3 🛁 -		
	MIN £ 15.00	MAX £ 18.00	MIN £ 30.00	MAX £ 36.00	OPEN 3-10

GH	Old Vicarage

Erwood, Builth Wells,
Powys LD2 3SZ
Tel: (01982) 560680

Beautiful situation in peaceful grounds just off A470 near Erwood. Breathtaking views. Elegant decoration, spacious throughout. Beverage tray, hot and cold water all rooms, one with colour TV. Guests own bathroom and separate toilet. Private TV lounge, adequate comfort, indoor games, separate dining room. Farmhouse roasts with vegetables from our garden. Farm animals. Children and pets welcome. Ideal base for touring Mid and South Wales.

P 🛏️ 🐕 🍴 🍽️ T	SINGLE PER PERSON B&B	DOUBLE FOR 2 PERSONS B&B	🛁 3 🛁 -		
	MIN £ 12.50	MAX £ 13.00	MIN £ 25.00	MAX £ 26.00	OPEN 1-12

GH	Querida

43 Garth Road,
Builth Wells,
Powys LD2 3AR
Tel: (01982) 3642

Within easy reach of town centre with its craft shops, theatre, swimming pool, golf course, cricket etc Beautiful walks beside River Wye. Washbasin, shaver points, tea and coffee making facilities all rooms. Lounge with colour TV, dining room, full central heating. Guests welcome at all times.

P 🛏️ 🐕 🍴 T	TW	SINGLE PER PERSON B&B	DOUBLE FOR 2 PERSONS B&B	🛁 3 🛁 -		
		MIN £ 12.00	MAX £ 14.00	MIN £ 24.00	MAX £ 28.00	OPEN 1-12

FH	Gwern-y-Mynach

Llanafan Fawr,
Builth Wells,
Powys LD2 3PN
Tel: (01597) 860256

Gwern-y-Mynach has one en-suite family bedroom and one single. We are a working mixed sheep and dairy farm situated in the Heart of Wales near the three famous spa towns, within easy reach of the Elan Valley reservoirs which is a lovely walk across the mountains. A most friendly welcome awaits all guests. Nearby cricket, golf, bowling at Builth Wells.

🍽️ 🐕 🐴	TW	SINGLE PER PERSON B&B	DOUBLE FOR 2 PERSONS B&B	🛁 2 🛁 1		
		MIN £ 13.00	MAX £ 16.00	MIN £ 28.00	MAX £ 32.00	OPEN 1-12

GH	Orchard Cottage

Erwood,
Builth Wells,
Powys LD2 3EZ
Tel: (01982) 560600
HIGHLY COMMENDED

200 year old tastefully modernised cottage on banks of River Wye with wonderful views. Good value evening meals at inn next door. Colour TV in all rooms. Fishing available in Cletwr Brook. Ideal centre for exploring Mid Wales. Nearby canoeing, horseriding, gliding, swimming, local sports centres. Homely welcome from your well travelled hosts Pat and Alan Prior.

P 🛏️ 🐕 ♨️	SINGLE PER PERSON B&B	DOUBLE FOR 2 PERSONS B&B	🛁 3 🛁 1		
	MIN £ -	MAX £ -	MIN £ 30.00	MAX £ 35.00	OPEN 1-12

Heart of Wales

Knighton Llanbister Llandrindod Wells

H Castle Inn

Knucklas,
Knighton,
Powys LD7 1PW
Tel: (01547) 528150

Delightful family run Mid Wales village inn with oak beams, log fires. Renowned for home cooked food and comfort in en-suite rooms with colour TV and drinks tray. Situated in ideal walking country between Offa's Dyke and The Glyndwr Way. Guided walks and birdwatching our speciality.

SINGLE PER PERSON B&B		DOUBLE FOR 2 PERSONS B&B		🛏 5
				🛁 5
MIN £	MAX £	MIN £	MAX £	OPEN
17.50	17.50	35.00	35.00	1-12

GH Corven Hall

Howey,
Llandrindod Wells,
Powys LD1 5RE
Tel: (01597) 823368

 AWARD HIGHLY COMMENDED

Victorian country house in large grounds surrounded by beautiful countryside. 1¹/₂ miles south of Llandrindod Wells off A483 at Hundred House turn. The house is licensed, centrally heated and spacious. TV lounge, bar. Most bedrooms en-suite, TV, tea/coffee facilities. Ground floor accommodation. Traditional home-cooking, freshly prepared. Dinners by arrangement. Elan Valley, Brecon Beacons nearby.

SINGLE PER PERSON B&B		DOUBLE FOR 2 PERSONS B&B		🛏 10
				🛁 8
MIN £	MAX £	MIN £	MAX £	OPEN
16.00	18.00	32.00	36.00	2-11

FH Highbury Farm

Llanyre,
Llandrindod Wells,
Powys LD1 6EA
Tel: (01597) 822716

 AWARD HIGHLY COMMENDED

A small-holding situated 1¹/₂ miles west of Llandrindod Wells, where a warm welcome awaits you. Comfortable spacious rooms in our Victorian farmhouse. Beverage tray in bedrooms. Firm beds guaranteed. TV lounge. Separate dining room. Evening meal optional. Ideal base for bird watching and walking. Brochure and enquiries to Mrs Shirley Evans.

SINGLE PER PERSON B&B		DOUBLE FOR 2 PERSONS B&B		🛏 3
				🛁 1
MIN £	MAX £	MIN £	MAX £	OPEN
13.00	17.00	26.00	34.00	3-10

FH Cefnsuran

Llangunllo,
Knighton,
Powys LD7 1SL
Tel: (01547) 550219

 HIGHLY COMMENDED

15th/16th century farmhouse ideal for relaxing or a walking holiday (Offa's Dyke/Glyndwr's Way). Superb views. All rooms en-suite or private bath. Traditional farmhouse fare, vegetarian and special diets, all by prior arrangement. Games room, snooker and table tennis. Abundant wildlife. Inglenook fireplaces, oak beams throughout. Meticulously maintained, all modern comforts.

SINGLE PER PERSON B&B		DOUBLE FOR 2 PERSONS B&B		🛏 4
				🛁 4
MIN £	MAX £	MIN £	MAX £	OPEN
15.00	17.50	30.00	35.00	1-12

GH Ty Clyd

Park Terrace,
Llandrindod Wells,
Powys LD1 5PP
Tel: (01597) 822122

Tea and coffee making facilities in lounge. One bath, two showers, three toilets, to service maximum of eleven guests. Quiet cul-de-sac overlooking wooded park. Easy on road parking. Garage available for push bikes etc. Close to railway station.

SINGLE PER PERSON B&B		DOUBLE FOR 2 PERSONS B&B		🛏 7
				🛁 -
MIN £	MAX £	MIN £	MAX £	OPEN
14.00	14.00	28.00	28.00	1-12

FH Holly Farm

Howey,
Llandrindod Wells,
Powys LD1 5PP
Tel: (01597) 822402

 AWARD HIGHLY COMMENDED

Holly Farm set in beautiful countryside offers guests a friendly welcome. 1¹/₂ miles south of Llandrindod Wells, an excellent base for exploring lakes, mountains and bird watching. Full central heating, most rooms en-suite, beverage trays, TV lounge, log fire, dining room with separate tables and superb meals, using home produce. Safe car parking, evening meal by arrangement. AA Listed. Brochure Mrs Ruth Jones.

SINGLE PER PERSON B&B		DOUBLE FOR 2 PERSONS B&B		🛏 3
				🛁 3
MIN £	MAX £	MIN £	MAX £	OPEN
16.00	18.00	30.00	36.00	4-11

FH The Rhos

Llanbister,
Llandrindod Wells,
Powys LD1 6TL
Tel: (01597) 840691
Fax: (01597) 840691

AWAITING INSPECTION

Our farm is situated in the rolling Moelfre Hills. We are ideally located for exploring the ancient and mysterious Radnor Forest. Offa's Dyke wanders through Knighton just 15 miles away. The Victorian spa town of Llandrindod Wells is only 10 miles away. A leisure centre, golf course, riding school, fishing and birdwatching are within easy access. Guests' horses welcome. Dogs accepted by arrangement.

SINGLE PER PERSON B&B		DOUBLE FOR 2 PERSONS B&B		🛏 2
				🛁 -
MIN £	MAX £	MIN £	MAX £	OPEN
15.00	15.00	30.00	30.00	1-12

FH Brynhir Farm

Chapel Road,
Howey,
Llandrindod Wells,
Powys LD1 5PB
Tel: (01597) 822425

 AWARD HIGHLY COMMENDED

Charming olde worlde farmhouse situated 1 mile off A483, in magnificent mountain setting. Traditional inglenook fireplace, exposed oak beams. Ideal relaxing holiday, good walking area. Trout fishing lake. Pied flycatchers, Redstarts and Buzzards commonly seen. Conducted badger sett tours. Beverage trays. Delicious cuisine. 1 mile off A483 through Howey Village, turn right up Chapel Road. Evening meal by arrangement.

SINGLE PER PERSON B&B		DOUBLE FOR 2 PERSONS B&B		🛏 6
				🛁 5
MIN £	MAX £	MIN £	MAX £	OPEN
16.50	17.50	33.00	35.00	3-11

FH Three Wells Farm

Chapel Road,
Howey,
Llandrindod Wells,
Powys LD1 5PB
Tel: (01597) 824427
Fax: (01597) 822484

 AWARD HIGHLY COMMENDED

A working farm overlooking fishing lake in beautiful countryside. 1¹/₂ miles from Llandrindod Wells. All en-suite bedrooms offering tea/coffee facilities, TV, video, radio, telephone. Suites available. Licensed bar. Special breaks available, brochure Ron, Margaret and Sarah Bufton. AA/RAC Highly Commended. Best Small Hotel in Wales 1990. FHG Diploma. Rural Tourism Award for accommodation and catering. Safe parking.

SINGLE PER PERSON B&B		DOUBLE FOR 2 PERSONS B&B		🛏 15
				🛁 15
MIN £	MAX £	MIN £	MAX £	OPEN
17.00	19.00	34.00	38.00	1-12

67

Llanwrtyd Wells New Radnor Rhayader

GH	Cerdyn Country Guest House

Cerdyn Villa,
Llanwrtyd Wells,
Powys LD5 4RS
Tel: (01591) 610635

Peaceful location amidst mountains, lakes, rivers and forests. Family run guest house in large Victorian house with comfortable accommodation, log fires and plentiful, good home cooked food. Spectacular walking, cycling, riding and birdwatching country. Special rates for groups (8+) and 2 night breaks. Self-contained apartment available. Half a mile from A483, railway station 200 yards.

P	🐕	SINGLE PER PERSON B&B		DOUBLE FOR 2 PERSONS B&B		🛏 4
C	🍴					🛁 3
🏠	✂	MIN £	MAX £	MIN £	MAX £	OPEN
🐾	🍽	-	-	30.00	36.00	1-12

GH	Liverpool House

East Street,
Rhayader,
Powys LD6 5EA
Tel: (01597) 810706

A warm welcome awaits you at Liverpool House where friendliness and service go hand in hand. Secure private car parking on premises. Bedrooms have colour television, clock/radio, hairdryer, iron, beverage tray and most have en-suite. Full central heating. Spacious lounge. Reduced rates for children sharing with parents. Cot and highchair. Full fire certificate.

P	🐕	SINGLE PER PERSON B&B		DOUBLE FOR 2 PERSONS B&B		🛏 4
🏠	🏠					🛁 3
✂	🐾	MIN £	MAX £	MIN £	MAX £	OPEN
🍽		15.00	-	26.00	-	1-12

FH	Downfield Farm

Rhayader,
Powys LD6 5PA
Tel: (01597) 810394

Welcome to Downfield. Situated one mile east of Rhayader on the A44 road. 3 double bedrooms, all with hot and cold water plus beverage tray. 2 bathrooms, one with shower. Lounge with television, dining room with separate tables. Fully centrally heated. Surrounded by hills and lakes, ideal for touring, walking, birdwatching etc.

P	🐕	SINGLE PER PERSON B&B		DOUBLE FOR 2 PERSONS B&B		🛏 3
🏠	✂					-
🐾	🐾	MIN £	MAX £	MIN £	MAX £	OPEN
		15.00	16.00	28.00	28.00	2-11

H	Eagle Hotel

Broad Street,
New Radnor,
Powys LD8 2SN
Tel: (01544) 350208
Fax: (01544) 350208

Long established village coaching inn offering comfortable accommodation both for independent tourists and larger groups undertaking our many outdoor activities including walking, golf, canoeing, abseiling. Excellent food including vegetarian in bistro style restaurant and adjoining part covered terrace. Cosy lounge bar with log fire. Public bar, games area, live music. Unspoilt rural Mid Wales location.

P	🐕	SINGLE PER PERSON B&B		DOUBLE FOR 2 PERSONS B&B		🛏 6
🍷	🏠					🛁 1
🐾	🍽	MIN £	MAX £	MIN £	MAX £	OPEN
T	TV	17.00	19.00	34.00	38.00	1-12

FH	Beili Neuadd Farmhouse

Beili Neuadd,
Rhayader,
Powys LD6 5NS
Tel: (01597) 810211

HIGHLY COMMENDED

Set amidst glorious countryside, beside a trout pool, 2 miles from the market town of Rhayader, best known as the gateway to "The lakeland of Wales." The stonebuilt 16th century farmhouse has central heating, log fires, well appointed en-suite bedrooms with beverage trays. We offer good imaginative meals using farm and garden produce.

P	🐕	SINGLE PER PERSON B&B		DOUBLE FOR 2 PERSONS B&B		🛏 3
🏠	✂					🛁 3
🐾	🍽	MIN £	MAX £	MIN £	MAX £	OPEN
T		17.00	18.00	34.00	35.00	1-12

FH	Gigrin Farm

South Road,
Rhayader,
Powys LD6 5BL
Tel: (01597) 810243

L

Gigrin is a 17th century longhouse peacefully situated overlooking the Wye Valley, only $\frac{1}{2}$ mile from Rhayader with its numerous Inns and friendly welcome. The spectacular Elan Valley, home of the red kite is just 3 miles away. Aberystwyth 35 miles away. Our working farm offers a nature trail, RSPB Reserve and fishing. Walking, pony trekking and golf are available nearby. Three bedrooms.

P	🏠	SINGLE PER PERSON B&B		DOUBLE FOR 2 PERSONS B&B		🛏 3
✂	🐾					🛁 1
🐾		MIN £	MAX £	MIN £	MAX £	OPEN
		16.00	-	30.00	-	3-11

GH	Brynteg

East Street,
Rhayader,
Powys LD6 5EA
Tel: (01597) 810052

Friendly Edwardian guest house overlooking hills and gardens, close to town centre. We have double twin/family or single rooms with en-suite, central heating, tea/coffee facilities, TV lounge and separate breakfast room. Special rates 5 nights or more, children half price. We are ideally situated for exploring the beautiful Elan Valley and Cambrian Mountains. Croeso.

P	🐕	SINGLE PER PERSON B&B		DOUBLE FOR 2 PERSONS B&B		🛏 3
🏠	🏠					🛁 3
🐾		MIN £	MAX £	MIN £	MAX £	OPEN
		-	-	28.00	28.00	3-10

Llanwrtyd Wel...

This region, which extends from the borderland Wye Valley across to the western tip of Pembrokeshire, is full of contrasts.

The changing face of the historic waterfront along Cardiff Bay

South and West Wales

For a start, there are two very different National Parks, the Pembrokeshire Coast and the Brecon Beacons. Add to these the splendid Gower Peninsula, Carmarthen Bay, the Glamorgan Heritage Coast, the characterful Welsh Valleys and the wooded Wye Valley, and you have a multiplicity of holiday choices.

Pembrokeshire is one of Europe's finest stretches of coastal natural beauty. Stay at Tenby or Saundersfoot (you'll find an excellent choice of holiday accommodation here) or at one of the many smaller resorts along this magnificent coastline. Wherever you travel in South and West Wales, you'll come across attractive seashores – the cliffs and dunes of Glamorgan's Heritage Coast, the popular resorts of Barry Island and Porthcawl, Gower's sheltered bays and spectacular headlands, and the endless sands of Carmarthen Bay.

Inland, the Brecon Beacons National Park is an exhilarating landscape of open spaces, grassy summits and big skies, popular with walkers and pony trekkers. Abergavenny, Llandovery and, of course, Brecon, are good centres from which to explore the Park.

St. David's Cathedral

Cardiff, Wales's capital, is a cosmopolitan city of museums, theatres and green spaces, with an architecturally magnificent Civic Centre, ornate castle and exciting new waterfront development. Swansea's stylish marina and Maritime Quarter have been praised for bringing new life to old docklands. The city's success story is one of the many surprises you'll come across in South and West Wales, a region of grand castles and 'Great Little Trains', wildlife parks and showcaves, Roman remains and mining museums.

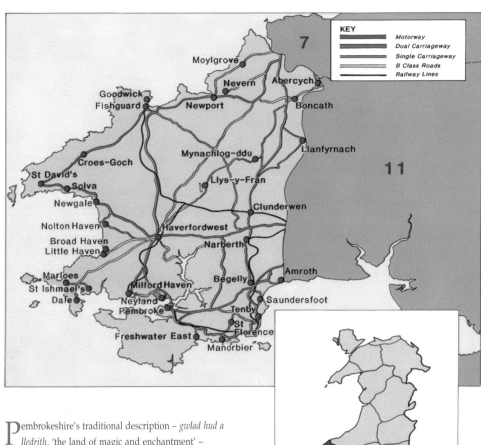

Pembrokeshire's traditional description – *gwlad hud a lledrith*, 'the land of magic and enchantment' – perfectly captures the qualities of its outstanding coastline. Almost all of this special shoreline falls within the Pembrokeshire Coast Park, Britain's only coastal-based National Park.

The Park's 225 square miles, running from near Tenby in the south to Cardigan in the north, are indeed extraordinary – they contain everything from towering cliffs to sheltered harbours, huge beaches to secluded coves, wildlife sanctuaries to wooded creeks. The Park's boundary, which shadows the coastline for most of the way, even ventures inland between Fishguard and Cardigan to encompass the Preseli Hills, a haunting area scattered with prehistoric sites.

Much of the holiday accommodation is found around stylish Tenby and Saundersfoot. If you're looking for somewhere smaller, there's an excellent choice – Broad Haven, Dale, Solva or St David's to name but a few. There are also many places to stay inland – the old county town of Haverfordwest, for example – which are convenient for exploring all parts of the coast.

Jb5 Broad Haven

Sand and green hills cradle this holiday village on St Bride's Bay in the Pembrokeshire Coast National Park. Beautiful beach and coastal walks. National Park Information Centre.

Jb3 Croes-goch

Small village, useful spot for touring Pembrokeshire Coast National Park - especially its peaceful, rugged northern shores and nearby centres of St David's and Fishguard. Llangloffan Farmhouse Cheese Centre nearby.

Jc2 Fishguard

Lower Fishguard is a cluster of old wharfs and cottages around a beautiful harbour. `Under Milk Wood' with Richard Burton was filmed here in 1971. Shopping in Fishguard town. Good walks along Pembrokeshire Coast Path and in the country. Nearby Goodwick is the Irish ferry terminal, with a direct link from London. Excellent range of craft workshops in area including Tregwynt Woollen Mill. Music Festival in July.

Jd6 Freshwater East

Sheltered sandy bay south-east of Pembroke backed by dunes. Good swimming, access for boats, limited car parking.

Jc2 Goodwick

Goodwick is harbour for Fishguard - Irish ferries sail from here. Rugged and spectacular coastal scenery a short distance to the north at Carreg Wastad Point, scene of the last invasion of Britain (an unsuccessful attempt by French forces) in 1797

Jc5 Haverfordwest

Ancient town - now a good base for exploring the Pembrokeshire Coast National Park - and the administrative and shopping centre for the area. Medieval churches and narrow streets. Museum in the castle grounds, which occupy an outcrop overlooking the town. Attractive redeveloped riverside and old wharf buildings. Graham Sutherland art collection in Picton Castle, a few miles east. Many other attractions nearby, including Scolton Manor Country Park, `Motormania' exhibition, Selvedge Farm Museum and Nant-y-Coy Mill.

Jb5 Little Haven

Combines with Broad Haven - just over the headland - to form a complete family seaside holiday centre in the Pembrokeshire Coast National Park. The village dips down to a pretty sandy beach. Popular spot for sailing, swimming and surfing.

Ka1 Llanfyrnach

Village in maze of peaceful, unexplored country lanes between Carmarthen and Cardigan. Handy for Pembrokeshire's north coast and Preseli Hills as well as Telfi Valley.

Jb5 Marloes

Village near Marloes Sands, a remote stretch of the Pembrokeshire Coast National Park - and one of its finest beaches - overlooking Skomer Island, a haven for puffins and other seabirds. Good swimming and surfing; boat trips to the island from nearby Martin's Haven.

Jc6 Milford Haven

Important port on edge of Pembrokeshire Coast National Park; Nelson called it one of the best natural harbours he had seen. Marina in redeveloped docks has maritime museum and other attractions. Fine walks and gardens. Torch Theatre, maritime museum and leisure centre. Excellent touring base.

Je5 Narberth

Small market town, ancient castle remains (private). Charming local museum. Convenient for beaches of Carmarthen Bay and resorts of Tenby and Saundersfoot. Many attractions nearby, including activity-packed Oakwood Park, Canaston Centre, Heron's Brook Country Park, Folly Farm and Blackpool Mill.

Jd2 Newport

Ancient castled village on Pembrokeshire coast. Fine beaches - bass and sea trout fishing. Pentre Ifan Burial Chamber is close by. Backed by heather-clad Preseli Hills and overlooked by Carn Ingli Iron Age Fort.

Jc6 Neyland

Old seafaring village on northern bank of Milford Haven waterway opposite Pembroke Dock. Attractive new marina. Superb sailing centre. Easy access to Pembrokeshire's south and west coasts.

Jd6 Pembroke

Ancient borough built around Pembroke Castle, birthplace of Henry VII. Fascinating Museum of the Home and next-door Sea Historic Gallery. In addition to impressive castle, well-preserved sections of old town walls. Sandy bays within easy reach, yachting, fishing - all the coastal activities associated with estuaries. Plenty of things to see and do in the area, including visit to beautiful Upton Castle Grounds.

Ja4 St David's

Smallest cathedral city in Britain, shrine of Wales's patron saint. Magnificent ruins of a Bishop's Palace beside ancient cathedral nestling in hollow. Set in Pembrokeshire Coast National Park, with fine beaches nearby; superb scenery on nearby headland. Craft shops, sea life centres, painting courses, boat trips to Ramsey Island, farm parks and museums; ideal for walking and birdwatching.

Jb6 St Ishmael's

Village in far-flung south-west of the Pembrokeshire Coast National Park, close to sailing centre of Dale on the Milford Haven waterway. Some of Pembrokeshire's loveliest coastline close by - the unexplored Dale Peninsula, Marloes Sands, and boat trips to Skomer Island from Martin's Haven.

Je6 Saundersfoot

Popular resort on South Pembrokeshire coast within the National Park. Picturesque harbour and sandy beach. Very attractive sailing centre. Good sea fishing. In the wooded hills to the north is the fascinating Stepaside Industrial Heritage Centre.

Whitesand Bay, near St David's

Jb4 Solva

Picturesque Pembrokeshire coast village with small perfectly sheltered harbour and excellent craft shops. Pembrokeshire Coast Path offers good walking. Famous cathedral at nearby St David's.

Je6 Tenby

Popular, picturesque South Pembrokeshire resort with two wide beaches. Fishing trips from the attractive Georgian harbour and boat trips to Caldy Island. The medieval walled town has a maze of charming narrow streets and fine old buildings, including Tudor Merchant's House (National Trust). Galleries and craft shops, excellent museum on headland, good range of amenities. Attractions include Manor House Leisure Park and `Silent World' Aquarium.

Broad Haven   Croes-goch   Fishguard   Freshwater East   Goodwick   Haverfordwest

---

GH   Glenfield

5 Atlantic Drive,
Broad Haven,
Pembrokeshire,
Dyfed SA62 3JA
Tel: (01437) 781502

A warm welcome awaits you at my comfortable guest house, with ample home cooked meals and friendly service. Hot and cold, tea making facilities in all rooms. Full central heating, colour television, own key. 300 yards to beach and Coastal Path.

P 🖳 T	🐾	SINGLE PER PERSON B&B		DOUBLE FOR 2 PERSONS B&B		🛏 4
		MIN £ 12.50.	MAX £ 12.50	MIN £ -	MAX £ 25.00	OPEN 4-11

GH   Heathfield

Mathry Road,
Letterston,
Dyfed SA62 5EG
Tel: (01348) 840263

Our exclusive Georgian country house in its tranquil setting of pastures and woodlands is the perfect place to relax and be spoilt. It is ideally situated to explore Pembrokeshire's treasures. The comfortable rooms with beautiful views over rolling countryside, the friendly atmosphere and the excellent food and wines make for a truly enjoyable holiday.

P 🖳 🐾	🐾 ✂ 🍽	SINGLE PER PERSON B&B		DOUBLE FOR 2 PERSONS B&B		🛏 3
		MIN £ 16.50	MAX £ 18.00	MIN £ 33.00	MAX £ 36.00	OPEN 4-10

H   The Hope and Anchor Inn

Goodwick,
Dyfed SA64 0BP
Tel: (01348) 872314

Small family run inn overlooking Fishguard Bay, two minutes from Sealink Ferry and Sea Lynx. Restaurant, fresh seafood. All en-suite rooms with TV. Parking. Located on Coastal Path. Ramblers Guide. Cycling Touring Club, Les Routiers.

🐾 ♀ 🖳 🍽	SINGLE PER PERSON B&B		DOUBLE FOR 2 PERSONS B&B		🛏 3
	MIN £ -	MAX £ 16.00	MIN £ -	MAX £ 32.00	OPEN 1-12

FH   Trearched Farm Guest House

Croes-goch,
Haverfordwest,
Dyfed SA62 5JP
Tel: (01348) 7831310

HIGHLY COMMENDED

Enjoy a relaxing break in our 18th century listed farmhouse on arable farm. Long drive, entrance by lodge on A487 in village. Sorry no dogs or smoking please. Spacious grounds with small lake. Double, twin or single rooms. B&B only. Footpath link to coast, approximately 2¼ miles. Ideal walking and birdwatching area. Also self-catering for two.

P 🖳 ✂ 🐾 🏍 T	SINGLE PER PERSON B&B		DOUBLE FOR 2 PERSONS B&B		🛏 6
	MIN £ 15.00	MAX £ 16.00	MIN £ 30.00	MAX £ 32.00	OPEN 1-12

FH   Berry-Hill

Goodwick,
Nr Fishguard,
Pembrokeshire,
Dyfed SA64 0HG
Tel: (01348) 872260

 AWARD   HIGHLY COMMENDED

Small-holding with various pets overlooking Fishguard Harbour and Preseli Mountains. 2 minutes walk from Coastal Path. Breathtaking views from both en-suite rooms. Tea/coffee facilities, hairdryer, shaver etc. TV lounge, separate dining tables. Parking. Sorry no children and no pets.

P 🖳 ✂ 🐾 🍽 T	SINGLE PER PERSON B&B		DOUBLE FOR 2 PERSONS B&B		🛏 2
	MIN £ 17.00	MAX £ 18.00	MIN £ 34.00	MAX £ 36.00	OPEN 4-10

GH   Glanmoy Lodge

Tref-Wrgi Road,
Goodwick, Fishguard,
Pembrokeshire,
Dyfed SA64 0JX
Tel: (01348) 874333
Fax: (01348) 874333

HIGHLY COMMENDED

Totally private accommodation in our guest suite. One booking per night, nothing shared. Choice of double, twin, family accommodation with en-suite facilities. All rooms have alarm radio and TV. A telephone is available. Choice of breakfast. Beautiful gardens and views. Very quiet. Ferry, beaches and town 1 mile. Late night travellers welcome.

P 🖳 ✂ T	SINGLE PER PERSON B&B		DOUBLE FOR 2 PERSONS B&B		🛏 2
	MIN £ 19.00	MAX £ 19.00	MIN £ 30.00	MAX £ 35.00	OPEN 1-12

H   Penlan Oleu

Llanychaer,
Fishguard,
Dyfed SA65 9TL
Tel: (01348) 881314
Freephone: (0500) 118037

Peaceful Penlan Oleu is a small friendly hotel on a converted Welsh hill farm. Rural hilltop setting with super views and 6 acres of ground. Traditional Welsh home cooking with a selection of fine wines. Only 4 miles from Fishguard and clean beaches. Ideal for walkers, birdwatchers and mountain bikers. Siaredir Gymraeg yma.

P C 🖳 ✂ 🐾 🍽	🐾 🖳	SINGLE PER PERSON B&B		DOUBLE FOR 2 PERSONS B&B		🛏 4
		MIN £ -	MAX £ 19.00	MIN £ -	MAX £ 38.00	OPEN 1-12

FH   East Trewent Farm

East Trewent,
Freshwater East,
Pembrokeshire,
Dyfed SA71 5LR
Tel: (01646) 672127

Birds, flowers, fresh air in abundance. East Trewent Farm adjoins the Coastal Path. Beach 400 yards. Fishing and riding nearby. Ideal for those who love the outdoor life. In the evening relax in the bar and enjoy the excellent cuisine in the Chough Restaurant. Open all the year round.

P 🐾 ♀ 🖳 🍽 TW	SINGLE PER PERSON B&B		DOUBLE FOR 2 PERSONS B&B		🛏 5
	MIN £ 15.50	MAX £ 19.00	MIN £ 31.00	MAX £ 38.00	OPEN 1-12

GH   College Guest House

93 Hill Street,
Haverfordwest,
Pembrokeshire,
Dyfed SA61 1QX
Tel: (01437) 763710

Family run Georgian guest house established 22 years. 5 minutes from centre of town. Ideal for touring, beaches, coastal paths, Preseli Mountains, fishing, shooting, water sports or for relaxing. Car parking available opposite.

🐾 C 🖳 ✂ 🐾	SINGLE PER PERSON B&B		DOUBLE FOR 2 PERSONS B&B		🛏 10
	MIN £ 16.00	MAX £ 19.00	MIN £ 30.00	MAX £ 38.00	OPEN 1-12

Haverfordwest   Little Haven   Llanfyrnach   Marloes   Milford Haven

---

GH | The Fold

Cleddau Lodge,
Camrose,
Haverfordwest,
Pembrokeshire,
Dyfed SA62 6HY
Tel: (01437) 710640

Converted 15th century farmhouse in secluded garden overlooking River Cleddau. Private fishing available. Central to Pembrokeshire coast 6 miles. Double bedroom, hot and cold water, TV, tea/coffee, own shower, toilet, separate entrance. Homely welcome, as one of the family. Part of 50 acre estate with gardens, woodlands and river. View of the Preseli Hills.

		SINGLE PER PERSON B&B		DOUBLE FOR 2 PERSONS B&B		🛁 1
		MIN £	MAX £	MIN £	MAX £	OPEN
		15.00	15.00	26.00	30.00	4-10

FH | Cuckoo Mill

Pelcombe Bridge,
St David's Road,
Haverfordwest,
Pembrokeshire,
Dyfed SA62 6EA
Tel: (01437) 762139

Ideally situated peacefully in central Pembrokeshire on working family farm. Two miles out of Haverfordwest. Nearby to coastline walks, sandy beaches, golf course, riding stables. Real home comfort in pretty rooms with heating, H&C, tea trays, radio. Good home cooked meals of home produce. Evening meal. Personal attention. Senior citizens and children welcome.

		SINGLE PER PERSON B&B		DOUBLE FOR 2 PERSONS B&B		🛁 3
		MIN £	MAX £	MIN £	MAX £	OPEN
		14.00	16.50	28.00	33.00	1-12

GH | Bron-y-Gaer

Llanfyrnach,
Pembrokeshire,
Dyfed SA35 0DA
Tel: (01239) 831265

Our peaceful smallholding just three miles off the A478 near Crymych offers an ideal touring base for exploring West Wales. Accommodation is in pretty en-suite bedrooms, all with tea/coffee making facilities. Guests have their own lounge with colour TV. We have a craft shop, hand spun garments, beautiful gardens and friendly farm animals.

		SINGLE PER PERSON B&B		DOUBLE FOR 2 PERSONS B&B		🛁 2
		MIN £	MAX £	MIN £	MAX £	OPEN
		15.00	15.00	30.00	30.00	1-12

GH | Greenways

Shoals Hook Lane,
Haverfordwest,
Pembrokeshire,
Dyfed SA61 2XN
Tel: (01437) 762345

HIGHLY COMMENDED

Set in two acres, picturesque gardens, picnic area, sun terrace, overlooking golf course, Preseli mountains. Greenways is an ideal touring base. We are twenty minutes drive from ferry terminals. Relax in comfort. All bedrooms are ground floor, with en-suite facilities, service tray, hairdryer and colour TV. Private parking. A quiet retreat home from home. Children, pets welcome.

		SINGLE PER PERSON B&B	DOUBLE FOR 2 PERSONS B&B	🛏 4
		MIN £	MAX £	MIN £	MAX £	OPEN
		15.00	19.00	30.00	38.00	1-12

FH | Knock Farm

Camrose,
Haverfordwest,
Pembrokeshire,
Dyfed SA62 6HW
Tel: (01437) 762208

Our working dairy farm is peacefully situated in a scenic valley ten minutes from Pembrokeshire's sandy beaches and coastline walks. Pretty centrally heated bedrooms, hot and cold water, tea/coffee facilities. Large family room en-suite. Good home cooking and homely atmosphere. TV lounge with central heating. Log fires in winter available all day. Children welcome at reduced rates.

		SINGLE PER PERSON B&B	DOUBLE FOR 2 PERSONS B&B	🛏 2
		MIN £	MAX £	MIN £	MAX £	OPEN
		14.00	16.50	28.00	33.00	1-11

GH | Foxdale

Glebe Lane,
Marloes, Haverfordwest,
Pembrokeshire,
Dyfed SA62 3AX
Tel: (01646) 636243

HIGHLY COMMENDED

Foxdale is a large comfortable detached house. Three spacious rooms, one en-suite, all with tea/coffee making facilities. TV lounge. Ideal base for all seawater sports, walking, birdwatching and spectacular coastal scenery and flora. Close to Skomer and Grassholm islands and Marloes Sands. B&B, camping facilities, campers' breakfasts and swimming pool. Fully licensed, B&B and campsite. OS Ref. SM 796 083.

		SINGLE PER PERSON B&B	DOUBLE FOR 2 PERSONS B&B	🛏 3
		MIN £	MAX £	MIN £	MAX £	OPEN
		18.00	18.00	32.00	36.00	3-10

FH | Bicton Farm

St Ishmael's,
Haverfordwest,
Pembrokeshire,
Dyfed SA62 3DR
Tel: (01646) 636215

Comfortable farmhouse one mile from the village of St Ishmael's, with easy access to Coastal Path, several beaches and the bird sanctuaries of Skomer and Skokholm. Two double rooms, one with WC, shower en-suite, one twin. Sitting room with TV, central heating.

		SINGLE PER PERSON B&B	DOUBLE FOR 2 PERSONS B&B	🛏 3
		MIN £	MAX £	MIN £	MAX £	OPEN
		14.00	15.00	28.00	30.00	3-10

GH | Whitegates

Settlands Hill,
Little Haven,
Pembrokeshire,
Dyfed SA62 3LA
Tel: (01437) 781552
Fax: (01437) 781552

COMMENDED

On the Pembrokeshire Coastal Path in lovely fishing village. Beautiful sea views, heated swimming pool, en-suite most rooms, tea/coffee, radio in all rooms. TV lounge, access at all times. Ideal walking, windsurfing, birdwatching on four islands or family beach holidays. Local sea food/produce in several reasonably priced pubs - restaurants within comfortable walking distance.

		SINGLE PER PERSON B&B	DOUBLE FOR 2 PERSONS B&B	🛏 4
		MIN £	MAX £	MIN £	MAX £	OPEN
		-	-	34.00	38.00	1-12

FH | The Old Dairy

Castle Pill Farm,
Steynton,
Milford Haven,
Dyfed SA73 1HE
Tel: (01646) 692906

A warm welcome over a cup of tea (or something stronger!) awaits you at Castle Pill Farm. Our secluded sheep, arable and fruit farm adjacent to woodland and tidal estuary. The end of lane location belies our nearness to Pembrokeshire's beaches, walks and historical towns. Beverage tray, colour TV. Ample private parking and own access.

		SINGLE PER PERSON B&B	DOUBLE FOR 2 PERSONS B&B	🛏 2
		MIN £	MAX £	MIN £	MAX £	OPEN
		15.00	15.00	28.00	30.00	1-12

Narberth   Newport   Neyland   Pembroke   St David's

FH | Highland Grange Farm Guest House

Robeston Wathen,
Narberth, Pembrokeshire,
Dyfed SA67 8EP
Tel: (01834) 860952
Fax: (01834) 860952

Lovely family home centrally situated on A40 amidst beautiful countryside. Ideal for touring West Wales. Ground floor accommodation, 2 en-suites, comfort assured. Delicious home cooking. Panoramic views, pleasant walks within surrounding area. Beach 8 miles. Fishing, riding, cycling, Oakwood Park nearby. Local information provided by helpful host. A warm welcome awaits you. Enquiries to Naomi Jones.

	SINGLE PER PERSON B&B		DOUBLE FOR 2 PERSONS B&B		4
	MIN £	MAX £	MIN £	MAX £	OPEN
	16.50	-	28.00	33.00	1-12

GH | Church Lakes Guest House

88 Church Road,
Llanstadwell, Neyland,
Milford Haven, Pembrokeshire,
Dyfed SA73 1EA
Tel: (01646) 600840

Comfortable, detached house alongside the Cleddau Estuary foreshore and Coastal Path. Haven views from all rooms and terrace with yachts from nearby Neyland Marina, the Irish Ferries etc, often adding interest. In bedrooms. Good food. Near Haven Bridge linking Preseli and South Pembrokeshire. Details from Barry and Sylvia Fieldhouse.

	SINGLE PER PERSON B&B		DOUBLE FOR 2 PERSONS B&B		3
	MIN £	MAX £	MIN £	MAX £	OPEN
	14.00	15.00	28.00	30.00	1-12

GH | Awel-Môr Guest House

Penparc, Tre-fin,
Nr St David's,
Pembrokeshire,
Dyfed SA72 5AG
Tel: (01348) 837865

Luxury 'non-smoking' accommodation. Magnificent views overlooking sea and Pembrokeshire Coast National Park. Comfortable seating, colour TV, tea/coffee facilities in each bedroom. Delicious food from breakfast/dinner menu. Optional evening meal. Taste of Wales member. "The Best Guest House in Wales" - Wales Tourist Board Hospitality Award. Free brochure available.

DE LUXE

	SINGLE PER PERSON B&B		DOUBLE FOR 2 PERSONS B&B		3
					2
	MIN £	MAX £	MIN £	MAX £	OPEN
	17.50	-	35.00	-	4-10

FH | Lower End Town House

Lampeter Velfrey,
Narberth,
Dyfed SA67 8UJ
Tel: (01834) 83738

Victorian farmhouse on working farm. Recent refurbishment has been aimed at comfort in traditional surroundings. Ideal for walking, cycling, touring or just relaxing. Two rooms, one double, one twin, both en-suite with colour TV and tea making facilities. Both luxuriously appointed. Breakfast when you want it. A home from home is what we want for you.

	SINGLE PER PERSON B&B		DOUBLE FOR 2 PERSONS B&B		2
					2
	MIN £	MAX £	MIN £	MAX £	OPEN
	15.00	15.00	30.00	30.00	1-12

FH | Bangeston Farm

Stackpole,
Pembroke,
Dyfed SA71 5BX
Tel: (01646) 683986

Homely farmhouse in peaceful country side with view of Stackpole and St Govan's Head, three miles from Pembroke. Good walking area and a base from which to explore the Pembrokeshire Coast National Park. Early reservations are advised. Home cooked hearty breakfasts. Tea making facilities, hot & cold in all bedrooms. Colour TV in lounge. Brochure from Mrs Mathias.

	SINGLE PER PERSON B&B		DOUBLE FOR 2 PERSONS B&B		3
					-
	MIN £	MAX £	MIN £	MAX £	OPEN
	12.50	12.50	25.00	25.00	4-9

GH | Ramsey House

Lower Moor,
St David's,
Pembrokeshire,
Dyfed SA62 6RP
Tel: (01437) 720321

HIGHLY COMMENDED

Great value dinner, B&B featuring our award winning Welsh cuisine using traditional recipes and local produce. Catering exclusively for adults, our tastefully appointed rooms offer quiet relaxation with congenial hospitality. Cosy bar and TV lounge. Convenient location for touring/walking, $\frac{1}{2}$ mile from Cathedral and Coast Path. Dogs welcome. En-suite supplement. Les Routiers. AA QQQ. RAC Acclaimed.

	SINGLE PER PERSON B&B		DOUBLE FOR 2 PERSONS B&B		7
					6
	MIN £	MAX £	MIN £	MAX £	OPEN
	-	-	38.00	-	1-12

GH | Grove Park Guest House

Grove Park,
Pen-y-Bont,
Newport,
Dyfed SA42 0LT
Tel: (01239) 820122

HIGHLY COMMENDED

Grove Park is situated on the outskirts of Newport, 100 yards from Pembrokeshire Coastal Path. 19th century house which has been completely refurbished, but retains original character. Estuary and mountain views, easy distance from large sandy beach and Preseli Mountains. Imaginative four course dinner menu. Winter breaks, log fires, hearty casseroles. Colour TV all bedrooms.

	SINGLE PER PERSON B&B		DOUBLE FOR 2 PERSONS B&B		4
					2
	MIN £	MAX £	MIN £	MAX £	OPEN
	18.00	-	36.00	-	1-12

FH | Poyerston Farm

Cosheston,
Pembroke,
Dyfed SA72 4SJ
Tel: (01646) 651347

HIGHLY COMMENDED

Peaceful surroundings on working dairy farm approached by private drive. Set in picturesque unspoilt countryside. Our centuries old farmhouse has antique marble fireplaces and window seats in dining room. Well appointed bedrooms all with en-suite facilities, beverage trays and full central heating. Regret no smoking in farmhouse. Basic food hygiene certificate. AA Selected QQQQ.

	SINGLE PER PERSON B&B		DOUBLE FOR 2 PERSONS B&B		2
					2
	MIN £	MAX £	MIN £	MAX £	OPEN
	16.50	18.00	33.00	36.00	4-10

H | Ynys Barry Holiday Centre

Porthgain,
St David's
Pembrokeshire,
Dyfed SA62 5BH
Tel: (01348) 831180
Fax: (01348) 831800

COMMENDED

Located adjacent to famous Pembrokeshire Coastal Path. Facilities include lounge bar, games room, restaurant, snacks, cream teas. Home cooking. Self-contained holiday cottages, Motel room. All in the midst of Pembrokeshire with glorious rugged coastline and sweeping beaches is literally on your doorstep. B&B available and room only.

	SINGLE PER PERSON B&B		DOUBLE FOR 2 PERSONS B&B		14
					14
	MIN £	MAX £	MIN £	MAX £	OPEN
	19.00	19.00	38.00	-	1-12

St Ishmael's   Saundersfoot   Solva   Tenby

FH   Skerryback

Sandy Haven,
St Ishmael's
Haverfordwest,
Pembrokeshire,
Dyfed SA62 3DN
Tel: (01646) 636598

HIGHLY COMMENDED

A traditional Pembrokeshire welcome on Coastal Path. A haven for walkers and bird lovers. Ideal for exploring Pembrokeshire's beautiful coast. Children welcome. Central heating, drying facilities. Open fires in winter. TV lounge. Double and twin rooms with hot and cold water, tea/coffee facilities.

SINGLE PER PERSON B&B		DOUBLE FOR 2 PERSONS B&B		🛏 2 🛁
MIN £	MAX £	MIN £	MAX £	OPEN
-	-	30.00	-	1-12

H   Pleasant Valley House

Pleasant Valley,
Stepaside,
Nr Saundersfoot,
Dyfed SA67 8NY
Tel: (01834) 813607

HIGHLY COMMENDED

Small friendly countryside hotel, set in its own grounds. Located in picturesque wooded valley. 32' x 16' heated swimming pool, children's swing. Few minutes walk Wiseman's Bridge beach, 30 minutes stroll along flat coastal path into Saundersfoot. Tenby 5 miles. Ample parking within hotel grounds. Licensed, tea making, home cooking, varied menu. Personal service.

SINGLE PER PERSON B&B		DOUBLE FOR 2 PERSONS B&B		🛏 8 🛁 3
MIN £	MAX £	MIN £	MAX £	OPEN
13.00	15.00	26.00	30.00	3-9

FH   Llanddinog Old Farmhouse

Solva,
Haverfordwest,
Pembrokeshire,
Dyfed SA62 6NA
Tel: (01348) 831224

Peaceful 16th century farmhouse, situated only 3 miles from sandy beaches and coastal paths. Excellent facilities including roaring fires, substantial country food, using local ingredients. Children enjoy the large garden, rope swings, aerial slide, small animals. Riding, golf, mountain bikes nearby. Picnics prepared. Pets welcome. Close to Solva harbour, St David's Cathedral, castles, beaches, Preseli Hills. SAE please Mrs S Griffiths.

SINGLE PER PERSON B&B		DOUBLE FOR 2 PERSONS B&B		🛏 2 🛁 2
MIN £	MAX £	MIN £	MAX £	OPEN
16.00	16.00	32.00	32.00	1-12

H   Cliff House

Wogan Terrace,
Saundersfoot,
Pembrokeshire,
Dyfed SA69 9HA
Tel: (01834) 813931

HIGHLY COMMENDED

Quality, comfort, service, welcome - words our guests tell us really mean something at Cliff House. In the heart of the village, one minute from beach, with outstanding sea and harbour views. Ideal accommodation for relaxation, sporting holidays or exploring beautiful Pembrokeshire. Quality en-suite facilities in several rooms, supplement payable. Personal service from resident proprietors. Prices quoted relate to 3 rooms only.

SINGLE PER PERSON B&B		DOUBLE FOR 2 PERSONS B&B		🛏 6 🛁 3
MIN £	MAX £	MIN £	MAX £	OPEN
-	-	30.00	36.00	1-12

GH   Pinewood

Cliff Road,
Wiseman's Bridge,
Narberth, Pembrokeshire,
Dyfed SA67 8NU
Tel: (01834) 811082

HIGHLY COMMENDED

Comfortable, large dormer bungalow in peaceful, rural surroundings 350 yards from the beach. Lounge with sea view. Adjacent to Pembrokeshire Coastal Path, halfway between Saundersfoot and Amroth. Twin and double rooms are en-suite with colour TV and tea/coffee facilities - two are on the ground floor. Ideal for relaxing, sightseeing and walking. Brochure Mrs Gwen Grecian.

SINGLE PER PERSON B&B		DOUBLE FOR 2 PERSONS B&B		🛏 3 🛁 3
MIN £	MAX £	MIN £	MAX £	OPEN
13.00	16.00	26.00	32.00	1-12

FH   Upper Vanley Farm

Llandeloy,
Solva,
Haverfordwest,
Pembrokeshire,
Dyfed SA62 6LJ
Tel: (01348) 831418

COMMENDED

Friendly farmhouse, central for St David's Peninsula. Three miles from Coastal Path, Solva harbour, safe sandy beaches. Spectacular walks, birdwatching, wild flowers, water sports. Pretty rooms all en-suite, colour TV, tea making. Children welcome. Delicious traditional and vegetarian dishes. Licensed. Dogs welcome free of charge. Ample parking.

SINGLE PER PERSON B&B		DOUBLE FOR 2 PERSONS B&B		🛏 7 🛁 6
MIN £	MAX £	MIN £	MAX £	OPEN
16.50	19.00	33.00	38.00	2-11

H   The Grange Hotel

Wooden,
Saundersfoot,
Dyfed SA69 9DY
Tel: (01834) 812809

COMMENDED

Family run licensed hotel close to Saundersfoot, Tenby and the Pembrokeshire Coastal Path. All rooms have tea/coffee, colour TV and central heating. There is a large car park. An ideal base for beach and water sports holidays, birdwatching, walking and fishing. Reductions are available for weekly bookings and children. Brochure: Mrs S Griffin - Proprietor.

SINGLE PER PERSON B&B		DOUBLE FOR 2 PERSONS B&B		🛏 6 🛁 2
MIN £	MAX £	MIN £	MAX £	OPEN
-	-	26.00	38.00	2-11

FH   Carne Mountain Farm

Reynalton,
Kilgetty,
Pembrokeshire,
Dyfed SA68 0PD
Tel: (01834) 860546

COMMENDED

A warm welcome awaits you at our lovely 200 year old farmhouse. Set amidst the peace and tranquility of the beautiful Pembrokeshire countryside. Distant views of Preseli Hills, yet only 3½ miles from Saundersfoot. Picturesque bedrooms with TV, tea/coffee, wash hand basins, central heating. Separate dining room with interesting plate collection. Delicious farmhouse food. SAE Mrs Joy Holgate.

SINGLE PER PERSON B&B		DOUBLE FOR 2 PERSONS B&B		🛏 2 🛁 -
MIN £	MAX £	MIN £	MAX £	OPEN
13.00	14.50	26.00	29.00	1-12

H   Buckingham Hotel

Esplanade,
Tenby,
Dyfed SA70 7DU
Tel: (01834) 842622

Superbly situated overlooking the sunny South Beach and only 5 minutes from Tenby town centre. Relaxing family run hotel offering fine food, wine and service. All rooms heated, colour TV, beverage facilities and en-suite. Two day breaks from £45, weekly rates from £157.00 above rates include dinner.

SINGLE PER PERSON B&B		DOUBLE FOR 2 PERSONS B&B		🛏 8 🛁 8
MIN £	MAX £	MIN £	MAX £	OPEN
17.00	19.00	32.00	38.00	4-11

Tenby

H	Clarence House Hotel

Esplanade,
Tenby,
Pembrokeshire,
Dyfed SA70 7DU
Tel: (01834) 844371
Fax: (01834) 844372

COMMENDED

Tenby Town, Centre Esplanade, South Beach sea front.

Send for free colour brochure. Full information. All you need to know.

		SINGLE PER PERSON B&B		DOUBLE FOR 2 PERSONS B&B			29
							29
		MIN £	MAX £	MIN £	MAX £	OPEN	
		17.00	19.00	30.00	36.00	4-9	

GH	Flemish Court

St Florence,
Tenby,
Dyfed
Tel: (01834) 871413

COMMENDED

Lovely home of June and Eric, where you will find a real Welsh welcome. All rooms en-suite. Sumptious breakfast. All day access. Parking. Situated in the floral village. Norman church opposite. Easy access to all attractions, coastal walks etc. Try us first for that restful relaxing holiday you all deserve. Evening meals available. Telephone June Taylor for brochure. Safe parking.

P		SINGLE PER PERSON B&B		DOUBLE FOR 2 PERSONS B&B			3
							3
TW	T	MIN £	MAX £	MIN £	MAX £	OPEN	
		13.00	16.00	26.00	32.00	1-12	

GH	Sutherlands

3 Picton Road,
Tenby,
Pembrokeshire,
Dyfed SA70 7DP
Tel: (01834) 842522

Small family run guest house, ideally situated for all the delights of this attractive walled town. Golf links, bowling green and beautiful unspoilt beaches all within easy reach. Noted for our hospitable and 'rich' breakfasts. The discerning palate will also appreciate our evening meals.

		SINGLE PER PERSON B&B		DOUBLE FOR 2 PERSONS B&B			3
							1
T		MIN £	MAX £	MIN £	MAX £	OPEN	
		14.00	18.00	28.00	36.00	1-12	

H	Pen-Mar

New Hedges,
Tenby,
Dyfed SA70 8TL
Tel: (01834) 842435

HIGHLY COMMENDED

Comfortable relaxing atmosphere awaits, offering 'a touch of Italy' at Pen-Mar, our friendly fully licensed family run hotel. Excellent choice of menu. British and continental cuisine. All diets catered for. Rooms have tea/coffee, hairdryer, TV. Betwixt Tenby and Saundersfoot in Pembrokeshire National Park. Recommended by the Guild of Master Caterers/Hoteliers. For more information please enquire to Mrs R Romeo.

P		SINGLE PER PERSON B&B		DOUBLE FOR 2 PERSONS B&B			10
							6
		MIN £	MAX £	MIN £	MAX £	OPEN	
		15.00	19.00	30.00	38.00	1-10+12	

GH	High Seas

8 The Norton,
Tenby,
Dyfed SA70 8AA
Tel: (01834) 843611 or 842491

COMMENDED

This Georgian town house is in an ideal position with beautiful views of the beach and harbour. Close to the town centre and only a few steps from the sands and safe bathing of the North Beach. There are six bedrooms, five with private bathroom. All rooms have colour TV and tea-making facilities.

C		SINGLE PER PERSON B&B		DOUBLE FOR 2 PERSONS B&B			6
							5
		MIN £	MAX £	MIN £	MAX £	OPEN	
		14.00	19.00	28.00	38.00	4-10	

GH	The Coach Guest House

11 Deer Park,
Tenby,
Dyfed SA70 7LE
Tel: (01834) 842210

Family run fully licensed guest house, ideally situated two minutes from town centre and beaches. Comfortable en-suite bedrooms with tea/coffee facilities, colour TV, central heating and access at all times. Oak beamed dining room and well stocked cosy bar. Special price short breaks available out of main season. Private parking by arrangement. Please telephone for brochure.

P		SINGLE PER PERSON B&B		DOUBLE FOR 2 PERSONS B&B			9
							9
		MIN £	MAX £	MIN £	MAX £	OPEN	
		15.00	18.00	25.00	32.00	1-12	

Tenby harbour

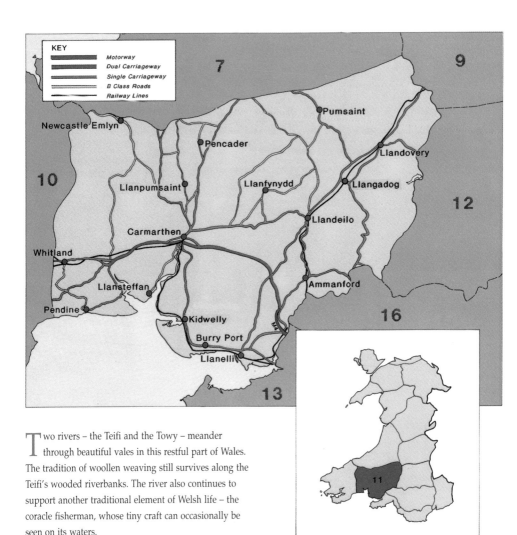

Two rivers – the Teifi and the Towy – meander through beautiful vales in this restful part of Wales. The tradition of woollen weaving still survives along the Teifi's wooded riverbanks. The river also continues to support another traditional element of Welsh life – the coracle fisherman, whose tiny craft can occasionally be seen on its waters.

The Towy's broad vale cuts a swathe through rich farming country, flowing past the pleasant country towns of Llandovery, Llandeilo and Carmarthen. Don't miss Carmarthen's busy market (Wednesday is the best day) when farmers and shoppers pour in for the livestock sales and the fresh food stalls. Flanking the vale are the brooding Black Mountain, western outpost of the Brecon Beacons National Park, and the silent Brechfa Forest.

The Towy meets the sea at Carmarthen Bay. This sandy coastline, and the sleepy little seatown of Laugharne, inspired some of Dylan Thomas's best work (the poet's Boathouse home at Laugharne is open to the public). Elsewhere along this uncrowded coastline there's more sand – miles and miles of it – at Pendine and the splendid Pembrey Country Park.

Ke2 Ammanford

Bustling valley town, good for Welsh crafts and products, on western edge of Brecon Beacons National Park. Spectacular mountain routes over nearby Black Mountain to Llangadog.

Kc2 Carmarthen

County town of Dyfed in pastoral Vale of Towy. Lively market and shops, livestock market. Carmarthen Castle was an important residence of the native Welsh princes but only the gateway and towers remain. Golf, fishing, tennis and well-equipped leisure centre. Remains of Roman amphitheatre. Immaculate museum in beautiful historic house on outskirts of town. Gwili Railway and ornamental Middleton Hall Amenity Area nearby.

Ga7 Llandeilo

Farming centre at an important crossing on River Towy, and handy as touring base for Carreg Cennen Castle, impressively set on high crag, and remains of Dryslwyn Castle. Limited access to Dinefwr Castle in parklands on edge of town. Gelli Aur Country Park nearby has 90 acres, including a nature trail, arboretum and deer herd.

Gb6 Llandovery

An important market town on the A40 with a ruined castle; its Welsh name Llanymddyfri means 'the church among the waters'. In the hills to the north is the cave of Twm Siôn Cati - the Welsh Robin Hood. Good touring centre for Brecon Beacons and remote Llyn Brianne area.

Ga6 Llangadog

Small market town set on two tributaries of the nearby Towy. Convenient for walking and touring the Black Mountain in the west of the Brecon Beacons National Park. The road over the mountain to Brynaman is one of the most scenic in South Wales. Bethlehem, a few miles south, has a famous Christmas postmark.

Carreg Cennen Castle

Fc7 Llanpumsaint

Small village off the main A485 Carmarthen-Lampeter road, nestling in a quiet valley between Cynwyl Elfed and the western edge of the Brechfa Forest. Take a ride on the steam-powered Gwili Railway from Bronwydd Arms.

Ka2 Whitland

Market town with remains of 12th-century abbey. Touring centre. Canolfan Hywel Dda is a visitors' centre, with thematic gardens, which tells the story of the Welsh King Hywel the Good, who devised a famous legal code. Two popular attractions - Pemberton's Victorian Chocolates and Grove Land Adventures - nearby.

River Towy at Carmarthen

79

Ammanford Carmarthen Llandeilo

GH	Mount Pleasant

Pontardulais Road,
Garnswllt,
Ammanford,
Dyfed SA18 2RT
Tel: (01269) 591722
Fax: (01269) 591722

L
COMMENDED

Enjoy the best of both worlds. Relax in peaceful surroundings with magnificent views over Loughor Valley and enjoy the convenient location. Situated 2¹/₂ miles from Ammanford market town and 5 miles from M4 junction 48. In easy reach of Swansea shopping and leisure facilities and many tourist attractions. A warm welcome awaits you.

		SINGLE PER PERSON B&B	DOUBLE FOR 2 PERSONS B&B	🛏 5 / 🛁 2
		MIN £ 16.00	MAX £ 18.00	MIN £ 28.00	MAX £ 32.00	OPEN 1-12

FH	Coedhirion Farm Guest House

Llanddarog,
Carmarthen,
Dyfed SA32 8BH
Tel: (01267) 275666

COMMENDED

Conveniently situated just off A48 9 miles west J49 M4. Near the village of Llanddarog with two 17th century Inns for evening meals. A warm Welsh welcome awaits you with a Welsh breakfast. Pets welcome by arrangement. An ideal centre to tour Pembrokeshire and the Gower Peninsula. Ask for our brochure (it's in English!) and free.

		SINGLE PER PERSON B&B	DOUBLE FOR 2 PERSONS B&B	🛏 2 / 🛁 2
		MIN £ 19.00	MAX £ 19.00	MIN £ 38.00	MAX £ 38.00	OPEN 1-12

FH	Trebersed Farmhouse

Travellers Rest,
St Peter's,
Carmarthen,
Dyfed SA31 3RR
Tel: (01267) 238182

HIGHLY
COMMENDED

A warm welcome awaits you at our working dairy farm overlooking the thriving market town of Carmarthen, only two miles from its centre. Plenty of parking space. Excellent touring base, just off main A40. Three comfortable rooms, all en-suite with tea/coffee facilities. Full central heating, radio alarms and colour TV lounge. Enquiries Mrs Rosemary Jones.

		SINGLE PER PERSON B&B	DOUBLE FOR 2 PERSONS B&B	🛏 3 / 🛁 3
		MIN £ 16.00	MAX £ 18.00	MIN £ 32.00	MAX £ 32.00	OPEN 1-12

GH	Glasfryn Guest House

Brechfa,
Carmarthen,
Dyfed SA32 7QY
Tel: (01267) 202306

HIGHLY
COMMENDED

Situated at the edge of Brechfa Forest surrounded by moss covered hills. A small family owned guest house ideally located for fishing, pony trekking, walking, birdwatching, forest mountain bike trails. All rooms en-suite, recently refurbished. Excellent home cooking, licensed restaurant 20 minutes from Carmarthen, 45 minutes blue flag beach, 1¹/₄ hours Fishguard ferry. Colour brochure available.

		SINGLE PER PERSON B&B	DOUBLE FOR 2 PERSONS B&B	🛏 3 / 🛁 3
		MIN £ 18.00	MAX £ -	MIN £ 36.00	MAX £ -	OPEN 1-12

FH	Pantgwyn Farm

Whitemill,
Carmarthen,
Dyfed SA32 7ES
Tel: (01267) 290247
Fax: (01267) 290247

DE LUXE
AWARD

Our 200 year old farmhouse offers extremely comfortable accommodation. The lounge with its inglenook fireplace, the beamed dining room and the traditionally furnished en-suite bedrooms. Meals at Pantgwyn are something special - not surprising from the Wales' winners of the "Best Breakfast in Britain". Beach 8 miles. Fishing nearby. Ideally situated for touring West Wales. "Taste of Wales" member.

		SINGLE PER PERSON B&B	DOUBLE FOR 2 PERSONS B&B	🛏 3 / 🛁 3
		MIN £ -	MAX £ -	MIN £ 38.00	MAX £ -	OPEN 1-12

GH	Brynawel Guest House

17 New Road,
Llandeilo,
Dyfed SA19 6DD
Tel: (01558) 822925

COMMENDED

Family run guest house in the centre of town. Buses and railway station close by. Centrally located for Gower and Pembroke coasts and Brecon Beacons National Park. National Trust park within town. Gelli Aur Country Park, Pembrey Country Park and Oakwood theme park within 1 hour drive. Easy access to M4.

		SINGLE PER PERSON B&B	DOUBLE FOR 2 PERSONS B&B	🛏 5 / 🛁 3
		MIN £ 19.00	MAX £ 24.00	MIN £ 29.00	MAX £ 35.00	OPEN 1-12

GH	Old Priory Guest House

20 Priory Street,
Carmarthen,
Dyfed SA31 1NE
Tel: (01267) 237471

L

Family run guest house with 15 bedrooms all with central heating, television and hand basins in all bedrooms. Bath and showers available. Television lounge. A la carte restaurant, and bar. We are situated five minutes walk from the shopping centre and market.

		SINGLE PER PERSON B&B	DOUBLE FOR 2 PERSONS B&B	🛏 15 / 🛁
		MIN £ 17.50	MAX £ 18.50	MIN £ 29.00	MAX £ 31.00	OPEN 1-12

FH	Plas Farm

Llangynog,
Carmarthen,
Dyfed SA33 5DB
Tel: (01267) 211492

L

A warm welcome awaits you at this family run working farm, with very comfortable farmhouse. All rooms have hot and cold, tea/coffee facilities, colour TV and central heating. One room en-suite. Ideal base for touring South and West Wales with its many beaches and historical places of interest.. Golf course nearby. Good and varied evening meals available locally at restaurant or inn.

		SINGLE PER PERSON B&B	DOUBLE FOR 2 PERSONS B&B	🛏 2 / 🛁 1
		MIN £ 16.00	MAX £ 18.00	MIN £ 28.00	MAX £ 32.00	OPEN 1-12

Please note

All the accommodation in this guide has applied for verification/classification and in many instances for grading also. However, at the time of going to press not all establishments had been visited – some of these properties are indicated by the wording 'Awaiting Inspection' or 'Awaiting Grading'.

Llandeilo Llandovery Llangadog Llanpumsaint Whitland

GH	Ty Gwyn Bach

Gwynfe Road,
Ffairfach,
Llandeilo,
Dyfed SA19 6UY
Tel: (01558) 823546

 COMMENDED

Spacious, attractive and comfortable rooms. Central heating, hot and cold, tea making facilities. One bed-sitting room with en-suite shower. The house is set in an acre of landscaped gardens. Outdoor swimming pool, heated in summer. Ideally located for touring, walking, golf, birdwatching, fishing etc. Within easy reach of Brecon Beacons, Gower Peninsula and M4. Very peaceful location.

P C ✂ T	🐕 🏙 👤	SINGLE PER PERSON B&B		DOUBLE FOR 2 PERSONS B&B		🛏 2 🛁 1
		MIN £ 13.00	MAX £ 15.00	MIN £ 26.00	MAX £ 30.00	OPEN 1-12

FH	Pencrug Farm

Gwynfe,
Llangadog,
Dyfed SA19 9RP
Tel: (01550) 740686

From the comfort of a restored 17th century farmhouse in a superb setting, explore the attractions of the Brecon Beacons National Park and the rich beauty of West Wales. Walking, riding, fishing, golf, birdwatching all available in the area. Coast within easy reach.

P 🏙 🍽 🏠	🍳	SINGLE PER PERSON B&B		DOUBLE FOR 2 PERSONS B&B		🛏 3 🛁 -
		MIN £ 12.00	MAX £ 12.00	MIN £ 24.00	MAX £ 24.00	OPEN 1-12

FH	Brunant

Whitland,
Dyfed SA34 0LX
Tel: (01994) 240421

Relax in rural tranquillity, centrally situated for touring or beaches. Within easy reach of leisure parks, places of interest and ferries. All rooms en-suite with hospitality tray, TV and radio. Choice of menus, vegetarian by prior arrangement. "Never enough time to enjoy this to the full", John Carter, Thames TV.

P 🍽 ✂ 🍽	🍸 🏙 🍳	SINGLE PER PERSON B&B		DOUBLE FOR 2 PERSONS B&B		🛏 3 🛁 3
		MIN £ 16.00	MAX £ 18.00	MIN £ 30.00	MAX £ 32.00	OPEN 4-9

GH	Myrtle Hill Guest House

Llansadwrn,
Llanwrda,
Dyfed SA19 8HL
Tel: (01550) 777530

 COMMENDED

Old farmhouse with magnificent views in beautiful unspoilt countryside. All bedrooms with en-suite bathroom, tea/coffee facilities. Two sitting rooms, one "No Smoking". Access at all times. Excellent food, freshly prepared using own garden produce. Ideally situated for exploring South, West and Mid Wales. Abundant wildlife, fishing, pony trekking locally, lovely walking country.

P 🍸 ✂ 🍽	🐕 🏙 👤 📺	SINGLE PER PERSON B&B		DOUBLE FOR 2 PERSONS B&B		🛏 3 🛁 3
		MIN £ 17.00	MAX £ -	MIN £ 34.00	MAX £ -	OPEN 2-10

FH	Fferm-y-Felin

Llanpumsaint,
Dyfed SA33 6DA
Tel: (01267) 253498

A warm welcome awaits you at our very comfortable 18th century farmhouse with log fires, oak beams and traditional Welsh cooking. Situated in 15 acres of conserved countryside, with large lake and interesting woodland walks. This is where you can enjoy peace and tranquility. No television! No newspapers! What a find! Ideal for the discerning traveller. A delight! Pets by arrangement.

P 👤 🍽 🏠	C 🏙 ✂ 🍽	SINGLE PER PERSON B&B		DOUBLE FOR 2 PERSONS B&B		🛏 5 🛁 2
		MIN £ 15.00	MAX £ 18.00	MIN £ 30.00	MAX £ 36.00	OPEN 1-12

FH	Cwmgwyn Farm

Llangadog Road,
Llandovery,
Dyfed SA20 0EQ
Tel. (01550) 20410
From May 1995 Tel: (01550) 720410

 HIGHLY COMMENDED

Warm welcome to enjoy the country on our working livestock farm overlooking the river Towy, two miles from Llandovery on A4069. The 17th century farmhouse is full of charm and character with inglenook fireplace, exposed stonework and beams. Spacious luxury en-suite bedrooms with hairdryer, colour TV, tea/coffee. Ideally situated for touring Mid and South Wales.

P 👤 🍽	🏙 🍳	SINGLE PER PERSON B&B		DOUBLE FOR 2 PERSONS B&B		🛏 3 🛁 3
		MIN £ 18.00	MAX £ 19.00	MIN £ 36.00	MAX £ 38.00	OPEN 4-10

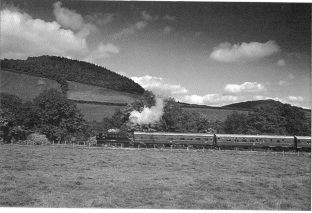

Gwili Narrow Gauge Railway

81

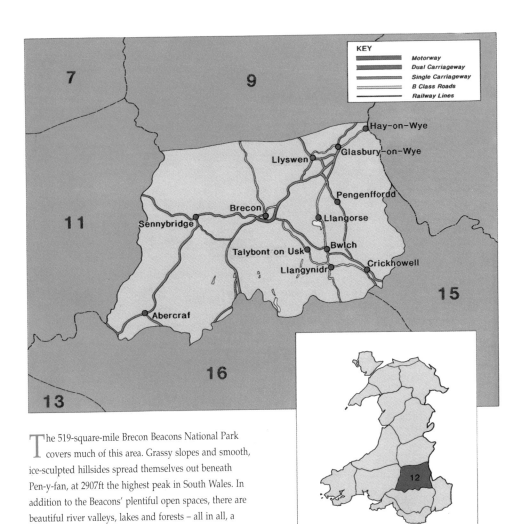

The 519-square-mile Brecon Beacons National Park covers much of this area. Grassy slopes and smooth, ice-sculpted hillsides spread themselves out beneath Pen-y-fan, at 2907ft the highest peak in South Wales. In addition to the Beacons' plentiful open spaces, there are beautiful river valleys, lakes and forests – all in all, a landscape which might have been purpose-built for lovers of the great outdoors.

Walking, pony trekking, fishing, watersports and canal cruising are all popular here – some visitors are even content just to look at the scenery! Explore Pen-y-fan, Llangorse Lake and the central Beacons from the charming old town of Brecon or pretty Crickhowell in the Usk Valley.

Further west, the moorlands of Fforest Fawr lead to the wildernesses of the Black Mountain. Don't confuse this Black Mountain with the Black Mountains at the other end of the park. This latter chain of hills straddles the Wales/England border, running almost to Hay-on-Wye, the world-famous 'town of books'. Hay is a magnet for bibliophiles, especially during its annual Festival of Literature. And music fans from far and wide flock to Brecon each summer for its Jazz Festival.

Ge6 Brecon

Main touring centre for the 519 square miles of the Brecon Beacons National Park. Handsome old town with thriving market, ruined castle, cathedral, priory and two interesting museums (Brecknock and South Wales Borderers'). Wide range of inns and good shopping. Centre for walking and pony trekking. Golf, fishing, and canal cruising also available. Very popular summer International Jazz Festival.

Hb7 Crickhowell

Small, pleasant country town beautifully situated on the River Usk. Good for walking, fishing, pony trekking and riding. Remains of Norman castle, 14th-century Tretower Court and earlier castle worth a visit.

Hb5 Hay-on-Wye

Small market town on the Offa's Dyke Path, nestling below the Black Mountains on a picturesque stretch of the River Wye. A mecca for book lovers - there are antiquarian and second-hand bookshops, some huge, all over the town. Attractive crafts centre. Literature Festival in early summer attracts big names.

Ha6 Pengenffordd

Tiny settlement on scenic road between Tretower and Talgarth, which cuts through the edge of the Black Mountains. Wonderful views from Castell Dinas Iron Age hillfort. Popular with walkers and pony trekkers - good selection of trekking centres locally. Llangorse Lake nearby,.

Talybont Falls

Ha7 Talybont on Usk

Village in pastoral setting on banks of River Usk and Monmouthshire and Brecon Canal. Within the Brecon Beacons National Park. Surrounding hills perfect for walking and pony trekking. Brecon nearby.

Crickhowell

Brecon

GH | Aberyscir Old Rectory

Aberyscir,
Brecon,
Powys LD3 9NP
Tel: (01874) 623457

AWARD — HIGHLY COMMENDED

Set in 6 acres of its own grounds, Aberyscir Old Rectory is only 2$\frac{1}{2}$ miles from Brecon. Two rooms are en-suite, one with private facilities and are centrally heated. Private lounge, home cooking. Glorious views of Brecon Beacons. Golf, fishing, trekking nearby.

		SINGLE PER PERSON B&B		DOUBLE FOR 2 PERSONS B&B		🛏 3 🛁 3
		MIN £	MAX £	MIN £	MAX £	OPEN
		-	-	36.00	36.00	1-12

GH | The Coach Guest House

Orchard Street,
Brecon,
Powys LD3 8AN
Tel: (01874) 623803

AWARD — HIGHLY COMMENDED

"Hotel standards at guest house prices". Six bedrooms all en-suite, three with bath, three with shower. Four double rooms, two twin. All have colour TV, hairdryer, clock, radio, telephone and beverage tray. Whole house completely non smoking. Ideal base for touring Brecon Beacons National Park. Close to town centre. RAC Highly Acclaimed. AA Listed QQQQ.

		SINGLE PER PERSON B&B		DOUBLE FOR 2 PERSONS B&B		🛏 6 🛁 6
		MIN £	MAX £	MIN £	MAX £	OPEN
		-	-	36.00	38.00	1-12

GH | Tir Bach Guest House

13 Alexandra Road,
Brecon,
Powys LD3 7PD
Tel: (01874) 624551

Comfortable, homely, family run guest house, on quiet road overlooking town. Two minutes walk from town centre. Panoramic view of Brecon Beacons. Loung with colour TV. Plentiful hot water, central heating, car parking, traditional British breakfast. Special rates for children. Well travelled friendly hosts.

		SINGLE PER PERSON B&B		DOUBLE FOR 2 PERSONS B&B		🛏 3 🛁
		MIN £	MAX £	MIN £	MAX £	OPEN
		14.50	16.00	28.00	30.00	2-10

GH | Beacons Guest House

16 Bridge Street,
Brecon,
Powys LD3 8AH
Tel: (01874) 623339

COMMENDED

A friendly atmosphere is assured in our Georgian guest house, close to town centre, river and Brecon Beacons. En-suite rooms with beverage tray and colour TV. Cosy bar, residents' lounge, car parking. Groups, pets and children welcome! Ideal location for attractions and outdoor activities. Excellent home cooking, "Taste of Wales" recommended. AA/RAC Acclaimed. Credit cards accepted. Brochure available on request.

		SINGLE PER PERSON B&B		DOUBLE FOR 2 PERSONS B&B		🛏 10 🛁 7
		MIN £	MAX £	MIN £	MAX £	OPEN
		16.50	-	33.00	-	1-12

GH | Glasfryn House

Church Street,
Brecon,
Powys LD3 8BY
Tel: (01874) 623014

L HIGHLY COMMENDED

Highly commended with warm and friendly atmosphere. Tastefully furnished rooms with colour TV, hairdryer, tea/coffee facilities. Close town centre and glorious countryside. Centrally situated for exploring National Park, Mid and South Wales. Many restaurants and pubs just minutes walk away. Ring Peter or Barbara Jackson for personal help and advice about Brecon and the surrounding area.

		SINGLE PER PERSON B&B		DOUBLE FOR 2 PERSONS B&B		🛏 9 🛁 -
		MIN £	MAX £	MIN £	MAX £	OPEN
		16.00	17.00	32.00	34.00	1-12

GH | The Tower

Scethrog,
Brecon,
Powys LD3 7YE
Tel: (01874) 87672
From May 1995 Tel: (01874) 676672
Fax: (0181) 960 8246

COMMENDED

Romantic, medieval house surrounded by meadows, mountains and river. Two spacious oak beamed bed-sitting rooms, each with own en-suite toilet and washbasin, colour TV, tea/coffee and fridge. Picnic in large garden overlooking kingfisher pool or by log fire in your room. Relaxed atmosphere, late breakfast, steep stone steps. Private trout fishing.

		SINGLE PER PERSON B&B		DOUBLE FOR 2 PERSONS B&B		🛏 2 🛁 2
		MIN £	MAX £	MIN £	MAX £	OPEN
		17.00	19.00	28.00	32.00	3-10

GH | Cambridge House Guest House

St David Street,
Brecon,
Powys LD3 8BB
Tel: (01874) 624699

HIGHLY COMMENDED

Small quiet family run guest house. Close to town centre and the Beacons. Clean and cosy. Activities arranged. Our en-suite room is equipped with dressing table, hairdryer. Superb views of the Beacons. Full fire certificate. Private parking. Pay phone. Ironing facilities available. Packed lunches.

		SINGLE PER PERSON B&B		DOUBLE FOR 2 PERSONS B&B		🛏 4 🛁 1
		MIN £	MAX £	MIN £	MAX £	OPEN
		15.00	-	28.00	32.00	1-12

GH | The Old Rectory

Llanddew,
Brecon,
Powys LD3 9SS
Tel: (01874) 622058

HIGHLY COMMENDED

Peacefully situated in 2 acres of its own grounds, The Old Rectory is 1$\frac{1}{2}$ miles from Brecon with magnificent views of the Brecon Beacons. Every comfort provided for. Central heating, colour TV, tea/coffee in all rooms. A warm welcome is assured and personal service with fresh food served. Pony trekking, golf, fishing nearby. Ample parking. RAC Acclaimed.

		SINGLE PER PERSON B&B		DOUBLE FOR 2 PERSONS B&B		🛏 3 🛁 2
		MIN £	MAX £	MIN £	MAX £	OPEN
		-	-	32.00	36.00	1-12

FH | Brynfedwen Farm

Trallong Common,
Sennybridge,
Brecon,
Powys LD3 8HW
Tel: (01874) 636505

AWARD — HIGHLY COMMENDED

Brynfedwen meaning "hill of the birch trees", is a family farm set high above the Usk Valley, commanding splendid views of the Brecon Beacons. Well situated for all country pursuits or just relaxing. Period, centrally heated farmhouse, all three rooms are en-suite, including self-contained flat for disabled visitors. Good home cooking. Children welcome.

		SINGLE PER PERSON B&B		DOUBLE FOR 2 PERSONS B&B		🛏 3 🛁 3
		MIN £	MAX £	MIN £	MAX £	OPEN
		16.00	-	32.00	-	1-12

Brecon

FH Cefncoedbach Farm

Sarnau,
Brecon,
Powys LD3 9PT
Tel: (01874) 623548

With beautiful views of Black Mountains and Brecon Beacons. Ideally situated for visiting main attractions. Centrally heated double and twin bedded rooms, one en-suite. Tea making facilities, TV and games room. Offers all modern comforts in friendly family atmosphere. Four miles north of Brecon, three miles golf course. Lovely walking country.

P ▥ ▥ ⚟ ☂ T	SINGLE PER PERSON B&B		DOUBLE FOR 2 PERSONS B&B		🛏 2 🛁 1
	MIN £ 14.00	MAX £ 16.00	MIN £ 28.00	MAX £ 32.00	OPEN 1-12

FH Llwyncynog Farm

Felinfach,
Brecon,
Powys LD3 0UG
Tel: (01874) 623475

Family farm set in peaceful countryside, 5 miles east of Brecon. Splendid views of Brecon Beacons and Black Mountains. 17th century farmhouse with guests' lounge and dining room with colour TV. Comfortable bedrooms each with tea/coffee making facilities, one family room en-suite, one twin en-suite and double room with private bathroom. Central for many leisure activities or quiet walks.

P ⚟ ▥ ⚟ ⚟ T	SINGLE PER PERSON B&B		DOUBLE FOR 2 PERSONS B&B		🛏 3 🛁 2 🛁 1
	MIN £ 15.00	MAX £ 15.00	MIN £ 28.00	MAX £ 30.00	OPEN 4-10

FH The Old Mill

Felinfach,
Brecon,
Powys LD3 0UB
Tel: (01874) 625385

Peacefully situated in its own grounds in the village of Felinfach, The Old Mill has a wealth of character with original features being retained. Friendly atmosphere. Large garden, TV lounge, tea/coffee facilities. Some en-suite bedrooms. Within easy reach Brecon Beacons, Black Mountains, Hay-on-Wye, pony trekking etc. Within walking distance of local pubs.

P ▥ ⚟ ⚟ T	SINGLE PER PERSON B&B		DOUBLE FOR 2 PERSONS B&B		🛏 3 🛁 1
	MIN £ 16.00	MAX £ 18.00	MIN £ 27.00	MAX £ 30.00	OPEN 3-11

FH Cwmcamlais Uchaf Farm

Cwmcamlais,
Sennybridge,
Brecon,
Powys LD3 8TD
Tel: (01874) 636376

HIGHLY COMMENDED

Cwmcamlais Uchaf is situated in the Brecon Beacons National Park, 1 mile off the A40 between Brecon and Sennybridge. Our spacious 16th century farmhouse has exposed beams, log fires and 3 tastefully decorated bedrooms. One double en-suite and one double and one twin with private bathrooms. Good food and a warm Welsh welcome of prime importance.

P ⚟ ▥ ⚟ ⚟	SINGLE PER PERSON B&B		DOUBLE FOR 2 PERSONS B&B		🛏 3 🛁 1
	MIN £ 16.50	MAX £ 18.00	MIN £ 30.00	MAX £ 34.00	OPEN 1-12

FH Llwynhir Farm

Crai,
Brecon,
Powys LD3 8YW   L
Tel: (01874) 636563

Mixed 500 acre hill farm. Panoramic mountain views. Peaceful, near Dan yr Ogof Caves, National Park Centre, waterfalls, Brecon Beacons, Black Mountains, National Trust properties, Penscynor Wildlife Park. Nearby attractions: fishing, pony trekking, dry ski slope, castles, pottery, art gallery, indoor swimming pool. Brecon 12 miles. Swansea, Gower 24 miles. Established over 20 years.

P ⚟ ⚟ ⚟ C ⚟ T	SINGLE PER PERSON B&B		DOUBLE FOR 2 PERSONS B&B		🛏 3 🛁 ·
	MIN £ 15.00	-	MIN £ 28.00	-	OPEN 3-10

FH Tre Graig Farm

Bwlch,
Brecon,
Powys LD3 7SJ   AWARD
Tel: (01874) 730973

HIGHLY COMMENDED

Excellent value accommodation in peaceful elevated position surrounded by breathtaking panoramic views within the Brecon Beacons National Park. The farm is ¾ mile off the A40 on the Crickhowell side of Bwlch village. Cosy centrally heated en-suite bedrooms with colour TV and tea/coffee facilities. Marjorie Morris welcomes you with good food and warm welcome. Brochure available. SAE please.

P ▥ ⚟ ⚟ ⚟	SINGLE PER PERSON B&B		DOUBLE FOR 2 PERSONS B&B		🛏 3 🛁 2
	MIN £ -	MAX £ -	MIN £ 32.00	MAX £ 38.00	OPEN 2-11

FH Llanbrynean Farm

Llanfrynach,
Brecon,
Powys LD3 7BQ   L
Tel: (01874) 665222

Traditional, spacious Victorian farmhouse. Large garden and wonderful pastoral views. Informal, friendly atmosphere. In the heart of the Brecon Beacons, beside quiet village, ideally situated for country pursuits and good pub food. Two double bedrooms (one en-suite) and one twin bedroom. Tea/coffee facilities. Sitting room, TV. Working family farm.

P ⚟ C ▥ ⚟ ⚟	SINGLE PER PERSON B&B		DOUBLE FOR 2 PERSONS B&B		🛏 3 🛁 1
	MIN £ 14.00	MAX £ 14.50	MIN £ 27.00	MAX £ 32.00	OPEN 2-12

FH Llwyn Neath Farm

Sennybridge,
Brecon,
Powys LD3 8HN
Tel: (01874) 636641

Working hill stock farm with beautiful scenic views of Brecon Beacons. One family room en-suite and double room with private bathroom. Fine central area for walking and all country pursuits, sightseeing etc. Warm welcome and good food assured.

P ⚟ ⚟ ⚟ ⚟	SINGLE PER PERSON B&B		DOUBLE FOR 2 PERSONS B&B		🛏 2 🛁 2
	MIN £ -	MAX £ 18.00	MIN £ -	MAX £ 32.00	OPEN 1-12

FH Trehenry Farm

Felinfach,
Brecon,
Powys LD3 0UN   AWARD
Tel: (01874) 754312

DE LUXE

A 200 acre mixed working farm east of Brecon. The impressive 18th century farmhouse with breathtaking views, inglenook fireplaces, exposed beams, offers select accommodation. Cosy rooms, TV lounge, central heating, separate tables. All rooms with private bathroom, tea/coffee facilities. Personal service and good food is assured. Come and sample for yourself. Open all year. Also self-catering farmhouse.

P ▥ ⚟ ⚟	SINGLE PER PERSON B&B		DOUBLE FOR 2 PERSONS B&B		🛏 3 🛁 3
	MIN £ -	MAX £ -	MIN £ 36.00	MAX £ 38.00	OPEN 1-12

Crickhowell   Hay-on-Wye   Pengenffordd   Talybont on Usk

GH	Castell Corryn

Llangenny,
Crickhowell,
Powys NP8 1HE
Tel: (01873) 810327

HIGHLY COMMENDED

Situated above the Usk Valley within the Brecon Beacons. Outstanding views with beautiful restful gardens. Walking, activity sports, golf, pony trekking nearby. Colour TV in all bedrooms, all rooms en-suite. Children welcome. Special diets catered for. Home cooking. A40 (Glangrwny) turning to Llangenny village. Do not cross river bridge. Keep right, up hill, first right.

![P][C]	SINGLE PER PERSON B&B		DOUBLE FOR 2 PERSONS B&B		🛏 2
					🛁 2
✂ ☕	MIN £	MAX £	MIN £	MAX £	OPEN
🍴	17.50	19.00	35.00	38.00	4-10

GH	The Forge

Glasbury,
Nr Hay-on-Wye,
Powys HR3 5LN
Tel: (01497) 847237

Comfortable 17th century Welsh longhouse. Interesting, civilised accommodation. Quality early/later breakfasts. Assistance excursions. Pony trekking, canoeing bookings arranged, Remote satellite TV, beverage trays, electric blanket, central heating in all bedrooms. Central village near river beach. 3¹/₂ miles Hay-on-Wye book town, 12 miles east of Brecon. Superior restaurants nearby. Overwhelming natural beauty surrounds the area. Ideal tranquil break. Safe car parking.

![P]	SINGLE PER PERSON B&B		DOUBLE FOR 2 PERSONS B&B		🛏 3
					🛁 1
	MIN £	MAX £	MIN £	MAX £	OPEN
	16.00	18.00	32.00	36.00	4-11

H	Castle Inn

Pengenffordd,
Nr Talgarth,
Powys LD3 0EP
Tel: (01874) 711353

COMMENDED

This traditional country Inn lies at the top of an unspoilt valley in a peaceful part of Southern Powys. Grass covered mountains ascend on all sides. The Inn has its own spring water drinking supply. All rooms have colour TV, easy chairs, tea/coffee. Both en-suite and non en-suite are available.

![P]	SINGLE PER PERSON B&B		DOUBLE FOR 2 PERSONS B&B		🛏 5
					🛁 2
	MIN £	MAX £	MIN £	MAX £	OPEN
🍴	18.00	18.00	36.00	36.00	1-12

GH	The Firs

Tretower,
Crickhowell,
Powys NP8 1RF
Tel: (01874) 730780

HIGHLY COMMENDED

300 year old country house with cottage style characteristics, set in a secluded position surrounded by farmland just off A40. Close to small town of Crickhowell. Good views of surrounding area. Medieval Tretower Court and castle nearby. Personal service and good food is of prime importance. Hairdryer and tea/coffee tray in bedroom. AA/RAC Award.

![P]	SINGLE PER PERSON B&B		DOUBLE FOR 2 PERSONS B&B		🛏 4
					🛁 2
☕ T	MIN £	MAX £	MIN £	MAX £	OPEN
	-	-	34.00	38.00	1-12

GH	The Old Post Office

Llanigon,
Hay-on-Wye,
Powys HR3 5QA
Tel: (01497) 820008

COMMENDED

17th century character house in a quiet rural position only two miles from the famous second-hand book town of Hay-on-Wye and set in the lovely Brecon Beacons National Park. Black Mountains and Offa's Dyke Path close by. Superb vegetarian breakfast, early or late. Relaxed atmosphere. Guest's own sitting room and lovely bedrooms.

![P]	SINGLE PER PERSON B&B		DOUBLE FOR 2 PERSONS B&B		🛏 3
					🛁 2
	MIN £	MAX £	MIN £	MAX £	OPEN
	-	-	30.00	38.00.	3-11

GH	Belvedere

Station Road,
Talybont on Usk,
Brecon,
Powys LD3 7JE
Tel: (01874) 87264

Situated between the beautiful Brecon Beacons and the Black Mountains. A modern, friendly and very clean family run business. All rooms have hot and cold, colour TV, shaver points. A short walk from canal and a selection of restaurants and public houses. Local activities include pony trekking, cycling, walking, fishing, leisure centre, show caves and golf.

![P][C]	SINGLE PER PERSON B&B		DOUBLE FOR 2 PERSONS B&B		🛏 3
					🛁 -
✂ ☕ 🍴	MIN £	MAX £	MIN £	MAX £	OPEN
	15.00	19.00	28.00	32.00	1-12

GH	White Hall

Glangrwny,
Crickhowell,
Powys NP8 1EW
Tel: (01873) 811155 or 840267

Comfortable accommodation in Georgian house in ideal walking country between Black Mountains and Brecon Beacons National Park. Canal trips, pony trekking, riding nearby. Also, Norman castles, ancient churches and industrial heritage (Big Pit mine and museums). Extensive library of books for all ages. Bank holidays, minimum 2 nights; reduced rates 3 nights or more. En-suite supplement payable.

![P] 🐕	SINGLE PER PERSON B&B		DOUBLE FOR 2 PERSONS B&B		🛏 4
🍺 ✂					🛁 2
☕ 🍴	MIN £	MAX £	MIN £	MAX £	OPEN
T	13.00	13.00	30.00	30.00	1-12

Llangorse Lak

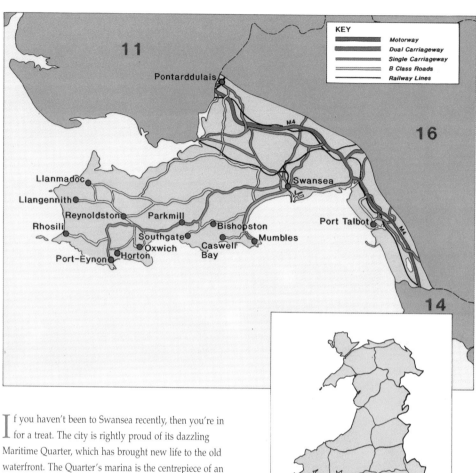

If you haven't been to Swansea recently, then you're in for a treat. The city is rightly proud of its dazzling Maritime Quarter, which has brought new life to the old waterfront. The Quarter's marina is the centrepiece of an award-winning development which includes a Leisure Centre and Maritime and Industrial Museum. Swansea successfully mixes traditional and modern influences. One of its most celebrated features is its fresh foods market – one of the best in Wales – where you can buy everything from Welshcakes to laverbread.

Swansea's setting is another of its strong points. The city is located on the grand sweep of Swansea Bay, close to the unspoilt Gower Peninsula. Mumbles, a pretty little resort and sailing centre, stands at Gower's gateway. From here, Gower's stubby peninsula points westwards, ending spectacularly at Rhosili's dizzy headland.

The peninsula was Britain's first 'Area of Outstanding Natural Beauty'. Most of its little seaside centres – they are too small to be called resorts – are located along the sandy, south-facing coast. But also visit the atmospheric saltings and cockle beds of North Gower.

La4 **Mumbles**

Small resort on Swansea Bay with attractive waterfront and headland pier; centre for watersports and sailing. On fringe of Gower Peninsula, a designated `Area of Outstanding Natural Beauty'. Oystermouth Castle and Clyne Valley Country Park and Gardens nearby.

Kd5 **Oxwich**

Popular Gower Peninsula beach with 3 miles of glorious sand and extensive dunes; easily accessible. Nature trail and visitor centre.

Ke5 **Parkmill**

Gower Peninsula village with easy access to beaches and Swansea. Visit Y Felin Ddwr Craft and Countryside Centre. Three Cliffs Bay - one of the finest stretches of Gower - and historic sites nearby.

Lb4 **Port Talbot** ⇌

Extensive sands at Aberavon Beach. Afan Lido sports centre. Margam Country Park has a deer herd, sculpture park, orangery, maze and children's fairytale village. The fascinating Welsh Miners' Museum is in the wooded Afan Argoed Country Park.

Kd5 **Reynoldston**

Gower Peninsula village near the sandy beaches of Oxwich, Port-Eynon and Rhosili

Ke5 **Southgate**

Gower Peninsula village; fine beaches at Three Cliffs Bay and Oxwich, and popular Caswell and Langland bays just to the east. Close to Swansea with its leisure centre, Maritime Quarter, museums and shopping.

La4 **Swansea**

Wales's second city and gateway to the Gower Peninsula, Britain's first designated `Area of Outstanding Natural Beauty'. Superb modern marina complex and Maritime Quarter - excellent leisure centre, with Maritime and Industrial Museum alongside. Art gallery, cultural/literature centre, Superbowl, dry ski slope and marvellous `Plantasia' exotic plants attraction. Good shopping. Covered market with distinctively Welsh atmosphere: try the cockles, laverbread and Gower potatoes. Swansea Festival and `Fringe' Festival in October. Theatres and cinemas, parks and gardens, restaurants and wine bars.

Three Cliffs Bay, Gower

88

Mumbles Oxwich Parkmill Port Talbot Reynoldston Southgate

GH | The Coast House

708 Mumbles Road,
Mumbles,
Swansea,
West Glamorgan SA3 4EH
Tel: (01792) 368702

COMMENDED

We are a well established family run guest house with a very high standard of accommodation. All our rooms are clean and modern with TV, tea making, radio/alarm and hairdryer. Most rooms are en-suite with sea views. Reductions for children.

SINGLE PER PERSON B&B		DOUBLE FOR 2 PERSONS B&B		5 / 4	
MIN £	MAX £	MIN £	MAX £	OPEN	
17.00	19.00	28.00	36.00	1-12	

FH | Parc Le Breos House

Parkmill,
Gower,
West Glamorgan SA3 2HA
Tel: (01792) 371636

COMMENDED

Spacious 18th century farmhouse in the heart of beautiful Gower Peninsula. Ideal base for a wide range of holiday activities around Gower. Riding holidays and day rides available, paddock rides for children. TV lounge, games room, safe lawn play area. Home grown cooked food, warm welcome. BHS approved. AA Listed. SAE for colour brochure.

SINGLE PER PERSON B&B		DOUBLE FOR 2 PERSONS B&B		10 / 8	
MIN £	MAX £	MIN £	MAX £	OPEN	
15.50	18.00	31.00	36.00	1-12	

FH | Sunnyside Farm

Llanddewi,
Reynoldston,
Gower,
West Glamorgan SA3 1AU
Tel: (01792) 390194

L

Family holiday on working farm. One family and twin bedded room. Reduced rates for children. TV lounge. Sandy beaches and pony trekking nearby. Easy reach of Swansea. Farm produce and home cooking. Guests welcome to look round farm. Plenty of parking space.

SINGLE PER PERSON B&B		DOUBLE FOR 2 PERSONS B&B		2	
MIN £	MAX £	MIN £	MAX £	OPEN	
14.00	14.00	28.00	28.00	1-11	

GH | Tides Reach

388 Mumbles Road,
Mumbles,
Swansea,
West Glamorgan SA3 5TN
Tel: (01792) 404877

The warmest of welcomes and an excellent standard of accommodation awaits you at Tides Reach. The elegant lounge furnished with antiques, overlooks the bay. Seafront location on level ground close to frequent public transport and all local amenities. En-suite rooms, some ground floor or sea view. Free accommodation and a warm welcome for your pet.

SINGLE PER PERSON B&B		DOUBLE FOR 2 PERSONS B&B		8 / 4	
MIN £	MAX £	MIN £	MAX £	OPEN	
17.50	19.00	31.00	37.00	1-12	

GH | Ty'n-y-Caeau

Margam Village,
Port Talbot,
West Glamorgan
SA13 2NW
Tel: (01639) 883897

COMMENDED

Originally 17th century vicarage for Margam Abbey, set in walled garden and fields. En-suite bedrooms with mountain and garden views. Close to Margam Park, Kenfig Nature Reserve and golf courses. Easy access off dual carriageway near J38. Fresh produce in season and always a warm Welsh welcome. Brochure from Mrs Rhiannon Gaen.

SINGLE PER PERSON B&B		DOUBLE FOR 2 PERSONS B&B		7 / 6	
MIN £	MAX £	MIN £	MAX £	OPEN	
18.00	-	34.00	36.00	1-11	

GH | Heatherlands

1 Hael Lane,
Southgate,
Gower,
West Glamorgan SA3 2AP
Tel: (01792) 233256

HIGHLY COMMENDED

Delightfully situated, Heatherlands is an immaculate residence in its own secluded garden near cliffs and sea. Short walk to Pobbles and Three Cliffs bays. Bedrooms with hot and cold, shaver points, tea making facilities. One bedroom with private bath. Two bedrooms share shower room with toilet. TV lounge. Separate tables in dining room. Excellent breakfast. Parking. Warm welcome.

SINGLE PER PERSON B&B		DOUBLE FOR 2 PERSONS B&B		3 / 1	
MIN £	MAX £	MIN £	MAX £	OPEN	
17.00	18.50	32.00	35.00	3-11	

GH | Little Haven Guest House

Oxwich,
Gower,
Swansea,
West Glamorgan SA3 1LS
Tel: (01792) 390940

Family run guest house situated in Oxwich village located near beach, which is ideal for most water sports. All rooms have tea/coffee facilities and hot/cold water. Children under 12 years reduced rates. Self-catering bungalow also available. Sorry no pets allowed in either property. Large garden with table, chairs and sun beds.

SINGLE PER PERSON B&B		DOUBLE FOR 2 PERSONS B&B		3	
MIN £	MAX £	MIN £	MAX £	OPEN	
17.00	17.00	30.00	30.00	1-12	

FH | Greenways Hills Farm

Reynoldston,
Gower,
West Glamorgan SA3 1AE
Tel: (01792) 390125

L

This 120 acre working farm in the beautiful village of Reynoldston is adjacent to "Cefn Bryn", a walker's paradise. Central to all Gower bays. Full central heating, hot and cold water in bedrooms. Separate tables, TV lounge. Pets by arrangement. Car park. Bowling green, tennis courts and squash courts available within reasonable distance. Enquiries to D W John.

SINGLE PER PERSON B&B		DOUBLE FOR 2 PERSONS B&B		3	
MIN £	MAX £	MIN £	MAX £	OPEN	
16.00	18.00	28.00	32.00	2-11	

Swansea

GH	Cwmdulais House

Cwmdulais,
Pontarddulais,
Swansea,
West Glamorgan SA4 1NP
Tel: (01792) 885008

HIGHLY
COMMENDED

"Arrive as a stranger, leave as a friend". Exceptional friendly welcome, relaxing homely atmosphere, with superb home cooking. Peaceful country house. Only three miles off M4, Swansea nine miles, Gower on doorstep. Local golf, fishing, walking. Artizan Recommended. Licensed bar, fire certificate. "Stay more than one day, less to pay". Brochure available.

🅿 🐎 ♟ 🍽	SINGLE PER PERSON B&B	DOUBLE FOR 2 PERSONS B&B	🛏 5 🛏 2
MIN £ 18.00	MAX £ -	MIN £ 36.00	MAX £ -	OPEN 1-12

FH	Coynant Farm

Felindre,
Swansea,
West Glamorgan SA5 7PU
Tel: (01269) 595640 or 592064

COMMENDED

Gower coast and Black Mountain only 7 miles from this idyllic 17th century farmhouse in 200 acres set in the heart of spectacular scenery. 7 bedrooms all with private bathroom, TV video and tea making. Riding, lake fishing, games room, licensed bar, log fires, pay phone. Renowned for good food. Probably the best value accommodation in the area. 'Which'? Best B&B. AA QQQ. RAC.

🅿 ♟ 🍽	SINGLE PER PERSON B&B	DOUBLE FOR 2 PERSONS B&B	🛏 7 🛏 5
MIN £ 18.00	MAX £ 18.00	MIN £ 36.00	MAX £ 36.00	OPEN 1-12

Mini posters

You may have noticed that we enlisted the help of celebrities such as *Sir Anthony Hopkins*, *Tom Jones and Ian Woosnam* to promote Wales on poster sites. Now you can purchase smaller versions of these attention-grabbing posters. See "Guide Books" page for details.

Swansea Marina

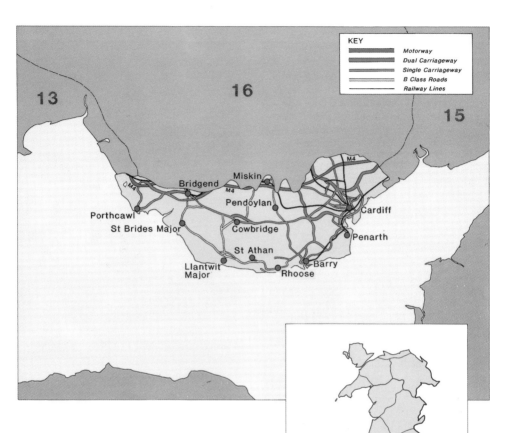

C ardiff, Wales's capital, is full of surprises – a vast, city-centre castle, neoclassical Civic Centre, lavish areas of parkland, Victorian arcades and covered market, stylish shopping centres, exciting new Cardiff Bay waterfront development, theatres and world-class museums. More and more visitors are now discovering Cardiff, thanks also to its excellent road and rail communications – it's less that two hours by train from London.

The city stands on a coastline where you'll find everything from towering cliffs to candy floss. Barry Island and Porthcawl are two popular family seaside resorts which offer great beaches and all the fun of the fair. In between is the untouched Glamorgan Heritage Coast, a beautiful area of cliffs, tiny bays and huge sand dunes. And on Cardiff's doorstep is Penarth, a delightful little Victorian resort complete with pier and modern marina.

Cardiff is also located on the doorstep of the Vale of Glamorgan, a pastoral area dotted with historic sites, pretty villages and handsome towns such as Cowbridge. Take time to explore the Vale's country lanes – and call in at the open-air Welsh Folk Museum, St Fagans.

Ld5   Bridgend

Bustling industrial and market town on edge of rural Vale of Glamorgan. Lively resort of Porthcawl and unspoilt Heritage Coast with cliffs and dunes nearby. Beautiful Bryngarw Country Park and ancient Ewenny Priory on doorstep. Three ruined Norman castles in the area - Coity, Newcastle and Ogmore.

Mb5   Cardiff   ⇌

Capital of Wales, business, trade and entertainment centre. Splendid Civic Centre, lovely parkland, modern pedestrianised shopping centre, new waterfront development, good restaurants, theatres, cinemas, clubs and sports facilities, including ice-rink and Superbowl. Visit St David's Hall for top-class entertainment. Ornate city-centre castle. National Museum of Wales has a fine collection of Impressionist paintings. Industrial and Maritime Museum and Techniquest Science Centre in docklands. National Stadium is home of Welsh rugby. Llandaff Cathedral close by and fascinating collection of old farmhouses and other buildings at Welsh Folk Museum, St Fagans.

Le6   Cowbridge

Picturesque town with wide main street and pretty houses - the centre of the Vale of Glamorgan farming community. Fine old inns, shops selling high-class clothes and country wares. 14th-century town walls. Good touring centre for South Wales. Visit nearby Beaupre Castle.

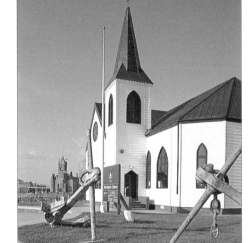

Norwegian Church, Cardiff Bay

Le5   Pendoylan

Vale of Glamorgan village surrounded by pleasant countryside, yet convenient for Cardiff and the South Wales coast. Llanerch Vineyard open to the public - visitor centre, vineyard trail, wine tasting. Welsh Folk Museum, St Fagans, nearby.

Lc6   Porthcawl

Traditional seaside resort - beaches, funfair, promenade. Attractive harbour and quieter coast along Rest Bay. Summer entertainment at the Grand Pavilion. Sailing and windsurfing. Famous golf course. Kenfig Pool and Dunes. Convenient for visiting the unspoilt Ogwr countryside, Bryngarw Country Park and Vale of Glamorgan with its attractive villages set amid leafy lanes.

Ld6   St Brides Major

Attractive village in the Vale of Glamorgan; spectacular Heritage Coast to the south. Close to Bridgend and ideal for visiting Ogmore Castle and Ewenny Priory. Golf at Southerndown.

Bryngarw Country Park

Bridgend Cardiff Cowbridge Pendoylan Porthcawl

GH | St Andrews Guest House

21 West Farm Road,
Brig-y-Don,
Ogmore-by-Sea,
Mid Glamorgan CF32 0PW
Tel: (01656) 880183

COMMENDED

Overlooking the sea. Quiet and secluded location. Easy reach of most sports facilities, including golf course 1¹/₂ miles. Vanity units, tea and coffee in all bedrooms. Full central heating. Family, double and single bedrooms. Lounge, colour TV, comfortable and decorative surroundings. Proven record of good food and hospitality. 7 miles off Junction 35 M4 motorway.

		SINGLE PER PERSON B&B		DOUBLE FOR 2 PERSONS B&B			3
		MIN £	MAX £	MIN £	MAX £	OPEN	
		17.00	17.00	32.00	32.00	1-12	

GH | Annedd Lon Guest House

3 Dyfrig Street,
Off Cathedral Road,
Cardiff,
South Glamorgan CF1 9LR
Tel: (01222) 223349

Completely smoke-free bed and breakfast in a Victorian town house furnished in keeping with the period, but with modern comforts. In a quiet close off Cathedral Road, within walking distance of the shopping centre, castle, sports centre and Arms Park, and on a frequent bus route. En-suite rooms available. Renowned for its generous breakfasts.

		SINGLE PER PERSON B&B		DOUBLE FOR 2 PERSONS B&B			4
							2
		MIN £	MAX £	MIN £	MAX £	OPEN	
		18.00	18.00	32.00	35.00	1-12	

FH | Llanerch Vineyard

Hensol, Pendoylan,
Vale of Glamorgan,
South Glamorgan CF7 8JU
Tel: (01443) 225877
Fax: (01443) 225546

HIGHLY COMMENDED

Traditional Welsh farmhouse overlooking six acre vineyard. Extensive grounds with ten acres of landscaped gardens, woodlands and lakes. All bedrooms with en-suite bathroom. Signposted from J34 of M4. Only fifteen minutes from Cardiff. Convenient for coast and Brecon Beacons. Ideal centre for touring South and West Wales. One of "Wales' Great Little Places".

		SINGLE PER PERSON B&B		DOUBLE FOR 2 PERSONS B&B			3
							3
		MIN £	MAX £	MIN £	MAX £	OPEN	
TW		-	-	-	38.00	1-12	

H | Austins

11 Coldstream Terrace,
Cardiff,
South Glamorgan CF1 8LJ
Tel: (01222) 377148

Situated in the centre of Cardiff 300 yards from the castle. Over the river bridge, turn left along the river. 10 minutes walk from the central bus and train stations, over the bridge and up the river. Small friendly hotel offering a warm welcome to all nationalities. Close to all amenities. Full English breakfast included.

		SINGLE PER PERSON B&B		DOUBLE FOR 2 PERSONS B&B			11
							3
		MIN £	MAX £	MIN £	MAX £	OPEN	
		14.00	-	26.00	32.00	1-12	

GH | Farthings

Lisvane Road,
Lisvane,
Cardiff,
South Glamorgan CF4 5SG
Tel: (01222) 756404

Close to Cardiff centre, yet in the heart of the village of Lisvane, Farthings offers double and single bedrooms with private bathroom in lovely family house. A few minutes walk from local inn serving meals. Also on main bus and rail routes to city centre and close to M4 motorway link. Secure parking. Own lounge.

		SINGLE PER PERSON B&B		DOUBLE FOR 2 PERSONS B&B			2
							-
		MIN £	MAX £	MIN £	MAX £	OPEN	
		19.00	19.00	35.00	35.00	1-12	

H | Penoyre Hotel

29 Mary Street,
Porthcawl,
Mid Glamorgan CF36 3YN
Tel: (01656) 784550

Penoyre is a family run licensed hotel 100 yards from beach and shopping centre. All rooms have colour TV, tea and coffee making facilities. En-suite available. Small friendly bar and TV lounge with satellite provided for guests' enjoyment. Children and pets welcome. Excellent home cooking, vegetarian and special diets on request. A la carte menu. RAC Acclaimed.

		SINGLE PER PERSON B&B		DOUBLE FOR 2 PERSONS B&B			6
							4
		MIN £	MAX £	MIN £	MAX £	OPEN	
		14.00	19.00	28.00	38.00	1-12	

H | Wynford Hotel

Clare Street,
Cardiff,
South Glamorgan CF1 8SD
Tel: (01222) 371983
Fax: (01222) 340477

Very close to the city centre, train and bus stations, the Wynford, privately owned and personally supervised, offers a comfortable lounge, two cosy bars, occasional music and dancing, bistro and restaurant. All rooms have colour TV and telephone. Many have private bathroom. French, Spanish, German spoken. Night porter, video linked security car park. Price quoted relates to 7 rooms only.

		SINGLE PER PERSON B&B		DOUBLE FOR 2 PERSONS B&B			29
							20
		MIN £	MAX £	MIN £	MAX £	OPEN	
		-	-	36.00	-	1-12	

FH | Cartreglas Farm

Welsh St Donats,
Cowbridge,
South Glamorgan CF7 7SX
Tel: (01446) 772368
Fax: (01446) 775553

HIGHLY COMMENDED

A warm welcome awaits you at Cartreglas, where we grow flowers for drying and rear cattle in the lovely Vale of Glamorgan. Conveniently situated for Cardiff, coast and mountains, just 3 miles from M4 and 4 miles from Cowbridge. A fully equipped kitchen where guests can cook own evening meal. Children and pets welcome.

		SINGLE PER PERSON B&B		DOUBLE FOR 2 PERSONS B&B			3
							2
		MIN £	MAX £	MIN £	MAX £	OPEN	
		16.00	18.00	32.00	36.00	1-12	

Prices

Please note that all prices are PER PERSON, based on TWO PEOPLE sharing a double or twin room. SINGLE OCCUPANCY will usually be charged extra, and there may be supplements for private bath/shower. All prices include VAT. Daily rates are for bed and breakfast. Weekly rates are for dinner, B&B. Please check all prices and facilities before confirming your booking.

Porthcawl   St Brides Major

GH	Rockybank Guest House

15 De Breos Drive,
Porthcawl,
Mid Glamorgan CF36 3JP
Tel: (01656) 785823

A warm welcome awaits you at the first guest house off Junction 37 (M4). Situated between two excellent golf courses, quiet spot, ample parking, near village inns, walking distance beaches, funfair and town centre. Large family room with balcony. Children welcome, half price. All rooms en-suite, hostess tray and TV. Proprietors Jean and John Lewis.

P ▥ ▥ ✂ ♨ T	SINGLE PER PERSON B&B	DOUBLE FOR 2 PERSONS B&B	🛏 2 🛏 2		
	MIN £ -	MAX £ -	MIN £ 36.00	MAX £ 38.00	OPEN 4-10

FH	Penuchadre Farm

St Brides Major,
Bridgend,
Mid Glamorgan CF32 0TE
Tel: (01656) 880313 ♨

15th century historic farmhouse. High quality accommodation comprising one family bedroom. M4 motorway 5 miles (farmhouse easily found). Real farm atmosphere, wonderful for children. Heritage coast, Southerndown Bay within walking distance. 18 hole championship golf course nearby. Evening meals available in local public houses. Idyllic countryside surroundings. A warm welcome awaits you at Penuchadre Farm.

P ▥ ♨ 🚜	SINGLE PER PERSON B&B	DOUBLE FOR 2 PERSONS B&B	🛏 1 🛁 -		
	MIN £ 18.00	MAX £ 18.00	MIN £ 36.00	MAX £ 36.00	OPEN 1-12

Slide sets

Ask about our attractive range of 35mm colour slides showing views of Wales, available at 75p per slide. For a complete list of subjects please contact the Photographic Librarian, Wales Tourist Board, Davis Street, Cardiff CF1 2FU (tel 01222-475215).

Dunraven Bay, south of St Brides Major

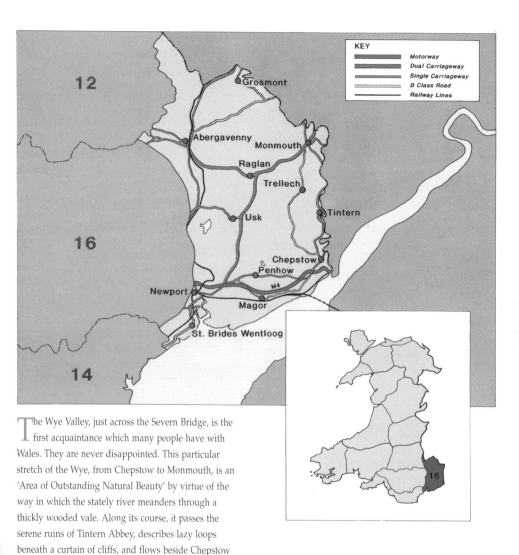

The Wye Valley, just across the Severn Bridge, is the first acquaintance which many people have with Wales. They are never disappointed. This particular stretch of the Wye, from Chepstow to Monmouth, is an 'Area of Outstanding Natural Beauty' by virtue of the way in which the stately river meanders through a thickly wooded vale. Along its course, it passes the serene ruins of Tintern Abbey, describes lazy loops beneath a curtain of cliffs, and flows beside Chepstow Castle, Britain's first stone-built fortress.

Chepstow is rich in history. So too is the other gateway town of Monmouth, with its fortified bridge, Henry V associations and wealth of period buildings. Historic sites are plentiful in these parts. Visit the outstanding late-medieval castle at Raglan and Caerleon's Roman remains, which include an amphitheatre, barracks and bath-house.

The Usk – like the Wye a celebrated fishing river – flows in a lovely valley past Abergavenny and the eponymous little town of Usk to meet the sea at Newport. On Newport's outskirts there's yet more history – the splendid 17th-century Tredegar House, set in its own country park.

Mc1 Abergavenny

Flourishing market town with backdrop of mountains at south-eastern gateway to Brecon Beacons National Park. Pony trekking in nearby Black Mountains. Castle, Museum of Childhood. Leisure centre. Monmouthshire and Brecon Canal runs just to the west of the town. Excellent touring base for the lovely Vale of Usk and Brecon Beacons.

Me1 Monmouth

Historic market town in picturesque Wye Valley - birthplace of Henry V and Charles Rolls (of Rolls-Royce). Interesting local history museum with collection of Nelson memorabilia. Rare fortified gateway still spans the River Monnow. Ruined castle close to town centre. Well located for touring Wye Valley and borderland Wales.

Me3 Chepstow

Attractive hilly town with substantial remains of a great stone castle - reputedly the first to be built in Britain - above the Wye. Fortified gate still stands in main street and medieval walls remain. Good shopping. Museum, Stuart Crystal Engraving Workshop. Sunday market, fine racecourse, excellent walks - beginning of the Wye Valley Walk and Offa's Dyke Path. Ideal for touring beautiful Wye Valley.

Mc4 Newport

Busy industrial, commercial and shopping centre. Interesting murals in main hall of Civic Centre. Newport Museum and Art Gallery in John Frost Square (named after Chartist leader) and leisure centre with wave machine. On the outskirts, magnificently restored Tredegar House with extensive country park, and 14 Locks Canal Visitor Centre. St Woolos Cathedral on hill overlooking town centre. Ruined castle on riverside near shops and attractive Victorian market hall.

Hd7 Grosmont

Border village with key medieval stronghold, one of the 'Three Castles' of Gwent. Church of St Nicholas is large and interesting. Set in lovely, restful countryside, ideal for walking and touring.

Md4 Penhow

Village between Chepstow and Newport with fascinating restored castle. Another impressive historic site nearby - Caerwent's Roman walls. Easy access to Wye Valley.

Vale of Usk, near Abergavenny

Md2   Raglan

Historic village dominated by Raglan Castle, noted for its impressive Great Tower of Gwent. Convenient for touring the Usk and Wye valleys and eastern Brecon Beacons.

Mc5   St Brides Wentloog

Settlement on mouth of Usk close to Newport overlooking Severn Estuary. Splendid Tredegar House and Country Park nearby; Cardiff only a short distance away.

Me3   Tintern

Riverside village in particularly lovely stretch of Wye Valley. Impressive ruins of Tintern Abbey not to be missed. The former railway station has a visitors' interpretive centre and picnic site with refreshments. Excellent walks and good fishing.

Md3   Usk

Ancient borough on River Usk; excellent salmon fishing and inns. Good walks. Rural Life Museum, grass skiing. Great castle of Raglan 5 miles north. Sailing and other watersports on nearby Llandegfedd Reservoir. Good central location for sightseeing.

Tredegar House, near Newport

Abergavenny Chepstow Grosmont Monmouth

H | Rock and Fountain Hotel

Main Road,
Clydach,
Abergavenny,
Gwent NP7 0LL
Tel: (01873) 830393

16th century family run hotel. Beautiful setting with spectacular views over the breathtaking Clydach Gorge. Charming restaurant with home cooked meals using local produce. "Taste of Wales " member. All rooms are en-suite with colour television and tea/coffee facilities. The route of a lovely walk used by many ramblers passes the door. Pony trekking, fishing and golf is nearby. RAC.

	SINGLE PER PERSON B&B		DOUBLE FOR 2 PERSONS B&B		🛏 9
					9
	MIN £	MAX £	MIN £	MAX £	OPEN
	16.00	19.00	35.00	38.00	1-12

GH | Pentre House

Brecon Road,
Abergavenny,
Gwent NP7 7EW
Tel: (01873) 853435
Fax: (01873) 853435

HIGHLY COMMENDED

Small period country house situated at the turning for Sugar Loaf just off the A40. Set in one acre of award winning gardens. Guest bathroom and separate shower room. Very comfortably furnished, peaceful surroundings. River Usk just down the lane. Pony trekking, lovely walks. Brochure on request.

	SINGLE PER PERSON B&B		DOUBLE FOR 2 PERSONS B&B		🛏 3
					-
	MIN £	MAX £	MIN £	MAX £	OPEN
	17.00	19.00	30.00	36.00	1-12

FH | Cribau

The Cwm,
Llanvair Discoed,
Chepstow,
Gwent NP6 6RD
Tel: (01291) 641528

16the century farmhouse at the end of no through road. TV, tea/coffee making. 1 twin bedded room, own patio. 1 double bedded room. Both have shower room en-suite. Good pub food. Golf, walking, scenic drive close by. Six miles from Severn Bridge. Take A48 Caerwent right turn Llanvair Discoed, right Cwm, Cribau sign at T junction.

	SINGLE PER PERSON B&B		DOUBLE FOR 2 PERSONS B&B		🛏 3
					2
	MIN £	MAX £	MIN £	MAX £	OPEN
	18.00	18.00	30.00	30.00	1-12

GH | Heathfield

Nant y Derry,
Abergavenny,
Gwent NP7 9DP
Tel: (01873) 880675

HIGHLY COMMENDED

Country house set in a large garden, views of the Blorenge Mountain. Comfortable and spacious rooms, all centrally heated with tea/coffee facilities. Quality evening and vegetarian meals on request. Relax in the TV lounge or play game of croquet on the lawn. Golf course two minutes away, scenic walks, national gardens, Big Pit, iron works to visit.

	SINGLE PER PERSON B&B		DOUBLE FOR 2 PERSONS B&B		🛏 3
					1
	MIN £	MAX £	MIN £	MAX £	OPEN
	-	-	26.00	34.00	4-11

FH | Great Tre-Rhew Farm

Llanvetherine,
Abergavenny,
Gwent NP7 8RA
Tel: (01873) 821268

Warm welcome on a family working sheep and cattle farm. Good home cooking in 15th century farmhouse. Quiet situation near Offa's Dyke and White Castle. Fishing in farm stream and river. Ideal for touring Wye Valley, Black Mountains and Brecon Beacons. Lovely walks and pony trekking. TV lounge, games room and dining room with separate tables.

	SINGLE PER PERSON B&B		DOUBLE FOR 2 PERSONS B&B		🛏 2
					-
	MIN £	MAX £	MIN £	MAX £	OPEN
	14.00	19.00	28.00	34.00	1-12

FH | Lawns Farm

Grosmont,
Abergavenny,
Gwent NP7 8ES
Tel: (01981) 240298

COMMENDED

A beautiful 17th century farmhouse set in peaceful Monnow Valley, central to several towns, walks, castles and only 20 minutes from the Brecon Beacons or Wye Valley. All rooms have en-suite or private bathroom, including 4 poster, colour TV, tea making facilities and central heating. Games room, lounge, large garden and several pub restaurants within easy walking distance.

	SINGLE PER PERSON B&B		DOUBLE FOR 2 PERSONS B&B		🛏 4
					4
	MIN £	MAX £	MIN £	MAX £	OPEN
	15.00	-	36.00	-	3-10

GH | Park Guest House

36 Hereford Road,
Abergavenny,
Gwent NP7 5RA
Tel: (01873) 853715

COMMENDED

Attractive detached Georgian guest house, close town centre. All rooms with colour TV, beverage tray, handbasin and radio alarm. Two bathrooms, dining room with individual tables. Excellent four course evening meal available. Fully licensed, fire certificate, free private parking. Convenient Brecon Beacons, Big Pit, castles and museums. Detailed brochure available on request.

	SINGLE PER PERSON B&B		DOUBLE FOR 2 PERSONS B&B		🛏 7
					-
	MIN £	MAX £	MIN £	MAX £	OPEN
	18.00	19.00	32.00	34.00	1-12

FH | Wern Goch Lyn Farm

Llantilio Pertholey,
Abergavenny,
Gwent NP7 3UB
Tel: (01873) 857357

APPROVED

12th century farmhouse 2½ miles from market town of Abergavenny. Bedrooms are en-suite and private bathroom for family room, colour TV, coffee making facilities, indoor heated swimming pool, games room. Children half price. Many friendly farm animals, licensed riding centre, riding and instruction. Good walks through farm to mountain, golf course, golf range ½ mile. Brochure on request.

	SINGLE PER PERSON B&B		DOUBLE FOR 2 PERSONS B&B		🛏 2
					2
	MIN £	MAX £	MIN £	MAX £	OPEN
	-	18.00	30.00	36.00	I-12

GH | Church Farm Guest House

Mitchel Troy,
Monmouth,
Gwent NP5 4HZ
Tel: (01600) 712176

COMMENDED

A spacious and homely 16th century former farmhouse with oak beams and inglenook fireplaces. Set in large attractive garden with stream. Easy access to A40 and only 2 miles from historic Monmouth. Excellent base for Wye Valley, Forest of Dean and Black Mountains. Large car park, terrace, barbecue, colour TV, central heating, tea/coffee making facilities.

	SINGLE PER PERSON B&B		DOUBLE FOR 2 PERSONS B&B		🛏 7
					5
	MIN £	MAX £	MIN £	MAX £	OPEN
	16.50	19.00	33.00	38.00	1-12

FH   Mill House Farm

Llanvihangel-Ystern-Llewern,
Monmouth,
Gwent NP5 4HN
Tel: (01600) 85468

A 17th century farmhouse set in lovely gardens located between Monmouth and Abergavenny. The Wye and Usk valleys, Offa's Dyke, Forest of Dean and the Black Mountains are all close by. Activities include golf, fishing, walking, canoeing and pony trekking. Tea and coffee in all rooms. Evening meals available, vegetarians welcome.

P 🛏 ♨ ⚷	C ✂ 🍽	SINGLE PER PERSON B&B		DOUBLE FOR 2 PERSONS B&B		🛏 3 🛁 1
		MIN £ 16.00	MAX £ 16.00	MIN £ 32.00	MAX £ 38.00	OPEN 1-12

GH   Widecombe

Old Chepstow Road,
Langstone,
Newport,
Gwent NP6 2ND
Tel: (01633) 413311

HIGHLY COMMENDED

Small friendly family home in half acre pleasant garden. Comfortable accommodation in two double rooms with tea making facilities, clock radio, shaver points, ample off-road parking. Good home cooking, lounge, sun lounge. Ideal base for touring. Just off A48 3/4 mile east of Junction 24 M4 and A449, 3 1/2 miles east of Newport town centre.

P ♨ ⚷ 🍽	🐕 ♨ TW	SINGLE PER PERSON B&B		DOUBLE FOR 2 PERSONS B&B		🛏 2
		MIN £ 16.00	MAX £ 18.00	MIN £ 32.00	MAX £ 36.00	OPEN 1-12

GH   Stone Lodge (Old School)

Llandevaud,
Newport,
Gwent NP6 2AA
Tel: (01633) 400915

Therapeutic massage is offered by hostess who is ITEC, MTI qualified. This can be very relaxing or stimulating. Rural location is near Penhow off A48 between Chepstow and Newport, near Severn Bridge, Wye Valley. An ideal stop-over. Excellent restaurant nearby (100 yds). Colour TV in rooms. Secluded garden with rabbits, squirrels, pheasants, maybe occasionally a fox.

P ♨ ⚷	C T	SINGLE PER PERSON B&B		DOUBLE FOR 2 PERSONS B&B		🛏 2
		MIN £ 18.00	MAX £ 19.00	MIN £ 28.00	MAX £ 30.00	OPEN 1-12

H   Manor Hotel

147 Stow Hill,
Newport,
Gwent NP9 4HB
Tel: (01633) 264685

Five minutes from M4. Well established small family hotel convenient for town centre and ideal base for Wye Valley, South Wales coast etc. Family, double, twin and single rooms each with colour television. Separate residents' television lounge and dining room. Lovely well established garden. Forecourt car parking facilities. Bed and excellent breakfast. Genuine homely welcome.

P 🛏 ♨	🐕 T	SINGLE PER PERSON B&B		DOUBLE FOR 2 PERSONS B&B		🛏 7 🛁
		MIN £ 16.00	MAX £ 17.00	MIN £ 28.00	MAX £ 32.00	OPEN 1-12

GH   Westwood Villa Guest House

59 Risca Road,
Cross Keys,
Gwent NP1 7BT
Tel: (01495) 270336
Fax: (01495) 270336

HIGHLY COMMENDED

Six miles from Junction 28 M4. Originally a manse, beautiful bedrooms, tastefully decorated all with colour TV, hot and cold water, radio alarms. Two en-suite, two shower rooms, bathroom. Comfortable lounge/bar, garden, play area. First stop Cambrian Way. Close to Newport, Cardiff, Sirhowy, Wye Valley, Brecon Beacons. Convenient for tourists and commercial. Warmest welcome from Bob and Maureen.

P ♨ ⚷ 🍽	🐕 ♨	SINGLE PER PERSON B&B		DOUBLE FOR 2 PERSONS B&B		🛏 6 🛁 2
		MIN £ 18.00	MAX £ -	MIN £ 30.00	MAX £ 36.00	OPEN 1-12

FH   The Brooklands

Chepstow Road,
Raglan,
Gwent NP5 2EN
Tel: (01291) 690782

Family run dairy mixed farm 200 metres Raglan village centre. Historic farmhouse with excellent facilities. Beautifully presented bedrooms one en-suite, with tea/coffee facilities. Both TV lounge and dining room overlook gardens. An excellent touring centre convenient yet quiet position.

🛏 ⚷ 🐄	🛏 ♨	SINGLE PER PERSON B&B		DOUBLE FOR 2 PERSONS B&B		🛏 2 🛁 1
		MIN £ 16.00	MAX £ 19.00	MIN £ 28.00	MAX £ 36.00	OPEN 1-12

GH   Park Guest House

381 Chepstow Road,
Newport,
Gwent NP9 8HL
Tel: (01633) 280333

COMMENDED

We are a family run guest house, three miles from the M4, near Newport. We offer nine rooms, three en-suite, all with tea/coffee making facilities. We provide a friendly and welcoming atmosphere for either business or pleasure. The guest house is centrally placed for many areas of outstanding beauty and for sites of interest.

P ♨ ⚷ ♨		SINGLE PER PERSON B&B		DOUBLE FOR 2 PERSONS B&B		🛏 9 🛁 3
		MIN £ 15.00	MAX £ 20.00	MIN £ 25.00	MAX £ 30.00	OPEN 1-12

FH   Pentre-Tai Farm

Rhiwderin,
Newport,
Gwent NP1 9RQ
Tel: (01633) 893284

HIGHLY COMMENDED

Situated 3 miles from J28 M4, 12 miles Cardiff. Why not make this your first stop in Wales? Peaceful sheep and horse farm. Ideal for visiting Wye Valley, Brecon Beacons, wonderful Welsh castles, South Wales coast. En-suite rooms. Special rates for children. One family room. All rooms with colour TV. Excellent pub food nearby.

P ♨ ♨ 🐄	⚷	SINGLE PER PERSON B&B		DOUBLE FOR 2 PERSONS B&B		🛏 3 🛁 2
		MIN £ 19.00	MAX £ 19.00	MIN £ 30.00	MAX £ 32.00	OPEN 2-11

FH   Lower Pen-y-Clawdd Farm

Dingestow,
Monmouth,
Gwent NP5 4BG
Tel: (01600) 83223 or 83677

This tastefully converted cider mill nestles against a 17th century farmhouse set within attractive gardens. Two well presented bedrooms with hot and cold, tea/coffee making facilities. 2 bathrooms with shower. TV in dining area. A working sheep and beef farm. Situated between Raglan and Monmouth (A40). Raglan Castle 2 miles, Monmouth and Wye Valley 6 miles.

P 🛏 ♨	⚷ ♨ 🐄	SINGLE PER PERSON B&B		DOUBLE FOR 2 PERSONS B&B		🛏
		MIN £ 16.00	MAX £ 18.00	MIN £ 30.00	MAX £ 33.00	OPEN 1-12

Raglan   St Brides Wentloog   Tintern   Usk

FH	Ty-Gwyn Farm

Gwehelog,
Nr Usk,
Gwent NP5 1RT
Tel: (01291) 672878

AWARD   HIGHLY COMMENDED

Wake up and sit up to magnificent views of Brecon Beacons National Park, at this award-winning farmhouse. Hearty breakfasts including homemade preserves served in spacious dining room, or conservatory overlooking secluded lawns. Tea making facilities and TV in bedrooms. Explore castles, mountains, rivers, golf courses and fishing nearby. Excellent meals, vegetarians and own wine welcome. Brochure available.

P, 📺	🐕, 🚲	SINGLE PER PERSON B&B		DOUBLE FOR 2 PERSONS B&B		🛏 3 🛁 2
🚿, 🍴	🚲, T	MIN £ -	MAX £ -	MIN £ 29.00	MAX £ 35.00	OPEN 1-12

GH	Valley House

Raglan Road,
Tintern,
Gwent NP6 6TH
Tel: (01291) 689652

👑👑

18th century detached house in picturesque valley just 800m off A466, within one mile of Tintern Abbey. Beautiful en-suite rooms with colour TV. radio, tea/coffee facilities and telephone. Freshly cooked hearty breakfasts, packed lunches available. Ideal base for touring or take a forest walk from our doorstep. There are numerous places to eat nearby.

P, 📺	🐕, 🚲	SINGLE PER PERSON B&B		DOUBLE FOR 2 PERSONS B&B		🛏 3 🛁 3
🚿		MIN £ -	MAX £ -	MIN £ 35.00	MAX £ 36.00	OPEN 1-12

FH	Rhydwern Farm

Llangwm,
Usk,
Gwent NP5 1NQ
Tel: (01291) 650306

👑

Small and friendly farm tucked away in a peaceful valley, lovely countryside with a wide variety of wildlife, yet within easy reach of ancient towns, forests, castles. The Brecon Beacons and Severn Bridge. 18th century stone farmhouse, log fire, home cooking. Ideal for walkers and country lovers.

P, 🏠	🐕, 🚲	SINGLE PER PERSON B&B		DOUBLE FOR 2 PERSONS B&B		🛏 3 🛁 -
🚿	🍴	MIN £ -	MAX £ -	MIN £ 28.00	MAX £ 28.00	OPEN 1-12

GH	Chapel Guest House

Church Road,
St Brides Wentloog,
Gwent NP1 9SN
Tel: (01633) 681018

COMMENDED

Comfortable en-suite accommodation in converted chapel situated in village between Newport and Cardiff. Inn/restaurant adjacent. Pleasant walks, fishing, golf, horse-riding nearby. Guest TV lounge with pool table. Tea/coffee, TV in all rooms. Children welcome. Special rates. Leave M4 Junction 28, take A48 Newport, at roundabout take 3rd exit B4239 St Brides. Centre of village opposite Church House Inn.

P, C, 📺	🐕	SINGLE PER PERSON B&B		DOUBLE FOR 2 PERSONS B&B		🛏 3 🛁 3
🚲, 🚿, 🍴	T	MIN £ 16.00	MAX £ 18.00	MIN £ 28.00	MAX £ 32.00	OPEN 1-12

GH	The Old Rectory

Tintern,
Gwent NP6 6SG
Tel: (01291) 689519

👑

A free and easy welcome awaits at this imposing 18th/19th century house with its own spring water. Most bedrooms have beautiful views. hot and cold water, tea/coffee facilities. Central heating, log fires. Dining room serving good food, own bread and produce in season. Central for fishing, walking, golf, horse-riding. Tintern Abbey 1/2 mile. Ideal for touring the border country.

P, 🏠	🐕, 📺	SINGLE PER PERSON B&B		DOUBLE FOR 2 PERSONS B&B		🛏 5 🛁 -
🚲, 🚿	🍴	MIN £ 14.00	MAX £ 14.50	MIN £ 28.00	MAX £ 29.00	OPEN 1-12

Tintern Abbe

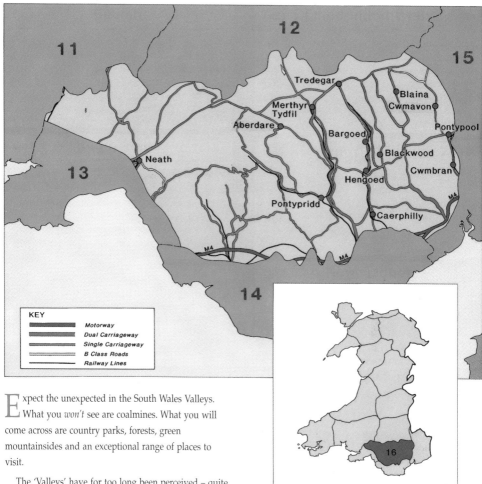

KEY
- Motorway
- Dual Carriageway
- Single Carriageway
- B Class Roads
- Railway Lines

E xpect the unexpected in the South Wales Valleys. What you *won't* see are coalmines. What you will come across are country parks, forests, green mountainsides and an exceptional range of places to visit.

The 'Valleys' have for too long been perceived – quite inaccurately – as a place despoiled by heavy industry. That picture is now changing, helped by the existence of country parks such as the Dare Valley and Sirhowy Valley, together with a host of attractions. Visit mighty Caerphilly Castle, one of Europe's greatest medieval fortresses, and the 'living history' manor house of Llancaiach Fawr. Travel along the spectacular Cwmcarn Scenic Forest Drive, or explore the 'Little Switzerland' of the wooded Afan Argoed Country Park. Near Neath, there's a famous wildlife park. And at Merthyr Tydfil,

you can ride a narrow-gauge railway into the foothills of the Brecon Beacons.

Bygone times have not been forgotten. The Valleys' rich industrial heritage is remembered at places such as the Big Pit Mining Museum, the Rhondda Heritage Park and the Cefn Coed Colliery Museum.

101

Ma4   Caerphilly

A sight not to be missed - 13th-century Caerphilly Castle is one of Europe's finest surviving medieval strongholds and has a famous leaning tower. Golf course, shopping, good centre for exploring the Valleys and visiting Cardiff. Fine views and pleasant walks from Caerphilly Mountain. Caerphilly cheese made at the Old Court.

Mc2   Cwmavon

Village a mile or so south of Blaenafon. Industrial heritage sites of Big Pit Mining Museum and Blaenafon Ironworks close by. Pontypool, just down the valley, has an attractive park with excellent dry ski slope. Well located for South Wales Valleys and Brecon Beacons National Park.

Mc3   Cwmbran

A `new town' development and administration centre for Gwent. Good leisure facilities. Llantarnam Grange Arts Centre. Shopping and sports centre with international athletics stadium. Theatre and cinemas. Good touring centre for the Vale of Usk and South Wales Valleys.

Le2   Merthyr Tydfil

Once the `iron capital of the world'. The museum in Cyfarthfa Castle, built by the Crawshay family of ironmasters and set in pleasant parkland, tells of those times. Visit the birthplace of hymn-writer Joseph Parry and the Ynysfach Engine House. The narrow-gauge Brecon Mountain Railway makes the most of the town's location on the doorstep of the Brecon Beacons National Park. Garwnant Forest Visitor Centre and scenic lakes in hills to the north.

Lb3   Neath

Busy town, now emerging from its industrial past. Museum and country park. The Vale of Neath has a wide variety of tourist attractions including an abbey, forests, Penscynor Wildlife Park and Aberdulais Falls and Canal Basin. Swansea and Gower nearby.

Aberdulais Falls, near Neath

Caerphilly Cwmavon Cwmbran Merthyr Tydfil Neath

GH	The Cottage

Pwllypant,
Caerphilly,
Mid Glamorgan CF8 3HW
Tel: (01222) 869160
Fax: (01222) 869160

A spacious, late 17th century cottage offering a homely welcome. Well situated on the edge of town with convenient access to main bus routes and established retaurants. Central location for Cardiff (9 miles), castles, hills and coastline. Owner is an Official Tour Guide and offers free touring advice.

P IIIII. ♦ ℒ⋇ T		SINGLE PER PERSON B&B		DOUBLE FOR 2 PERSONS B&B		🛏 3 🛏 1
		MIN £ 18.00	MAX £ -	MIN £ 30.00	MAX £ 36.00	OPEN 1-12

GH	Watford Fach Farm Guest House

Watford Road,
Caerphilly,
Mid Glamorgan CF8 1NE
Tel: (01222) 851500

👑

Caerphilly Castle. Rural setting. Close to town and railway. Discount for children.

P IIIII ♦	🍴 ℒ⋇ T	SINGLE PER PERSON B&B		DOUBLE FOR 2 PERSONS B&B		🛏 7 🛏 4
		MIN £ 15.00	MAX £ 19.00	MIN £ 30.00	MAX £ 30.00	OPEN 1-12

FH	Wern Ganol Farm

Nelson,
Treharris,
Mid Glamorgan CF46 6PS
Tel: (01443) 450413

👑 👑

Sixty acre dairy farm with pleasant views over surrounding countryside towards Llancaiach Fawr Manor House. Providing homely atmosphere for guests who may wish to relax in the lounge or on the patio. Easy access to Brecon Beacons and the South Wales coast. All rooms on ground floor. 20 minutes M4, Junction 32.

P IIIII ♦	🐕 ℒ⋇ 🐾 T	SINGLE PER PERSON B&B		DOUBLE FOR 2 PERSONS B&B		🛏 5 🛏 5
		MIN £ 17.00	MAX £ 17.00	MIN £ 34.00	MAX £ 34.00	OPEN 1-12

FH	Mill Farm

Cwmavon,
Nr Pontypool,
Gwent NP4 8XJ
Tel: (01495) 774588

 👑 👑

15th century farmhouse in idyllic setting. Oak beams, log fires, antique furniture, enhanced by all modern comforts including indoor heated pool. Each bedroom has private facilities, tea/coffee tray. TV lounge. Guests' lounge. Large garden and woodlands for guests enjoyment/bird watching. Ideal walking centre. Close to all major routes and amenities, yet secluded and tranquil.

P IIIII. ♦	🐕 ℒ⋇ 🐾	SINGLE PER PERSON B&B		DOUBLE FOR 2 PERSONS B&B		🛏 3 🛏 3
		MIN £ -	MAX £ -	MIN £ 34.00	MAX £ 38.00	OPEN 1-12

GH	Springfields Guest House

371 Llantarnam Road,
Cwmbran,
Gwent NP44 3BN
Tel: (01633) 482509

 👑 👑
HIGHLY COMMENDED

Family run for 22 happy years, 1¼ miles from Cwmbran. 2½ miles from M4. Central for touring Wye Valley, Caerleon, Big Pit, Brecon Beacons, Cardiff. My visitors have enjoyed "Springfields" and I have enjoyed their company. Come and see the beauty of South Wales, you will come again. "Thank you" old and new customers. Joan Graham and her staff.

P IIIII ℒ⋇ T	🐕 ♦	SINGLE PER PERSON B&B		DOUBLE FOR 2 PERSONS B&B		🛏 10 🛏 5
		MIN £ 13.50	MAX £ 16.00	MIN £ 26.00	MAX £ 30.00	OPEN 1-12

GH	Hillside House

1 Sunnybank,
Tirphil,
New Tredegar,
Gwent NP2 6EL
Tel: (01443) 834460

Ⓛ

A small family run guest house situated in the historic Rhymney Valley. Personal attention, relaxed atmosphere and home cooked food, with fresh produce from the garden whenever possible. Vegetarians welcome. Cosy TV lounge, central heating, hot and cold all rooms, fitted carpets, double glazing, tea/coffee making facilities. Car parking. Ideal base for touring South Wales.

P IIIII. ℒ⋇ 🍴		SINGLE PER PERSON B&B		DOUBLE FOR 2 PERSONS B&B		🛏 2 🛏 -
		MIN £ 14.00	MAX £ 14.00	MIN £ 28.00	MAX £ 28.00	OPEN 1-12

GH	Maes-y-Gwernen

School Road,
Abercraf,
Swansea,
West Glamorgan SA9 1XD
Tel: (01639) 730218
Fax: (01639) 730765

 👑 👑
HIGHLY COMMENDED

Country house in private grounds. All rooms en-suite, colour TV, trouser press, hairdryer, tea/coffee making facilities, direct dial telephone. Ample parking, licensed bar, conservatory, lounge, dining room, all exclusive to guests. Close to Show Caves, Black Mountains, pony trekking and fishing. Ideal walking area. Children welcome. Play area in grounds. Home cooking and friendly atmosphere.

P ℒ⋇ 🍴	🐕 IIIII. ♦ ♿	SINGLE PER PERSON B&B		DOUBLE FOR 2 PERSONS B&B		🛏 7 🛏 7
		MIN £ -	MAX £ -	MIN £ 37.00	MAX £ -	OPEN 1-12

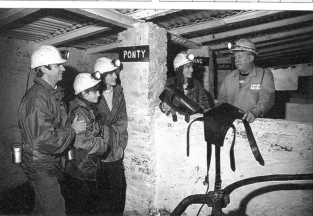

Big Pit, Blaenafon

Tourist Information Centres

Make the most of your stay in Wales by contacting one of our Tourist Information Centres for expert advice on all aspects of your holiday. TIC staff will be delighted to help you with:
• booking your accommodation •places to visit • places to eat • things to do • routes to take
• national and local events • maps, guides and books
Normal opening times are 10am-5.30pm. These hours may vary to suit local circumstances.

North Wales

Open all year

Betws-y-Coed
Royal Oak Stables,
Betws-y-Coed, Gwynedd
LL24 0AH
Tel (01690) 710426

Caernarfon
Oriel Pendeitsh, Castle Street,
Caernarfon, Gwynedd
LL55 2NA
Tel (01286) 672232

Colwyn Bay
40 Station Road, Colwyn Bay,
Clwyd LL29 8BU
Tel (01492) 530478

Conwy
Conwy Castle Visitor Centre,
Conwy, Gwynedd LL32 8LD
Tel (01492) 592248

Ewloe
Autolodge Services, Gateway
Services, A55 Westbound,
Northophall, Ewloe, Clwyd
CH7 6HE
Tel (01244) 541597

Holyhead
Marine Square,
Salt Island Approach, Holyhead,
Gwynedd LL65 1DR
Tel (01407) 762622

Llandudno
1-2 Chapel Street, Llandudno,
Gwynedd LL30 2YU
Tel (01492) 876413

Llanfairpwllgwyngyll
Station Site,
Llanfairpwllgwyngyll,
Gwynedd LL61 5UJ
Tel (01248) 713177

Llangollen
Town Hall, Castle Street,
Llangollen, Clwyd LL20 5PD
Tel (01978) 860828

Mold
Library, Museum and Gallery,
Earl Road, Mold, Clwyd
CH7 1AP
Tel (01352) 759331

Porthmadog
High Street, Porthmadog,
Gwynedd LL49 9LP
Tel (01766) 512981

Rhyl
The Promenade, Rhyl, Clwyd
Tel (01745) 355068

Ruthin
Ruthin Craft Centre, Park Road,
Ruthin, Clwyd LL15 1BB
Tel (01824) 703992

Wrexham
Lambpit Street, Wrexham,
Clwyd LL11 1AY
Tel (01978) 292015

Open seasonally

Blaenau Ffestiniog
Isallt, High Street, Blaenau
Ffestiniog, Gwynedd LL41 3HD
Tel (01766) 830360

Llanberis
41 High Street, Llanberis,
Gwynedd
Tel (01286) 870765

Prestatyn
Scala Cinema, High Street,
Prestatyn, Clwyd LL19 9LH
Tel (01745) 854365

Pwllheli
Min y Don, Station Square,
Pwllheli, Gwynedd LL53 5HG
Tel (01758) 613000

Rhos on Sea
The Promenade, Rhos on Sea,
Clwyd LL28 4EP
Tel (01492) 548778

Towyn
Sandbank Road, Towyn, Clwyd
LL22 9LB
Tel (01745) 332025

Mid Wales

Open all year

Aberaeron
The Quay, Aberaeron, Dyfed
SA46 0BT
Tel (01545) 570602

Aberystwyth
Terrace Road, Aberystwyth,
Dyfed SY23 2AG
Tel (01970) 612125

Builth Wells
Groe Car Park, Builth Wells,
Powys LD2 3BT
Tel (01982) 553307

Cardigan
Theatr Mwldan, Bath House
Road, Cardigan, Dyfed
SA43 2JY
Tel (01239) 613230

Dolgellau
Tŷ Meirion, Eldon Square,
Dolgellau, Gwynedd LL40 1PU
Tel (01341) 422888

Knighton
Offa's Dyke Centre,
West Street, Knighton, Powys
LD7 1EW
Tel (01547) 528753

Lake Vyrnwy
Unit 2, Vyrnwy Craft Workshop,
Lake Vyrnwy, Powys SY10 0LY
Tel (01691) 73346
(open Fri-Sun only in winter)

Llanidloes
Town Hall, Great Oak Street,
Llanidloes, Powys SY18 6BN
Tel (01686) 412605

Llandrindod Wells
Old Town Hall, Memorial
Gardens, Llandrindod Wells,
Powys LD1 5DL
Tel (01597) 822600

Machynlleth
Owain Glyndŵr Centre,
Machynlleth, Powys SY20 8EE
Tel (01654) 702401

Newtown
Central Car Park, Newtown,
Powys SY16 2PW
Tel (01686) 625580

Rhayader
Leisure Centre, North Street,
Rhayader, Powys LD6 5BU
Tel (01597) 810591

Tregaron
The Square, Tregaron, Dyfed
SY25 6JN
Tel (01974) 298144

Welshpool
Flash Leisure Centre, Salop
Road, Welshpool, Powys
SY21 7HD
Tel (01938) 552043

Open seasonally

Aberdovey/Aberdyfi
Wharf Gardens, Aberdovey,
Gwynedd LL35 0ED
Tel (01654) 767321

Bala
Penllyn, Bala, Gwynedd
LL23 7NH
Tel (01678) 521021

Barmouth
Old Library, Station Road,
Barmouth, Gwynedd LL42 1LU
Tel (01341) 280787

Borth
High Street, The Promenade,
Borth, Dyfed SY24 5HY
Tel (01970) 871174

Corris
Craft Centre, Corris, nr
Machynlleth, Powys SY20 9SP
Tel (01654) 761244

Elan Valley
Elan Valley Visitor Centre,
Elan Valley, Rhayader, Powys
LD6 5HP
Tel (01597) 810898

Canolfan
Croeso
Cymru
Tourist
Information
Centre

Harlech
Gwyddfor House, High Street,
Harlech, Gwynedd LL46 2YA
Tel (01766) 780658

Llanwrtyd Wells
Tŷ Barcud, The Square,
Llanwrtyd Wells, Powys
LD5 4RB
Tel (01591) 610666

New Quay
Church Street, New Quay,
Dyfed SA45 9NZ
Tel (01545) 560865

Presteigne
Old Market Hall, Broad Street,
Presteigne, Powys LD8 2AW
Tel (01544) 260193

Tywyn
High Street, Tywyn, Gwynedd
LL36 9AD
Tel (01654) 710070

South and West Wales

Open all year

Brecon
Cattle Market Car Park,
Brecon, Powys LD3 9DA
Tel (01874) 622485

Cardiff
Central Station, Central Square,
Cardiff, South Glamorgan
CF1 1QY
Tel (01222) 227281

Carmarthen
Lammas Street, Carmarthen,
Dyfed SA31 3AQ
Tel (01267) 231557

Cwmcarn
Visitor Centre, Cwmcarn Forest
Drive, nr Cross Keys, Gwent
NP1 7FA
Tel (01495) 272001

Fishguard
4 Hamilton Street, Fishguard,
Pembrokeshire, Dyfed
SA65 9HL
Tel (01348) 873484

Haverfordwest
Old Bridge, Haverfordwest,
Pembrokeshire, Dyfed
SA61 2EZ
Tel (01437) 763110

Llanelli
Public Library, Vaughan Street,
Llanelli, Dyfed SA15 3AS
Tel (01554) 772020

Magor
Granada Services
West, Junction 23 M4, Magor,
Gwent NP6 3YL
Tel (01633) 881122

Merthyr Tydfil
14a Glebeland Street,
Merthyr Tydfil, Mid Glamorgan
CF47 8AU
Tel (01685) 379884

Narberth
Town Hall, Narberth,
Pembrokeshire, Dyfed
SA67 7AR
Tel (01834) 860061

Newport
Newport Museum and Art
Gallery, John Frost Square,
Newport, Gwent NP9 1HZ
Tel (01633) 842962

Pembroke
Visitor Centre, Commons Road,
Pembroke, Pembrokeshire,
Dyfed SA71 4EA
Tel (01646) 622388

Pont Abraham
Pont Abraham Services,
Junction 49 M4, Llanedi, Dyfed
SA4 1FP
Tel (01792) 883838

Pont Nedd Fechan
nr Glyn Neath,
West Glamorgan SA11 5NR
Tel (01639) 721795
(open weekends only in winter)

Pontypridd
Pontypridd Historical and
Cultural Centre,
The Old Bridge, Pontypridd,
Mid Glamorgan CF37 3PE
Tel (01443) 409512

Porthcawl
Old Police Station, John Street,
Porthcawl, Mid Glamorgan
CF36 3DT
Tel (01656) 786639

Sarn
Sarn Services, Junction 36 M4,
nr Bridgend, Mid Glamorgan
CF32 9SY
Tel (01656) 654906

Swansea
PO Box 59, Singleton Street,
Swansea, West Glamorgan
SA1 3QG
Tel (01792) 468321

Tenby
The Croft, Tenby,
Pembrokeshire, Dyfed
SA70 8AP
Tel (01834) 842402

Open seasonally

Abergavenny
Swan Meadow, Monmouth
Road, Abergavenny, Gwent
NP7 5HH
Tel (01873) 857588

Barry
The Triangle, Paget Road,
Barry Island, South Glamorgan
CF62 8TJ
Tel (01446) 747171

Caerleon
Ffwrrwm Art and Craft Centre,
High Street, Caerleon, Gwent
NP6 1AG
Tel (01633) 430777

Caerphilly
Old Police Station, Park Lane,
Caerphilly, Mid Glamorgan
CF8 1AA
Tel (01222) 851378

Chepstow
Castle Car Park, Bridge Street,
Chepstow, Gwent NP6 5EY
Tel (01291) 623772

Crickhowell
Beaufort Chambers,
Beaufort Street, Crickhowell,
Powys NP8 1AA
Tel (01873) 812105

Kilgetty
Kingsmoor Common,
Kilgetty, Pembrokeshire, Dyfed
SA68 0YA
Tel (01834) 813672

Llandarcy
BP Club, Britannic House,
Llandarcy, Neath,
West Glamorgan SA10 6HJ
Tel (01792) 813030

Llandovery
Central Car Park, Broad Street,
Llandovery, Dyfed SA20 0AR
Tel (01550) 20693

Milford Haven
94 Charles Street, Milford
Haven, Pembrokeshire, Dyfed
SA73 2HL
Tel (01646) 690866

Monmouth
Shire Hall, Agincourt Square,
Monmouth, Gwent NP5 3DY
Tel (01600) 713899

Mumbles
Oystermouth Square, Mumbles,
Swansea, West Glamorgan
SA3 4DQ
Tel (01792) 361302

Newcastle Emlyn
Market Hall, Newcastle Emlyn,
Dyfed SA38 9AE
Tel (01239) 711333

Penarth
Penarth Pier, The Esplanade,
Penarth, South Glamorgan
CF64 3AU
Tel (01222) 708849

St David's
City Hall, St David's,
Pembrokeshire, Dyfed
SA62 6SD
Tel (01437) 720392

Oswestry on the Wales/England border

Open all year

Mile End Services, Oswestry,
Shropshire SY11 4JA
Tel (01691) 662488

Heritage Centre,
2 Church Terrace, Oswestry,
Shropshire SY11 2TE
Tel (01691) 662753

Wales in London's West End

If you're in London, call in at
the Wales Information Bureau,
British Travel Centre, 12 Lower
Regent Street, Piccadilly Circus,
London SW1Y 4PQ.
Tel (0171) 409 0969
Staff there will give you all the
information you need to plan
your visit to Wales.

Before you leave, contact your nearest BTA office for information and advice.

British Tourist Authority Overseas Offices

Australia
British Tourist Authority,
8th Floor,
The University Centre,
210 Clarence Street,
Sydney, NSW 2000
Tel: (02) 267 4555
Fax: (02) 267 4442

Argentina
British Tourist Authority,
Avenida Cordoba 645-2
Piso, 1054 Buenos Aires
Tel: (01) 314 5514
(open to the public
mornings only)

Belgium
British Tourist Authority,
Avenue Louise 306,
1050 Brussels
Tel: (02) 646 35 10
Fax: (02) 646 39 86

Canada
British Tourist Authority,
111 Avenue Road, Suite
450, Toronto, Ontario
M5R 3J8
Tel: (416) 925 6326
Fax: (416) 961 2175

Denmark
British Tourist Authority,
Møntergade 3,
1116 Copenhagen K
Tel: 33 33 91 88

France
Tourisme de Grande-
Bretagne, Maison de la
Grande-Bretagne,
19 rue des Mathurins,
75009 Paris
(entre les rues Tronchet
et Auber)
Tel: (1) 44 51 56 20
Minitel: 3615 BRITISH
Fax: (1) 44 51 56 21

Germany
British Tourist Authority,
Taunusstrasse 52-60,
60329 Frankfurt
Tel: 069-2380711
Fax: 069-2380717

Ireland
British Tourist Authority,
123 Lower Baggot Street,
Dublin 2
Tel: (01) 661 4188

Italy
British Tourist Authority,
Corso V.
Emanuele 337,
00186 Rome
Tel: 06/68806464
Fax: 06/6879095
(solo ricezione)

Japan
British Tourist Authority,
Tokyo Club Bldg,
3-2-6 Kasumigaseki,
Chiyoda-ku,
Tokyo 100
Tel: 03-3581 3603/4
Fax: 03-3581 5797

Netherlands
British Tourist Authority,
Stadhouderskade 2 (5e),
1054 ES, Amsterdam
Tel: 020-685 50 51

New Zealand
British Tourist Authority,
Ste 305, 3rd Floor,
Dilworth Building,
Corner Queen &
Customs Streets,
Auckland 1
Tel: (09) 303 1446
Fax: (09) 377 6965

Norway
Postbox 1554 Vika,
0117 Oslo 1
Tel: 095 468 212444

Singapore
British Tourist Authority,
24 Raffles Place,
#19-06 Clifford Centre,
Singapore 0104
Tel: 5352966
Fax: 5344703

South Africa
British Tourist Authority,
Lancaster Gate,
Hyde Lane,
Hyde Park,
Sandton 2196
Tel: (011) 325 0343
(for personal callers only)
Postal address:
PO Box 41896,
Craighall 2024

Spain
British Tourist Authority,
Torre de Madrid 6/5,
Pza. de España 18,
28008, Madrid
Tel: (91) 541 13 96
Fax: (91) 542 81 49

Sweden
British Tourist Authority,
Box 745,
S 101 35 Stockholm
(Postal address)
Klara Norra Kyrkogata
29, S 111 22 Stockholm
(Visitors)
Tel: 08-21 24 44
Fax: 08-21 31 29

Switzerland
British Tourist Authority,
Limmatquai 78,
CH-8001 Zurich
Tel: 01 261 42 77
Fax: 01 251 44 56

USA - Chicago
British Tourist Authority,
625 N Michigan Avenue,
Suite 1510,
Chicago IL 60611
(personal callers only)

USA - New York
British Tourist Authority,
551 Fifth Avenue,
New York,
NY 10176-0799
Tel: 1 800 G0 2 BRITAIN
Fax: (212) 986 1188

The following organisations and authorities will be pleased to provide any further information you require when planning your holiday to Wales.

Further Information

By rail

Please contact British Rail-appointed travel agents or principal stations:

Birmingham	Tel (0121) 643 2711
Cardiff	Tel (01222) 228000
London (to North Wales)	Tel (0171) 387 7070
London (to South Wales)	Tel (0171) 262 6767
Manchester	Tel (0161) 832 8353

Great Little Trains

There are eight members of Wales's narrow-gauge 'Great Little Trains':
Bala Lake Railway, Brecon Mountain Railway (Merthyr Tydfil), Ffestiniog Railway (Porthmadog), Llanberis Lake Railway, Talyllyn Railway (Tywyn), Vale of Rheidol Railway (Aberystwyth), Welsh Highland Railway (Porthmadog) and Welshpool and Llanfair Railway (Llanfair Caereinion).

'Great Little Trains' details are available from The Station, Llanfair Caereinion, Powys SY21 0SF (tel 01938-810441).

The railways operating independently of 'Great Little Trains' are:
Fairbourne and Barmouth Steam Railway (tel 01341-250362), Gwili Railway, nr Carmarthen (tel 01267-230666), Llangollen Railway (tel 01978-860951), Snowdon Mountain Railway, Llanberis (tel 01286-870223) and Teifi Valley Railway, nr Newcastle Emlyn (tel 01559-371077).

By coach

Contact your local travel agent or National Express office. National Express enquiries:

Birmingham	Tel (0121) 622 4373
Cardiff	Tel (01222) 344751
London	Tel (0171) 730 0202
Swansea	Tel (01792) 470820

By sea

Five services operate across the Irish Sea:

Cork to Swansea
Swansea-Cork Ferries   Tel 01792-456116

Dublin to Holyhead
B&I   Tel 01407-760222/760223

Dun Laoghaire to Holyhead
Provisionally for 1995 *Stena Sealink's* new high-speed 'superferry' service plus standard ferry.   Tel 01233-647047

Rosslare to Fishguard
Stena Sealink's high-speed catamaran service plus standard ferry.   Tel 01233-647047

Rosslare to Pembroke Dock
B&I   Tel 01646-684161

By air

There are direct flights from Aberdeen, Amsterdam, Belfast, Brussels, Dublin, Dusseldorf, Glasgow, Guernsey, Isle of Man, Jersey and Paris to Cardiff-Wales Airport (tel 01446-711111), 12 miles from the city centre. Connecting services worldwide are via Amsterdam. Manchester and Birmingham Airports are also convenient gateways for Wales.

Useful addresses

Wales Tourist Board
Dept WTS 5, Davis Street, Cardiff, South Glamorgan CF1 2FU
Tel (01222) 475226
(Holiday and travel information is available from this above address, together with a free leaflet explaining our 'Quest for Quality' inspection schemes)

Brecon Beacons
National Park
Park Office, 7 Glamorgan Street, Brecon, Powys
LD3 7DP
Tel (01874) 624437

Cadw: Welsh Historic Monuments
Brunel House, 2 Fitzalan Road, Cardiff, South Glamorgan CF2 1UY
Tel (01222) 465511

Football Association of Wales
3 Westgate Street, Cardiff, South Glamorgan
CF1 1DD
Tel (01222) 372325

Forestry Enterprise
(Forestry Commission)
Victoria House, Victoria Terrace, Aberystwyth, Dyfed
SY23 2DQ
Tel (01970) 612367

National Trust
North Wales Regional Office
Trinity Square, Llandudno, Gwynedd LL30 2DE
Tel (01492) 860123

South Wales Regional Office
The King's Head, Bridge Street, Llandeilo, Dyfed
SA19 6BB
Tel (01558) 822800

National Rivers Authority
(Fisheries and Conservation enquiries)
Plas-yr-Afon, St Mellons Business Park, St Mellons, Cardiff, South Glamorgan
CF3 0LT
Tel (01222) 770088

Offa's Dyke Centre
West Street, Knighton, Powys
LD7 1EW
Tel (01547) 528753

Pembrokeshire Coast
National Park
National Park Department
Council Offices, Haverfordwest, Dyfed
SA61 1QZ
Tel (01437) 764591

Ramblers' Association
in Wales
Ty'r Cerddwyr, High Street, Gresford, Wrexham, Clwyd LL12 8PT
Tel (01978) 855148

Surfcall Wales
(daily surf/weather conditions at all major beaches)
Tel (0839) 505697/360361
Calls cost 39p per minute cheap rate, 49p per minute at all other times

Taste of Wales -
Blas ar Gymru
Welsh Food Promotions, Cardiff Business Technology Centre, Senghenydd Road, Cardiff, South Glamorgan
CF2 4AY
Tel (01222) 640456

Wales Craft Council
Park Lane House, 7 High Street, Welshpool, Powys SY21 7SP
Tel (01938) 555313

Welsh Golfing Union
Powys House, Cwmbràn, Gwent NP44 1PB
Tel (01633) 870261

Welsh Rugby Union
Cardiff Arms Park, PO Box 22, Cardiff, South Glamorgan CF1 1JL
Tel (01222) 390111

Youth Hostels Association
1 Cathedral Road, Cardiff, South Glamorgan CF1 9HA
Tel (01222) 396766

We'll show you around

The Wales Official Tourist Guides offer an expert guiding service at very reasonable fees – from hourly tours by car or coach to extended tours of any duration throughout Wales. WOTG guides and driver/guides are the only qualified tourist guides in Wales, and the association is registered with the Wales Tourist Board. Further details from:

Derek Jones, Y Stabl, 30 Acton Gardens, Wrexham, Clwyd LL12 8DE
Tel (01978) 351212
Fax (01978) 363060

Information for visitors with disabilities

The wheelchair accessibility guidelines in the 'Where to Stay' sections of this guide are designed to provide reliable and consistent information through standardised inspection schemes. All properties in this book identified as being accessible to disabled visitors have been inspected by the Wales Tourist Board.

Accessible Wales is an information-packed guide for visitors with disabilities. The book, together with a factsheet listing suitable accommodation, is available free from the Wales Tourist Board. See 'Get Yourself a Guide' at the end of this publication for details.

For details of other wheelchair-accessible accommodation inspected to the same standards please contact the Holiday Care Service. This organisation also provides a wide range of other travel and holiday information for disabled visitors:

Holiday Care Service
2 Old Bank Chambers, Station Road, Horley, Surrey
RH6 9HW
Tel (01293) 774535

Other helpful organisations

Wales Council for the Blind
Shand House, 2 Fitzalan Place, Cardiff, South Glamorgan
Tel (01222) 473954

Wales Council for the Deaf
Maritime Offices, Woodland Terrace, Maes-y-Coed, Pontypridd, Mid Glamorgan
Tel (01443) 485687
Minicom (01443) 485686

Wales Council for the Disabled
Llys Ifor, Crescent Road, Caerphilly, Mid Glamorgan
CF8 1XL
Tel (01222) 887325/6/7/8

In many parts of Wales visitors may hear Welsh spoken as an everyday language. Here's a short introduction.

A Brief Guide to the Welsh Language

A few greetings

Welsh	English
Bore da	Good morning
Dydd da	Good day
Prynhawn da	Good afternoon
Noswaith dda	Good evening
Nos da	Good night
Sut mae?	How are you?
Hwyl	Cheers
Diolch	Thanks
Diolch yn fawr iawn	Thanks very much
Croeso	Welcome
Croeso i Gymru	Welcome to Wales
Da	Good
Da iawn	Very good
Iechyd da!	Good health!
Nadolig Llawen!	Merry Christmas!
Blwyddyn Newydd Dda!	Good New Year!
Dymuniadau gorau	Best wishes
Cyfarchion	Greetings
Penblwydd hapus	Happy birthday

The Welsh National Anthem

Mae hen wlad fy nhadau yn annwyl i mi,
Gwlad beirdd a chantorion enwogion o fri;
Ei gwrol ryfelwyr, gwladgarwyr tra mad,
Dros ryddid collasant eu gwaed.

Chorus

Gwlud! Gwlad! Pleidiol wyf i'm gwlad;
Tra môr yn fur i'r bur hoff bau,
O bydded i'r hen iaith barhau.

The ancient land of my fathers is dear to me,
A land of poets and minstrels, famed men.
Her brave warriors, patriots much blessed,
It was for freedom that they lost their blood.

Chorus

Homeland! I am devoted to my country;
So long as the sea is a wall to this fair beautiful land,
May the ancient language remain.

Pronunciation

There are some sounds in spoken Welsh which are very different from their English equivalents. Here's a basic guide.

Welsh		English equivalent
c	**c**ath *(cat)*	**c**at (never as in receive)
ch	**ch**waer *(sister)*	lo**ch**
dd	yn **dd**a *(good)*	**th**em
f	y **f**am *(the mother)*	o**f**
ff	**ff**enestr *(window)*	o**ff**
g	**g**ardd *(garden)*	**g**arden (never as in George)
h	**h**et *(hat)*	**h**at (never silent as in **h**onest)
th	by**th** *(ever)*	**Th**ree (never as in **th**e)
ll	**ll**aw *(hand)*	There is no equivalent sound. Place the tongue on the upper roof of the mouth near the upper teeth, ready to pronounce **l**; then blow rather than voice the **l**

The vowels in Welsh are **a e i o u w y**; all except **y** can be l-o-n-g or short:

long **a**	tad *(father)*	similar to h**a**rd
short **a**	mam *(mother)*	similar to h**a**m
long **e**	hen *(old)*	similar to s**a**ne
short **e**	pen *(head)*	similar to t**e**n
long **i**	mis *(month)*	similar to g**ee**se
short **i**	prin *(scarce)*	similar to t**i**n
long **o**	môr *(sea)*	similar to m**o**re
short **o**	ffon *(walking stick)*	similar to f**o**nd
long **w**	sŵn *(sound)*	similar to m**oo**n
short **w**	gwn *(gun)*	similar to l**oo**k

y has two sounds:

1. Clear
d**y**n *(man)* a long 'ee' sound almost like g**ee**se
c**y**n *(before)* a short 'i' sound almost like t**i**n

2. Obscure
something like the sound in English r**u**n, eg:
y *(the)*
yn *(in)*
d**y**nion *(men)*

It is well to remember that in Welsh the accent usually falls on the last syllable but one of a word, eg ca*d*air *(chair)*.

Get Yourself a Guide

Wales – Bed and Breakfast is one of a series of three official 1995 accommodation guides. All places listed have been checked out by the Wales Tourist Board.

Wales - Hotels, Guest Houses and Farmhouses £2.95

A wide cross-section of accommodation, with a great choice of places to stay throughout Wales. Something for all tastes and pockets.

Wales - Self-Catering £2.95

Thousands of self-catering properties, including cottages, flats, chalets and caravan holiday home parks. Also a huge range of parks for touring caravans, motorhomes and tents.

Wales Tourist Map £2

A best-seller – and now better than ever. Detailed 5 miles/inch scale, fully revised and updated. Also includes suggested car tours, town plans, information centres.

Wales - Castles and Historic Places £7

Describes more than 140 sites in full colour, including castles, abbeys, country houses, prehistoric and Roman remains. A historic introduction sets the scene, and detailed maps help visitors plan their routes.

Visitor's Guides to North, Mid and South Wales £3.55 each

Another series of best-sellers, written by Welsh author Roger Thomas. These three information-packed books give you the complete picture of Wales's holiday regions. In full colour – and fully updated. Don't think of visiting Wales without them!

- descriptions of resorts, towns and villages
- where to go and what to see
- hundreds of attractions and places to visit
- scenic drives, castles, crafts, what to do on a rainy day
- detailed maps and town plans

A Journey Through Wales £4.80

A magnificent production – 64 big-format pages of the best images in Wales, with descriptive text by Roger Thomas. The 90 photographs take the reader on a tour of Wales's mighty castles, spectacular mountains and coastline, country towns and colourful attractions. An ideal memento or gift.

Wales - A Touring Guide to Crafts £6.80

Specially devised tours in full colour take you to galleries, woodcarvers, potters, jewellers and woollen mills. Nearly 100 craft workshops are listed, together with other places to visit.

'By Car' Guides — £2.30 each

The Pembrokeshire Coast

The Brecon Beacons

Two of the 32-page White Horse series. Attractive routes, maps and photographs – the ideal car touring guides to these beautiful parts of Wales.

Ordnance Survey Pathfinder Guides — £8.45 each

Snowdonia Walks (including Anglesey/Llŷn Peninsula)

Pembrokeshire and Gower Walks

Brecon Beacons and Glamorgan Walks

80-page books with detailed maps, colour illustrations and descriptions which guide you safely along attractive walking routes.

Accessible Wales — Free

A 68-page guide for people with disabilities. Accommodation and travel information, where to eat, places to visit, local facilities, helpful organisations, etc.

Videos

The Wonder of Wales (VHS) — £10.50

The breathtaking beauty and myriad attractions of Wales encapsulated in 24 memorable minutes. Narrated by Siân Phillips. Also available in NTSC format at £12.50.

Heritage of a Nation (VHS) — £10

Narrated by Richard Burton, this 25-minute video presents the heritage of Wales from prehistoric to present times.

WALES CYMRU
LAND OF INSPIRATION

To order any of the items featured here, please write enclosing the appropriate remittance in the form of a cheque or postal/money order in £ sterling to: **Wales Tourist Board, Dept WTS 6, Davis Street, Cardiff CF1 2FU.**

All prices include postage and packing

			Videos:			Posters:	
☐	Wales - Hotels, Guest Houses and Farmhouses 1995	£2.95	☐ Wonder of Wales (VHS)	£10.50		☐ North Wales Scenes	£1.30
☐	Wales - Bed & Breakfast 1995	£2.95	☐ Wonder of Wales (NTSC)	£12.50		☐ Mid Wales Scenes	£1.30
☐	Wales Tourist Map	£2	☐ Heritage of a Nation (VHS)	£10		☐ South Wales Scenes	£1.30
☐	Wales - Castles & Historic Places	£7				☐ Llangrannog Beach	£1.20
☐	A Visitor's Guide to North Wales	£3.55				☐ Tom Jones (Tenby)	£2.50
☐	A Visitor's Guide to Mid Wales	£3.55				☐ Anthony Hopkins (Snowdonia)	£2.50
☐	A Visitor's Guide to South Wales	£3.55				☐ Ian Woosnam (Mid Wales)	£2.50
☐	A Journey Through Wales	£4.80				☐ Lewis Carroll (Conwy)	£2.50
☐	Wales - A Touring Guide to Crafts	£6.80				☐ Dylan Thomas (The Boathouse, Laugharne)	£2.50
	'By Car' Guides:					☐ Laura Ashley Products	£2.50
☐	The Pembrokeshire Coast	£2.30					
☐	The Brecon Beacons	£2.30					
	OS Pathfinder Guides:						
☐	Snowdonia Walks (incl Anglesey/Llŷn Peninsula)	£8.45					
☐	Pembrokeshire & Gower Walks	£8.45					
☐	Brecon Beacons & Glamorgan Walks	£8.45					
☐	Accessible Wales	Free					

Please send to:

BWRDD CROESO CYMRU
WALES TOURIST BOARD

Wales Tourist Board,
Dept WTS 5
Davis Street
Cardiff CF1 2FU

Total remittance enclosed: £ ___

Cheque/PO or Money Order No: ___

Name (please print): ___

Address (please print): ___

Post Code: ___

Maps of Wales

The maps which follow divide Wales into 12 sections, each with a slight overlap. The grid overlaying each map will help you find the town or village of your choice. Simply turn to the appropriate mapsheet, look for the grid square quoted in the code and pick out the place itself in that square.

The maps are at 5 miles or 8 kilometres to the inch.

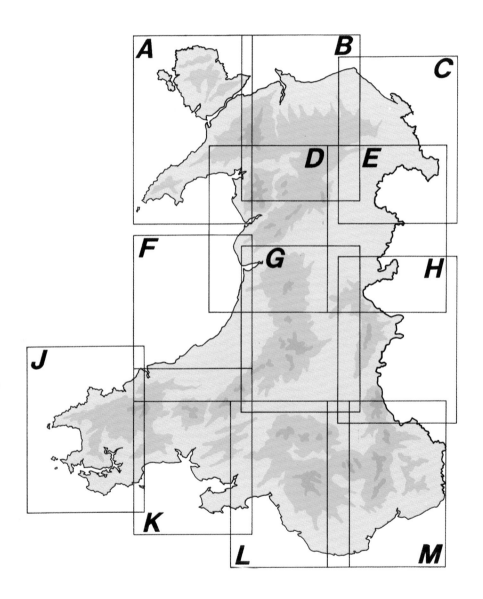

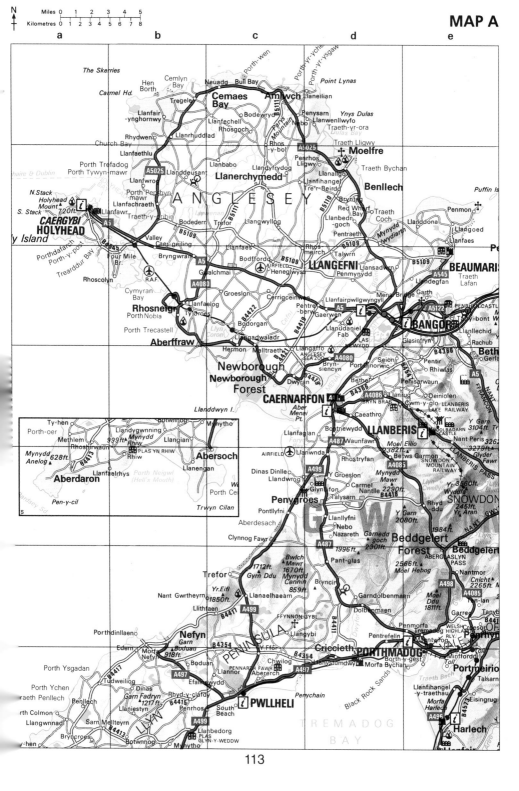

MAP A

113

MAP B

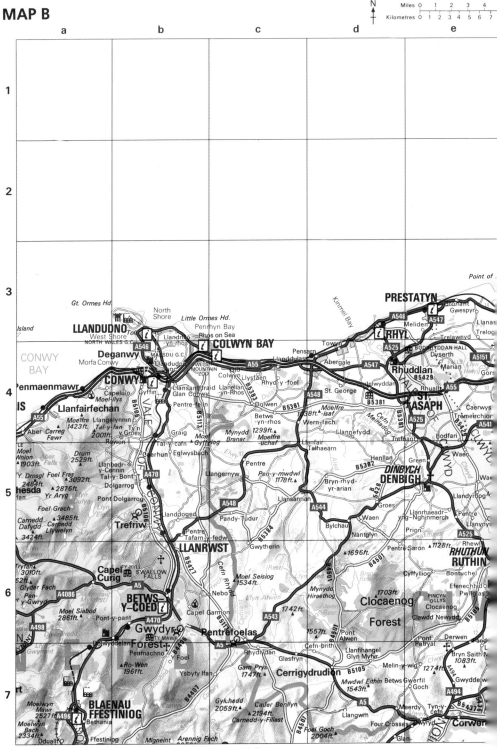

Point of

PRESTATYN

a b c d e

1

2

3

Gt. Ormes Hd.
North Shore
Little Ormes Hd.
Penrhyn Bay
Kinmel Bay
A548
Stronant
Gwespyr
Meliden
A547
Llanas
Trelawnyd
Trelog

Island
LLANDUDNO
West Shore
NORTH WALES G.C.
Llandrillo-yn-rhos
Rhos on Sea
COLWYN BAY
Towyn
RHYL
A525
BODRYDDAN HALL
Dyserth
A5151
Holy

CONWY BAY
Deganwy
Morfa Conwy
MAESDU G.C.
WELSH MOUNTAIN ZOO
Pensarn
Llanddulas
Abergale
A547
Rhuddlan
B5429
Marian
Gors

Penmaenmawr
CONWY
Cyffin
Llansantffraid
Glan Conwy
Llanelian-yn-Rhos
Colwyn
Rhyd-y-foel
Bodelwyddan
St. George
A548
B5381
ST. ASAPH
Rhuallt
A55
10

IS
Capelulo
Moel-llys
Pentre-felin
Dolwen
B5381
Betws-yn-rhos
1638ft.
Moelfre-isaf
Wern-fach
Caerwys
Trémeirchion
A541

Llanfairfechan
A55
Moelfre
Llangelynnin
1423ft.
Tal-y-fan
Ty'n-y-Groes
200ft.
Graig
Moel
Branar
Mynydd
1299ft.
Moelfre-uchaf
Llannefydd
Cefn Meiriadog
Trefnant
Bodfari
A525

Aber Carreg Fawr
Rowen
Tal-y-cafn
Gyffylliog
Llanfair Talhaearn
A470

Moel Wnion
1903ft.
Aber Falls
Drum
2529ft.
Caerhun
Eglwysbach
Elwy
Pentre
Henllan
Green
Waen
DINBYCH DENBIGH

Y. Drosgl Foel Fras
2484ft.
3092ft.
Llanbedr-y-Cennin
Tal-y-Bont
A470
Llangernyw
Pen-y-mwdwl
1178ft.
Bryn-rhyd-yr-arian
B5382

hesda
Yr Aryg
2876ft.
Dolgarrog
Groes
Llandyrnog
A525

lan
Foel Grach
Pont Dolgarrog
A548
Llansannan
Waen
Llanrhaeadr-yng-Nghinmerch
Prion
Pentre
Llanynys

Carnedd Dafydd
3485ft.
Carnedd Llywelyn
Trefriw
Llanddoged
Pentre Tafarn-y-fedw
Pandy-Tudur
Bylchau
Nantglyn
A544
A525

3424ft.
LLANRWST
Gwytherin
B5384
Resr.
1696ft.
Pentre Saron
1128ft.
RHUTHUN RUTHIN
Rhewl

Tryfan
3010ft.
62ft.
Capel Curig
TY-HYLL
SWALLOW FALLS
Moel Seisiog
1534ft.
Nebo
Cefn Rhydd
Llyn Alwen
Branin Reservoir
Cyffylliog
Bontuchel
Efenechtyd
Pwllglas

Glyder Fech
Pen-y-Gwryd
A4086
Moel Siabod
2861ft.
Pont-y-pant
BETWS-Y-COED
Capel Garmon
Mynydd Hiraethog
1703ft.
1742ft.
PINCYN OLLYS
Clocaenog
Clawdd Newydd
Clocaenog Forest

A498
Gwydyr Forest
TY MAWR
A470
Penmachno
Foel
Rhydlydan
A5
Rentrefoelas
Cefn-brith
A543
Pont Alwen
1557ft.
Derwen
Pont Petryal
Bryn Saith
1083ft.

Ro-Wen
1961ft.
Ysbyty Ifan
Garn Prys
1747ft.
Cerrigdrudion
Glasfryn
Llanfihangel Glyn Myfyr
Melin-y-wig
1274ft.
Gwyddelw

rt
Moelwyn Mawr
2527ft.
BLAENAU FFESTINIOG
A496
Bethania
Gylchedd
2059ft.
Cader Bronllyn
2194ft.
Carnedd-y-Filiast
Mwdwl Eithin
1543ft.
Betws Gwerfil Goch
A494
B5437

Moelwyn Bach
2334ft.
Dduallt
Ffestiniog
Migneint
Arennig Fach
Foel Goch
2004ft.
Llangwm
Four Crosses
Maerdy
Tyn-y-cefn
Dwyryd
Corwer
Glan-

114

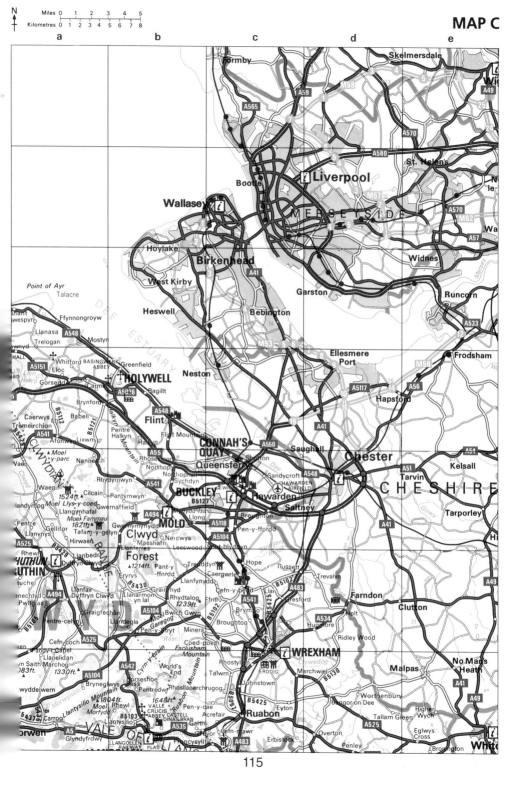

MAP C

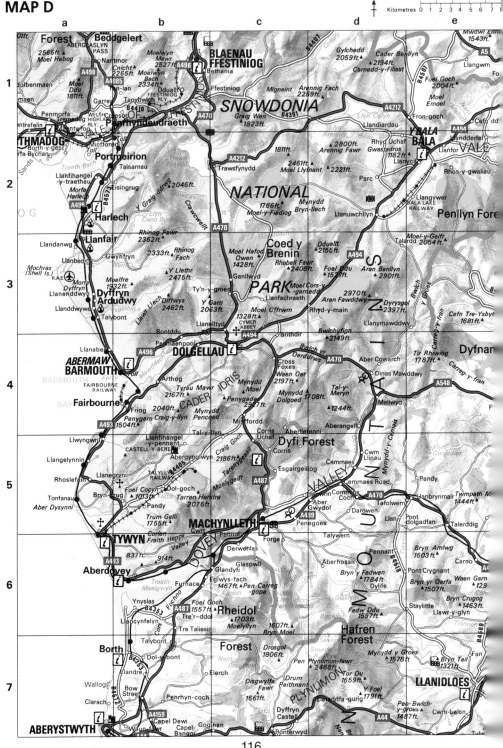

MAP D

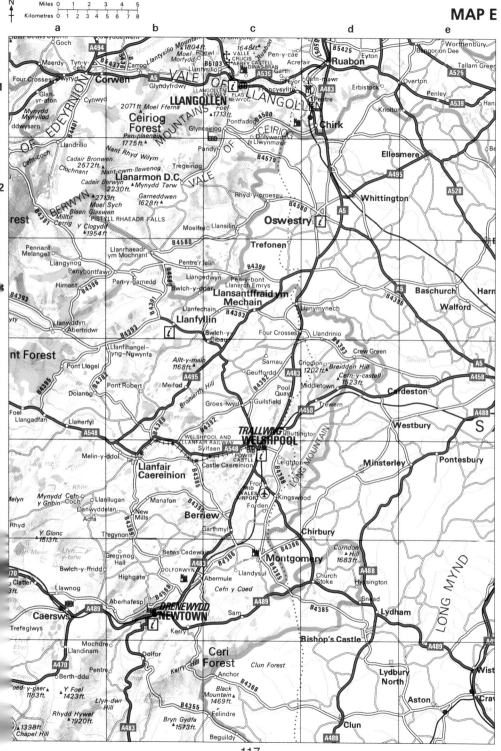

MAP F

N

Miles 0 1 2 3 4 5
Kilometres 0 1 2 3 4 5 6 7 8

a   **b**   **c**   **d**   **e**

B   A   Y

1

Borth ⓘ B4353 Dol-y-bont
Talybont
Co
Tr

Wallog Llandre
Bow Street Penrh
Clarach Capel Dew
Waun-fawr Cap
Ban
A4159

ABERYSTWYTH ⓘ
Llanbadarn
Pen-parcau A44 VALE OF
RHEIDOL RAILWAY

Rhyd-y-felin

2

Llanfarian
A487 Llanilar B43
Blaenplwyf Trav
B4275

Llanddeiniol

3

Llangwyryfon Lle
Llanrhystyd Trefenter Brc
B4337 A485
Aeron VYNYDD BACH
A487 Nebo Forest Blaenpennal
Aberarth Pennant Cross Inn Bethania
ABERAERON ⓘ B4577 Penuwch
A482 Cei Bach Ffos-y-ffin Llanaeron Cilcennin Llangeitho
B4578

4

New Quay ⓘ Llwyn-y-celyn Ciliau Bwlchllan B4342
B4342 Llanina Aeron Betws
Cwm Tudu Cross Inn Llanfihangel Leucu
Ynys Lochtyn A487 Dihewid Ystrad Tal-sarn Gartheli A485
A486 Temple Bar
Llwyn Dafydd B4342 Felinfach A482
Llangrannog Synod Inn Mydroilyn Llangybi
B4321 Bettws-
Mwnt FALLS Plwmp Cribyn Bledrws Llan
Traeth Penbryn Penbryn B4338 Gors-goch **LLANBEDR
Aberporth** Samau Brynhoffnant Talgarreg B4338 B4337 **PONT STEFFAN**
Tre-saith Capel 1062ft. Cwrt-newydd **LAMPETER**
Verwig M.o.D. Cynon B4459 Llanwnnen A475
5 Penparc Glyn Arthen Rhyd Cwm-sychpant Dre-fach Allt-y-blac Ram
Blaenannerch Lewis Pont-siân Rhyd Llanwenog Pencarreg Farm
Blaenporth Ffostrasol Owen Pen Tas-eithin Pur
Beulah B4570 A486 Tre-groes A475 Pren-gwyn **Llanybydder** 1361ft. A4
Brongest Maes-llyn Horeb B4337
ABERTEIFI Troed-y-raur A485
CARDIGAN ⓘ Aber-banc B4459 Maesycrugiau
Llangoedmor Cwm-cou bang Penrhiw-llan Llanllwni
A484 Llandygwydd Felindre Pentre-cwrt **Llandysul** Llanfihangel-ar-arth 1256ft.
Cilgerran Cenarth B4335 Pentre-cwrt 1256ft. Rhyd-
Aber Cych **Newcastle** Dre-fach Banc-y-ffordd Mynydd cymerau
A478 Newchapel **Emlyn** ⓘ Pencader Llanybydder Llansawel
6 Rhos-hill B4332 Pentre-drefelin Penboyr New Inn Mynydd Llanllwni Edwinsford
wysrwr Capel-Ifan 1209ft.
Blaenffos Bwlch-y-groes Moelfre A484 Rhos Gwyddgrug **Brechfa Forest** Abergorlech
Star 1100ft. 1080ft.
Treni-Faur Cwm Morgan Pencader B4459 Mynydd Cynr
1297ft. 1070ft. Cwm-duad Alltwalis Ha
Crymych Y Glog Tegryn B4333 827 ft. Mynydd Figyn
209ft. 869ft. Hermon Waun-deg Llanllawddog Brechfa
Drych Hermon Llanfyrnach Dinas Trelech Cynwyl Elfed Pont ar Sais Llanfynydd
7 Glandwr RAILWAY Llanpumsaint
Hebron Eglwys Trelech a'r Blaen-y-coed Sal
Fair a Chul Betws Talog Cwmdwyfran Rhyd-ar-gaeau Felin-gwm-uchaf Pen-y-banc
Llanglydwen A485
Coed Cwm-bach Peniel
Deufor

118

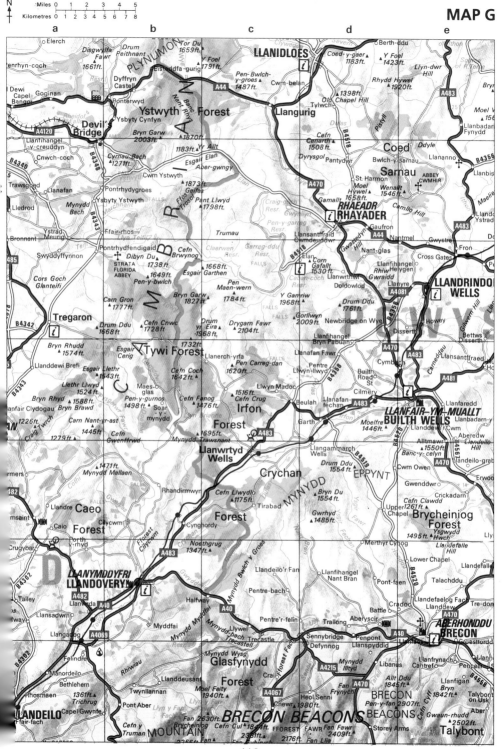

MAP H

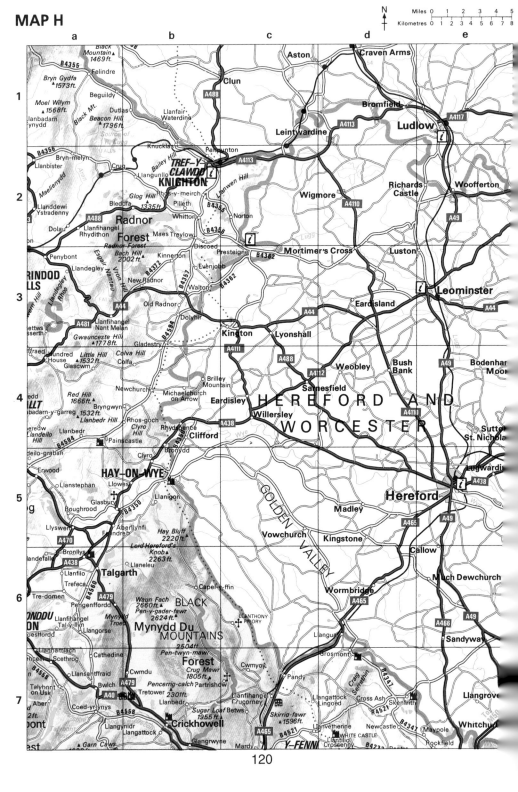

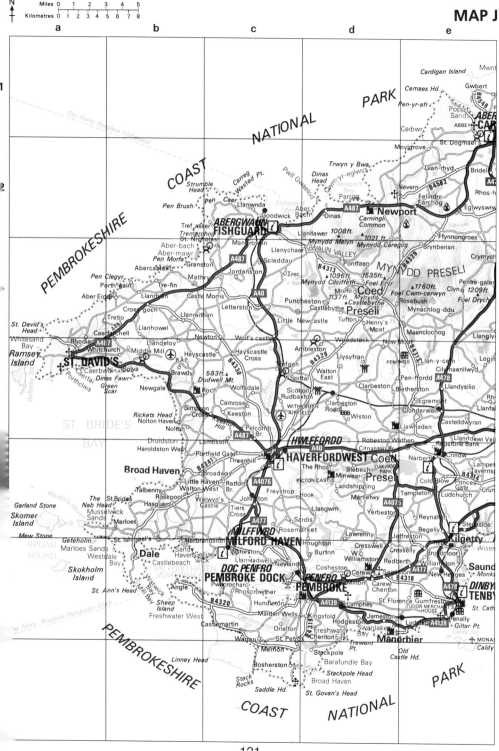

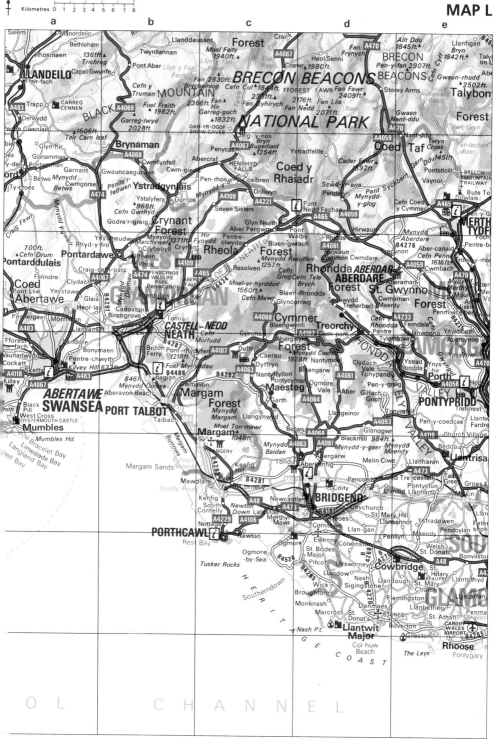

MAP L